Robert Hayden

UNDER DISCUSSION
David Lehman, General Editor
Donald Hall, Founding Editor

Volumes in the Under Discussion series collect reviews and essays about individual poets. The series is concerned with contemporary American and English poets about whom the consensus has not yet been formed and the final vote has not been taken. Titles in the series include:

Robert Hayden

Essays on the Poetry

Edited by Laurence Goldstein
and Robert Chrisman

Ann Arbor

THE UNIVERSITY OF MICHIGAN PRESS

Copyright © by the University of Michigan 2001
All rights reserved
Published in the United States of America by
The University of Michigan Press
Manufactured in the United States of America
⊖ Printed on acid-free paper

2004   2003   2002   2001   4   3   2   1

A CIP catalog record for this book is available from the British Library.

Library of Congress Cataloging-in-Publication Data

Robert Hayden : essays on the poetry / edited by Laurence
    Goldstein and Robert Chrisman.
        p.   cm. — (Under discussion)
    Includes bibliographical references.
    ISBN 0-472-11233-3 (acid-free paper)
      1. Hayden, Robert Earl—Criticism and interpretation.
    I. Goldstein, Laurence, 1943–   II. Chrisman, Robert.
    III. Series.
    PS3515.A9363 Z88   2002
    811'.52—dc21   2001001997

Contents

Chronology

1913 Born (as Asa Bundy Sheffey) in Detroit, Michigan, on 4 August.
Parents give him up for "adoption" to William and Sue Ellen Hayden.

1930 Graduates from Northern High School, Detroit.

1932 Enters Detroit City College (Wayne State University).

1936 Secures work as researcher and writer for the Detroit Writers Project Administration.

1938 Enters summer school at the University of Michigan.
Wins Hopwood Award (summer) for "Heart-Shape in the Dust."

1940 Publishes *Heart-Shape in the Dust*. Marries Erma Inez Morris.
Writes music and drama criticism for the *Michigan Chronicle*.
Studies with W. H. Auden at the University of Michigan (1941).

1942 Wins Hopwood Award (major) for "The Black Spear."
Daughter Maia born. Becomes a member of the Bahá'í World Faith.
Granted bachelor's degree, Detroit City College.

1944 Becomes teaching assistant in the Department of English at the University of Michigan. Awarded master's degree from the University of Michigan.

1946 Appointed Assistant Professor in English, Fisk University, Nashville, Tennessee.

1948 Publishes manifesto, "Counterpoise 3," and *The Lion and the Archer* (with Myron O'Higgins).

1954–55   Travels to Mexico on Ford Foundation Fellowship.
           Publishes *Figure of Time*.

1962   Publishes *A Ballad of Remembrance*.

1966   Awarded Grand Prix de la Poésie, First World Festival of
           Negro Arts, Dakar, Senegal. Publishes *Selected Poems*.

1968   Defends his art at the Black Writers' Conference, Fisk
           University.
           Records poems for Library of Congress.

1969   Resigns from Fisk University and teaches at the University
           of Louisville and University of Washington.
           Begins his tenure as Professor of English at the University
           of Michigan.

1970   Publishes *Words in the Mourning Time* (National Book
           Award nominee).
           Receives Russell Loines Award from the National Institute
           of Arts and Letters.

1971   Reads "The Night-Blooming Cereus" as the Phi Beta
           Kappa poem at the University of Michigan. Serves as
           Visiting Professor at the University of Connecticut and
           Denison University.

1972   Publishes *The Night-Blooming Cereus*.
           Serves on staff at Bread Loaf Writers' Conference in
           August.

1974   Visiting poet, Connecticut College.
           "In Memoriam Malcolm X," by composer T. J. Anderson
           with text by Hayden, sung by Betty Allen in Avery Fisher
           Hall, New York.

1975   Elected Fellow of the American Academy of Poets.
           Appointed consultant in poetry at the Library of Congress
           (serves two terms 1976–78).
           Publishes *Angle of Ascent*.

1978   Publishes *American Journal* (expanded edition published
           posthumously, 1982).

1979   Inducted into the Academy of American Poets and
           Institute of Arts and Letters.

1980   Included in a group of American poets honored by
        President Carter at the White House, 4 January.
        Dies 25 February. Buried in Fairview Cemetery, Ann
        Arbor, Michigan.

For a comprehensive chronology, see Fred M. Fetrow, *Robert Hayden* (Boston: Twayne, 1984); and Pontheolla T. Williams, *Robert Hayden: A Critical Analysis of His Poetry* (Urbana and Chicago: University of Illinois Press, 1987).

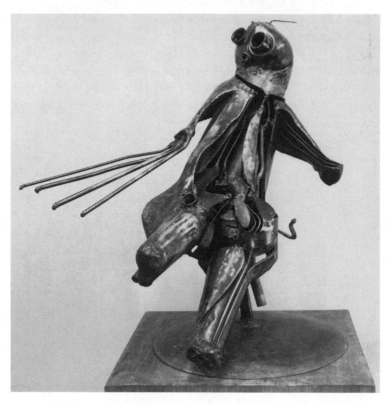

Richard Hunt, *Arachne,* 1956, welded steel. Photograph by
Soichi Sunami. Courtesy of the Museum of Modern Art,
New York.

LAURENCE GOLDSTEIN /
ROBERT CHRISMAN

Introduction

When Robert Hayden composed a poem about Richard Hunt's sculpture of Arachne, the mortal weaver who challenged the goddess Athena to a competition and was turned into a spider for her hubris, he fixed on the ultimate horror of her transformation: "mouth of agony shaping a cry it cannot utter." To be silenced in the act of protest, to be rendered inarticulate when the fierce spirit yearns to create language about the violation of one's humanity—this was a condition Hayden struggled against all his life. Despite personal and professional obstacles, he wrote poems throughout five decades with the clear purpose of shaping himself and his oeuvre into a triumphant testimony to the lasting power of passionate and well-wrought speech.

Every poetic career has something of the heroic about it, but Hayden's especially was forged and sustained against the grain of his native culture. An African-American poet who drew nourishment from a number of traditions—European, African, Latino, and Bahá'í, among others—he suffered from episodes of white bigotry and black hostility without succumbing to a speechless rage. He wrote some of the finest modern poems about African-American history, a kind of crypto-epic that would secure his immortality even if he had not also written a large number of near-perfect lyrics and verse narratives, on a variety of topics, still too little known even to students of late-twentieth-century poetry. Now that some of the furor over influences and reputation has abated and Hayden's *Collected Poems* has served a generation of readers, we can begin to see him as the champion of the creative life he aspired to become, a *becoming,* to cite the repeated word of his poem on Richard Hunt's *Arachne,* that places him in the front rank of poets of his generation.

Hayden has been the subject of four books at this writing (see "Selected Bibliography"), and a large number of essays, some in publications no longer in existence. The purpose of this book is to collect for convenient reference the most original and useful of the fugitive book reviews and essays extant and add to them some commentaries unpublished before this volume. No work in this anthology is excerpted from the books about Hayden, since they are easily accessible. The editors assume that the reader has Hayden's *Collected Poems* in hand, with its biographical essay by Arnold Rampersad, and does not require substantial quotation of poems being discussed. Nor have we selected materials that reiterate unduly the territory covered in Hayden's *Collected Prose*. The materials here extend what all these other writings provide. They deepen the discourse about Hayden's craft and the literary, historical, and cultural traditions in which he worked.

The book begins with some of Hayden's own previously uncollected work, including two interviews, a poem from *The Night-Blooming Cereus* he chose not to reprint in his *Collected Poems,* and a longer poem about Josephine Baker he left unfinished at his death in 1980. Hayden wrote only three book reviews of significance in his life, and they are all included in this section; they give us a further sense of his criteria for good poetry and for clear thinking on the most complex issues facing citizens of the modern world.

Reviews of Hayden's work are sparser and sparer than one might expect. His early books were published by small presses: Falcon, Counterpoise, Hemphill, Paul Breman, October House. Though grateful for the support of these struggling venues, Hayden remained bitter throughout his life about the fact that it took him some forty years of constant writing to secure a major East Coast publishing house. He recalled to one of the present editors how he had approached one well-known publisher in the early 1960s with a manuscript of his selected poems and enthusiastic letters of support from some of the most significant poets of his generation, only to be turned away by an acquisitions editor who explained to him, "We already publish a Negro poet." Reviews of volumes from small presses then and now tend to be brief, often a paragraph in an omnibus review of some dozen volumes of the season. The reviews collected here are the most substantial contributions to the evolution of Hayden's reputation.

A section of general essays on the work and one on individual poems round out the volume. Three poems by Hayden have received the lion's share of attention over the years: "Those Winter Sundays," a frequently anthologized personal lyric about his foster father; "Frederick Douglass," an encomium of high rhetoric and complex syntax in honor of the ardent foe of slavery; and "Middle

Passage," an evocation in collage form of slave ship experiences culminating in the mutiny aboard the *Amistad* in 1839. The present volume includes a suite of essays on "Middle Passage," in keeping with its status as central to Hayden's oeuvre, as well as essays on the other two poems. We have endeavored to include writings about the totality of his *Collected Poems,* however, and even a critical essay about poems that predate the earliest poems in that compendium. (Hayden requested that his "'prentice work" from the 1930s and early 1940s not be reprinted, but it is both right and inevitable that these poems see the light of day in the near future.) It remains a mystery to us that in the year 2001 so many of Hayden's best lyrics have received virtually no commentary at all.

Hayden's career, as Dennis Gendron points out, begins in the 1930s with poems displaying a mixture of influences. The hortatory, impassioned lyricism of Stephen Spender, C. Day Lewis, and Muriel Rukeyser attracted him, in part because of their radical politics. A pacifist poem like "In Time of War" catches the tone of their rhetoric:

> Though I be cast by war unto the rat, the dark,
> Though nightmare horrors mark my generation's end,
> Now while I live I'll not acknowledge death
> As Fuehrer to which the will must bend.
>
> O poets, lovers, eager-lipped young men,
> Say with me now that life is worthy—O give
> It affirmation; bring largesse of living,
> Make urgent now the will to live.

The balladry of Sterling Brown and the blues structures of Langston Hughes inform his best work of that period, as in his story-poem about a slave hanged for leading a slave revolt, "Gabriel":

> The black folk weep,
> The white folk stare:
> Gabriel is
> A sword in the air.
>
> His spirit goes flying
> Over the land
> With a song in his mouth
> And a sword in his hand.

W. H. Auden's more complicated poetry and the towering example of Yeats nourished Hayden's aesthetic of the 1940s. In order to make a clear break from the more formulaic "proletarian" phase of his work, he declared in a coauthored manifesto of 1948:"we believe experimentation to be an absolute necessity in keeping the arts vital and significant in contemporary life." In retrospect some of his experiments seemed to him too baroque or mannered, and he suppressed them, but this endorsement of modernist practice lies behind many of the masterpieces of his middle period, among them "Middle Passage" and "Runagate Runagate." Having entered his mature phase under the pressure of global events such as World War II and the Cold War, as well as the inception of the civil rights movement, Hayden wrote ever more capacious poems exploring, as if programmatically, every byway of the human condition he could imagine. One season might bring forth a comic poem about a woman reportedly abducted by extraterrestrials ("Unidentified Flying Object"), another might produce an elegy for Malcolm X or an appreciation of Monet's *Waterlilies* or a meditation on the philosophy of being, as in "Traveling through Fog." Many of the critics in this volume remark appreciatively on the manifold surprises of Hayden's volumes of poetry, as his attention turned alertly and artfully throughout the years to subjects of deep significance to any likely reader.

There is a range of methodologies at work in these essays, as is proper in a half-century's worth of considerations of a poet whose work invites large historical commentaries as well as minute observations on matters of idiom, lineation, stanza structure, and tone. Our criterion in selecting essays was straightforward: we asked whether the essay illuminated Hayden's artistry and his vision of human experience. We found that some early essays had become the victims of their own success—all of their insights had been thoroughly absorbed and extended by later essays. In recent years Hayden has attracted the notice of many poet-critics, an unsurprising turn of events for one who had been something of a poet's poet even when he spoke plainly on urgent matters of state. We welcomed a diversity of styles and approaches, from the most personal to the most scholarly.

Because Hayden's central concerns remain in the forefront of our attention as citizens, there is no danger that his work will lose its appeal to partisans; they will continue to cast their speculations on his work in the hermeneutical patterns popular in their time.

Nor do we doubt that his meditations on being and transcendence, the nature of artistic and religious experience, matters of racial and gender identity, and the ambiguities of time and temporal process, will continue to engage readers who find in verse the most satisfying enactments of profound thinking on those matters. Hayden is a poet for the ages, and we offer this collection of writings as an homage to one whose work repays all the scrutiny a conscientious reader can give to it.

This volume has benefited from the encouragement given the editors by many friends and colleagues. David Lehman, editor of the Under Discussion series, and LeAnn Fields, of the University of Michigan Press, have been exemplary monitors of our progress in bringing the book to completion. Maia Hayden Patillo, the poet's daughter, has graciously encouraged our efforts. The Special Collections libraries of the University of Michigan, including the Hopwood and Labadie holdings, as well as the Bentley Library on the same campus, have assisted us over a long period of time. We are especially grateful to Doris Knight for her Promethean labors in preparing the manuscript for publication.

A note on usage. Authors in these essays variously use the terms *Negro, Afro-American, Black, black,* and *African-American.* Because each term has some ideological and period significance, we have retained the original usage in each case.

PART ONE   *The Poet's Voice*

ROBERT HAYDEN

Statement on Poetics

From a letter of December 1970: "Every poem I write is for me, in Whitman's phrase, a 'language experiment' and a process of discovery. I value form and rhythm as having an organic relationship to the theme of a poem. I am as much concerned with the sounds and textures of words as I am with their meanings. I write slowly and painstakingly; often work on a poem several years, revising even after publication. Irony together with symbolism modified by realism are, I suppose, characteristic features of my poetry. I think of the writing of poems as one way of coming to grips with inner and outer realities—as a spiritual act, really, a sort of prayer for illumination and perfection. The Bahá'í Faith, with its emphasis on the essential oneness of mankind and its vision of world unity, is an increasingly powerful influence on my poetry today—and the only one to which I willingly submit."

From *Modern and Contemporary Afro-American Poetry* (Boston: Allyn and Bacon, 1972), 175.

ROBERT HAYDEN

Entrances and Tableaux for
Josephine Baker
[an unfinished draft]

I

> We see her in the next to final scene
> standing at the rainbow's end,
> Maya's darling still, and know the gold
> is real and all else brummagem.
>
> Once at the Casino de Paris
> she made her entrance—face agleam
> with diamond dust—descending invisible stairs
> whose treads unfolded to receive
>
> each glittering step just when it seemed
> that she must plunge through light and music
> to her death. Her Parisians gasped and cheered;
> such calculated risk exalted her;
>
> she sang J'ai deux amours, as now
> she sings it, grown old and ageless,
> triumphant in the sortilege of an art
> fleeting as rainbow fire, as durable.

II

> Oh, let us talk of happy things,
> she cried in those last years
> of her unhappiness, oh cherish, mon ami,
> illusions, do not look too close,
> believe in fairy tales and let us write

From *Michigan Quarterly Review* 31, no. 3 (Summer 1992): 318–20.

our own. By then the castle, rainbow
children—alas, for all my hopes
of human brotherhood—the exotic animals
in their diamond collars, the gold
all all was gone, had ended like

an idiot's tale. Whom had she offended,
God? Yet she had served Him in her way.
J'ai deux amours, one France and one
America, one had betrayed and one
had rejected her like some slavey stepchild.

Where then was La Belle France
that bitter day she never could quite
believe or understand when the ruffians came
to drag her from her fairy house foreclosed
and with vile names strike her down?

Where were de Gaulle, the Maquisards
with whom she braved the villains
of the Iron Cross? She had all
but died for France. But now her medals
were auctioned off as she lay in the mud.

There is no hope, she said, no hope
for France or anywhere. How could such things
happen here to me? I do not understand
the world any more. Why do we hate
each other so? My God, my God, I tried,

you know, as foster-mother to a brood
of homeless kids, to point a better way.
My rainbow children, ah, but they grew up
to call me whore; I gave them love
but failed. Was my love but vanity?

But let us talk no more today of trouble.
I am still Josephine, mon cher, these
fires have not consumed me, for I
am phoenix now, no longer bird of paradise.
Wait for me here. I'll climb those steps again.

III

Let down from the flies in gilt
baskets of cabbage roses, dancing
in ermined nudity from a Russian
Easter egg, borne upon hypnotic
mirrors by silverblack Nubians—
O Josephine O la Belle Sauvage

Dancing le Charleston le Blackbottom
singing whirling glittering to le jazz hot
L'Africane in jungle jewels by Cartier.
Baudelaire's ghost sighs in the wings,
Ah mon amour, fleur du mal retrouvée.

O washerwoman's daughter
from East St. Louis (and don't you forget it,
mes amis) walking her cheetahs on a diamond
leash vamping Vedette Americaine, conjure woman
with pranking familiars

Huckleberry Finn and Nigger Jim and
the voodoo empress Marie Laveau.
They laugh and bless her antic style, with sensuous
mockery, with something poignant
as down-home blues. . . .

ROBERT HAYDEN

Ballad of the True Beast

Enormous and greedily vicious. Four
        snapping heads. Reptilian
body exuding ichor of evil. Here
        lurking. There hiding. . . .

So the rumors went, the Stranger said.
        Relishing the worst, our villagers
believed. A few achieved status with tales
        of how narrowly they'd escaped it.

At first-dark returning from work
        in town one evening, we saw it,
my friend and I, at the edge of the pine-
        grove: beast-like child-like,

vaguely charming, if grotesque.
        And oh it was just as frightened
as we were. So nervous. Yet nodded its head
        to us in apparent greeting,

its four-tiered crown—all
        chime and sparkle—tumbling
off in the process. It scooped up
        the crown, murmured, skedaddled.

Not a soul in the village believed
        our story. Indeed, how could we
prove it? They gave us the haha in the streets
        and taverns, wrote us threatening

From *The Night-Blooming Cereus* (1975).

letters. More loutish than ever before—
    or so it appeared—they fed and
fattened the rumors like household pets.
    But worse much worse, the Stranger

said—we ourselves, this friend
    and I, fell to quarrelling
over what each of us had seen—
    and soon were bosom enemies.

ROBERT HAYDEN

An Interview with Dennis Gendron

What follows are excerpts from a long interview conducted by
Dennis Gendron at Connecticut College on 16–19 March 1974, and
appended to Professor Gendron's dissertation on Hayden's poetry.

HAYDEN: [I wrote a character-poem] about Prophet Jones ("Witch-
Doctor"), because there is a kind of drama there—even a kind of
mystery. There is something there for the imagination to work on.
When I say there is an element of mystery, I have to repeat myself
on that because I think that is precisely what I feel. I am trying to
think of some of the people I have written about. I like to write
about people, it must be clear to you. I like to write about people
who, to put it in a trite way, whose reality belies the superficial ap-
pearance. Like the woman in "Aunt Jemima of the Ocean Waves,"
who is really a composite of people that I knew at firsthand or read
about or saw on the stage when I was a young person. And I had a
certain distance from those kinds of people. . . . There are all kinds
of people, and there are all sorts of dramatic possibilities. Well, for
the reasons I have given, there is a kind of mystery—there is some-
thing that lies beneath the appearance they present. I like to try to
find what it is that gives them their unique and special qualities.

*You said you were very religious, if not in an organized, churchly way. It
seems to me that at times you have a frightening religion. For example, you
have healing spirits in some of your poems, but the healing spirit doesn't
seem to be tied in with your conception of God. Your conception of God
most of the time seems very frightening, as in the world created in "Mi-
rages." There is no healing spirit in that particular poem; all you have is
the stranger at the end who fools you. That seems to be the kind of view
that you have very often of what reality is like.*

From "Robert Hayden: A View of His Life and Development as a Poet" (Ph.D.
diss., University of North Carolina, 1975).

Well, it's because I am struggling toward belief and faith all the time. I am struggling with my own inner devils all the time, and we shall get to them, if not on the tape recorder, because I think we should be honest. So you can get certain clues you may or may not use; I don't care. But I am struggling, working toward being a believer. There is the part of my mind and the part of my being, part of my is-ness or my what-ness, that is convinced that there is transcendence, that there is a spiritual dimension and there is God, and that we do have obligations to God and that there is a divine plan for the world and so on. At the same time, there is the other side of me that finds it very hard to accept that, that finds it very hard to believe. And so I struggle with it. And I expressed it in a new poem that I hope to write and hope to finish. I have a persona in the poem who is really me speaking, and he says words to the effect that religion is a hair shirt. And in my own life it comforts me, but it harrows my soul at the same time. There is always a feeling of unworthiness on my part and the feeling that I am not living up to what I believe as a Bahá'í; yet I believe it, and I am getting blocked. That's all I can say about that.

I don't doubt anything. I am not a hypocrite, and that's one of those things that bothers me. I want to be honest; I won't lie to myself. I sometimes shy away from talking about religion and certainly shy away from writing about it sometimes because I am sure there are those people who would think, "He is a terrible hypocrite: he talks one way and acts another." But there is a kind of dualism in me. I feel sometimes as though, because I was pulled between two families, two sets of parents, that I have to this hour remained a divided person. One of my problems has been to make myself a whole person, and my faith has helped me to a certain extent. But then there is a point where I am not mature enough, I am not wise enough, to understand it fully so that it really could be a healing or unifying element in my life.

 ❧

Where did you get the title Heart-Shape in the Dust?

From Elinor Wylie. When I was young, I was much influenced by her. I willfully, consciously, submitted to her influence because she was such an exquisite craftsman. She is forgotten today, and she shouldn't be because she wrote some exquisite poems—marvelous craftsmanship—and I was much influenced by her.

 ❧

Yeats is also, obviously, a great influence on you. Is that because he is a kindred spirit?

Oh, yes, very much so. I keep a picture that Betsy [Graves Reyneau] made, a portrait of Yeats, a charcoal sketch, which, like all her work, is in the National Portrait Gallery. She gave me a photograph of her Yeats, and I had it framed. It sits in my room, and I look at it and wonder how he would feel about me. Yeats's life more than his poetry has had an influence on me. Yeats struggled with many of the things I have had to come to grips with: he struggled with being an artist and with being a man, and it's his approach to life, to these things, that I admire.

Your "Lear Is Gay" is a rather hopeful poem. But Lear is a fictional character, which is the point of Yeats's "Lapis Lazuli." Lady Gregory, Maud Gonne, those shrill women at the beginning of "Lapis Lazuli"—they cannot cope with reality; the people who cope with reality are Lear and Hamlet and the Chinamen, all make-believe characters.

Yes, but I hadn't thought of that. What I thought of was the fact of these old men and Lear in old age, having lost everything yet being able to see beyond that: finally seeing what reality is. That's what I had in mind. I always felt that life is a struggle. I used to say to students, "Living is the hardest thing you are going to have to do." They used to laugh and say, "What an old campus character," not knowing from what depth of feeling and suffering that had come. Living *is* the hardest thing you can do, and I always had that sense. And I think I have wrung a certain kind of affirmation and a certain kind of faith out of things that were really negative and troublesome, maybe. But I had to make an effort to do it.

ès

With this kind of vision and your idealism, and the way you manipulate images to emphasize life's struggle, do you think that you are primarily an ironist as a poet?

Maybe so, because I respond. That's another reason I have written about the people that are in my book. Yes, I respond to irony and consider myself something of an ironist. If I were more intellectual (and I am not apologizing, because I don't want to be that intellectual), but if I were more intellectual, I perhaps would be more of an ironist because it is, after all, a kind of intellectual movement. But I am aware of irony all the time. Life is shot through with ironies, and I think that if you have a sense of the dramatic then you have a sense of the ironical.

๛

That "Mystery Boy" in Nashville who was searching for kin seems to be a kind of Robert Hayden.

Oh, that's me, kid, looking for love. The original, the prototype of mystery boy, was a young woman. Yeah, that's definitely autobiographical.

๛

You seem to use everything that's a part of your experience. You have classical references because obviously classicism is a part of your background. You take from Yeats, Pound, and people like that because they are part of your background. You are not an average black poet. But, by being called a black poet, is that limiting? Do you think that's less than being a poet or more than being a poet?

Well, right now in America it has pejorative implications. Now I am trying to, I think, reach the point where I am finally indifferent to designations. I don't care whether I am called a poet or a black poet or whatever because I know in my own heart what I am. I think of myself as being a poet. I am afraid today that *black poet* carries the implication, has the connotation, that the poet is interested in one kind of thing and that he closes his mind upon the world and concentrates on the ethnocentric. I would hope that in time we will get away from that. I feel that *black poet* means you are over-specialized, you are concerned with one kind of thing, one kind of experience.

Does this bother you? The rest of the question I am trying to set up to indicate what your response should be. Does it bother you when a poem upon a subject that uses black history or black folklore, that really has universal application, to see that application stopped simply with its black implication?

Indeed so, and I have tried to write—early, before we were talking in terms of this nonsense, when I wrote "Middle Passage," for example—I tried to make that poem transcend narrow, racial, propagandistic implications. That's why I am very careful to allude to John Quincy Adams. And I wasn't conscious of this; I just did it because that's the way I am, because that's how I felt about things. I make it very clear that the black kings were in collusion with the traders. I feel that many people—I don't like to think in terms of black-and-white but you have to sometimes in this age—I think many white people put blinders on and read a poem by a Negro poet and would like to think it has no implications for them, that it's limited to the so-called black experience. But you are absolutely right. I think I always wanted to be a Negro poet or a black poet or an Afro-American poet—we'll use all the terms and be done with it—the same way Yeats is an Irish poet. To me this is what I learned from Yeats. This is what Yeats means to me. Yeats did not flinch from using materials from Irish experience, Irish myths. The whole Irish struggle has meaning for Yeats. He would have been astonished if anyone had told him to forget that he was Irish and just write his poetry. But he wrote as a poet; and I am not Irish, but I could read Yeats's poems, such as "Easter 1916," and relate to it. When I was teaching at Terre Haute one summer, teaching a course in contemporary poetry—it was right after the Detroit riots—I remember going to class one morning; we were working on Yeats, and we had that poem "Easter 1916." I began to read the poem and could not go on reading it: the tears welled up. I remember my old nun, who came to me after class and said, "We know exactly what you feel." It was a very moving experience reading that poem after the Detroit riots. Well, Yeats didn't write that poem for me particularly, but that is the kind of poetry I want to write. Yes, it may reflect a certain kind of experience, a certain kind of awareness, but it's human rather than racial. It speaks to other human beings, and it's not limited by time and place and not limited by the ethnic.

ॐ

Were those poems more part of prevalent attitudes, those Heart-Shape in the Dust *poems? They seem to be more racially orientated than later poems you wrote.*

Sure. That was because so many were written in the 1930s when I was very much involved in left-wing activities.

I can see Langston Hughes and Arna Bontemps in those poems.

Of course. Because I was young, and some of those poems were written while I was in my twenties, and some had been started in college and written afterwards. That was the zeitgeist. That was it, and it was the first book, and I had to start somewhere. I started with all those things. Also, I was called at one point "the people's

poet." The UAW-CIO was organizing in Detroit, and I well re-
member that one Sunday I was asked to come in and give a read-
ing. And, of course, in those days I read abominably, just abom-
inably. I was nervous, scared, and just read miserably. Anyway, a lot
of people were trying to put me down because, after all, it was De-
troit, and I wasn't being very practical. I was trying to be a poet,
and "Who in the hell do you think you are?" Anyhow I had writ-
ten these poems about working-class people, which was not to be
marveled at because, after all, I did come out of the working class.
I was very much aware of the labor struggle. I was very much aware
of the whole left-wing thing in Detroit, and so my poems attracted
some attention as propaganda more than anything else. So one
Sunday—at a big mass meeting—I was voted the people's poet of
Detroit [laughing].

I could have been the blackest of the blacks if I had wanted to
do it. Even then, as you can see, in that book I was trying to write
about all kinds of things. I was aware of a lot of things—uncertain
of myself but still aware of a lot of things. You know the poem
"These Are My People": oh, that was a great thing in the 1930s in
Chicago and Detroit. It was performed by groups. People talk
about influence, imitation, and so on. Sometimes it isn't a matter of
that at all: sometimes you are working in the same area and every-
body is doing the same thing, and that's true of the 1930s. Most of
us were writing like that. I had not seen Richard Wright's poem at
all. "These Are My People" was written for a Negro Congress cul-
tural event in Detroit. I got that poem together; and the emphasis
in those days was not apartheid or separatism, but the emphasis was
that black and white workers should come together. "Black and
white unite!" We used to have that slogan, you know, and "Black
and white stand up and fight!"

Weren't the mills trying to use the races against each other to break unions?

Sure, the factories in Detroit were. Black and white communists,
black and white union organizers, were working hand-in-glove to
bring the two together. You see, they were trying to use Negroes as
strikebreakers. They were trying to use them as anti-union forces.
I remember Paul Robeson's coming to Detroit speaking in behalf
of the union. When I wrote "These Are My People," it was con-
sidered a tremendous thing in Detroit, and then a group of people
from Chicago got copies of the poem [laughing]. The left-wing
people, socially conscious people, to this day think this was the best

poem I ever wrote and wonder why I ever did anything else. "What's all this jazz about *The Night-Blooming Cereus?*"

ॐ

Did you go to the services of those street preachers?

You couldn't miss it because we lived on the corner of Beacon Street and St. Antoine. St. Antoine was the parade ground for people from everywhere in the world. That was the place where the street preacher was most likely to attract an audience; so they'd get out on the corner to preach, sing, and shake their tambourines and all that.

Are they the prototype for your "Witch Doctor"?

Oh, that was Prophet Jones, but I wouldn't ever admit that when he was alive. I didn't want to get involved with him. But that's really Prophet Jones.

That's an effective poem because the form so fits the subject—both are baroque.

Others also like it; it's in some anthologies. LeRoi Jones criticized it way back there because it was full of fancy-pants big words and so on. Well, the fancy-pants big words are there to indicate something about the character I am writing about. It's meant to be a baroque poem. He is meant to be a very baroque personality; and, of course, it's all highfalutin and inflated because I am trying to say something about him.

I saw a review of your work by David Galler, who also objected to your big words, and the issue reminds me of Dunbar's complaint in "The Poet."

I never have used quite so many big words all in one poem as I did in that, but there was a purpose behind it.

Yes. The staircase sets the tone of the whole poem.

If you knew him, he was grandiose—the big baroque gesture. A friend of mine—I didn't get it into the poem, but you can't get everything into the poem—went to one of his services and said that when he came in, or before he appeared, some of his servitors placed a rose on the pulpit. All this ritualism and things to do, and his costume was, well, a costume.

Countee Cullen, you know, was adopted by a minister. But he was a bona fide minister at one of the big churches there in

Harlem. He was a very intellectual man, as a matter of fact. He made his trips to Europe and gave very cultivated sermons and so on. And he raised Countee in an atmosphere of learning and good living. No, he was nothing like that. This man was a charlatan, and I think that sex was all mixed up in what he was and what he did. He had a male secretary whom he was very close to, apparently. No one could get past that secretary. That secretary died, and Jones was very shattered by it. That I don't hold against him, and that we don't put into the record. But he was flamboyant; there was a lot of acting, a lot of prima donnaism. He was very much an androgynous character, and I indicated that in the poem. But I didn't come down hard on that because I didn't want people to think I was making a point of it. It's the kind of thing that, once you say anything, they think you are making a big point of it.

&

You said that Countee Cullen liked "The Falcon." Do you still like that poem?

Yes. Well, I did. So many of those poems—like "The Falcon" and "Sunflowers"—involve symbolism. But at that time, you see, the symbolism wasn't so carefully worked out as now I would do it. And I think that I did tend at that time to use what might be called, I guess, stock symbols. I didn't work it out carefully because I couldn't. I was developing. You know, those poems were written in my twenties, when I was in college. It was really early work, 'prentice work. It was what most young poets do.

You seem to get very passionate in Words in the Mourning Time *and lose all objectivity in that poem about Martin Luther King.*

Yes, I was very passionate about it; I was terribly worked up. I suppose that series of poems was my way to catharsis because in the 1960s I very often felt that I could not stand the horrors of that period. So much that was happening was distressing and dreadful. I felt I had to try to come to grips with it, and the only way I could bear it and understand it and handle it was to write out my feeling about it. So I did. Yes, it is very passionate. . . . It was my way toward resolving anxieties and fears and the great overwhelming sadness I found at that time.

Does section 2 of that poem echo the youth phrase, "Fighting for peace is like fornicating for chastity"?

[*Laughing*] No, but I think that's good. I did take from Shelley those two lines in section 5.

You also express the "kill a commie for Christ" idea in that section.

Yes, that's right. That's the idea. I was very much aware of that, as a matter of fact. Some of those poems were very deliberate, although many of those pieces were longer. They were full of rhetoric, and they were rather false. So I kept working at them and hacking them down so that they finally were very concentrated—and that's what I really wanted. I think that's one poem in there that may last now that the Vietnam War is over, if it is over: you know, "He comes to my table." That's a visionary poem. When I first began working on those Vietnam poems—that was one of the images from that poem, and the theme appeared early in the first rough drafts of the Vietnam poems—they were far from a success. So I cut everything out. When I got through hacking away, when I got through revising, cutting down the first Vietnam poem, those stanzas were left.

Those are horror-full images.

That's how I felt about the war. That poem has to do with the feeling of the horrors of war. The poem deals with war almost as a presence: the horror of war becomes a presence that you live with and you sit with. It might have been a result of the many times we would sit down to dinner and turn on the news and there would be reports about Vietnam. Sometimes we would get up and turn off the television because we couldn't stand it. I didn't think of that when I was writing the poem. But I was trying to convey the idea that the horrors of the war became a kind of presence, and they were with you in this most personal and intimate activity, having your meals and so on. Everything was touched by the horror and the brutality and criminality of war. I feel that's one of the best of the poems. I think it's a stronger poem than the one that usually wins a round of applause, or used to in the bad old days of the war, about the gook mother and the decent American boys lopping off Vietnamese ears and so on. I think that's rhetoric, but I don't care; and I didn't care when I wrote it that maybe the poem would disappear once the war was over, that it wouldn't be read as a poem so much as a statement or as a piece of propaganda. My friends warned me that I was taking a risk. So I said that I really didn't care, that I had to speak out, and that I had to speak now. And I felt better for having said it and having gotten it out. I slaved over those poems, and I don't think some of them are all that good. But, again, I did succeed in communicating something that used to move people profoundly. When I read those poems in the 1960s, people would cry, and they would come up to me afterwards and say, "Oh, God. Is that what we've become?"

How did you feel about Malcolm X? Why were you moved to write "El-Hajj" about him?

I began this series of poems on Malcolm X with a kind of Bahá'í prayer for his soul; I wrote it, and then I decided that it was rhetoric, rhetorical, and that the poem was much more effective if it ended as it did. So that's the story of Malcolm X. I read *The Autobiography* one summer, and I went to it rather reluctantly because I had not admired him in the early stages of his career. It was only toward the end of his life that I came to be a little more reconciled to him; and then, when the news and the circumstances of his death reached us, I can say that I am very thankful that I had a profound human reaction. I was full of anguish to think that he had been killed that way. Although I didn't agree with him, I recognized his ability and his sincerity, and I just was overwhelmed. I was horrified by his death and really regretted it. Later, when I read *The Autobiography,* I was won over to him. I realized what he represented, and the theme of metamorphosis took over in the poem because I guess that's what I became aware of as I read *The Autobiography:* you know, evolving, changing, and so on.

Where did the opening phrase, "O masks and metamorphoses of Ahab, Native Son," come from?

I made that up; it has to do with *Moby-Dick.* I think that in an early version of the Malcolm X poem—see, I had worked on the Malcolm X poem at various times: I had written drafts and never been able to finish it—in an early draft I think that was going to be the first stanza, or lines in the first stanza, and then I cut it out and used it as a kind of epigraph. I had in mind Richard Wright's *Native Son* and native son as a symbol—you know, the dispossessed Afro-American. And then, of course, Ahab in his desire to conquer evil as represented by the white whale and all that, his becoming somewhat diabolical in his desire to track down evil and destroy it. That's what the epigraph grew out of.

How about the section on "Lord Riot / naked / in flaming clothes"? You seem to portray Lord Riot as almost a new god in this age, to replace the old one. And his "I hate / I destroy / I am" is a topsy-turvy "I think, therefore I am."

Yes. I was trembling when I wrote that poem. And, again, I felt I had to do something about the riots: I felt that I understood why they were taking place, but I felt that there was an element of the absurd in them, that there was destructiveness and that they were a means of—they represented a quest for identity and, well, you know, I've said it in the poem. But I was trying—I was coming to grips with that reality, and I saw the absurdity in it and I saw all the things that were involved.

❧

Did you also make up the epigraph to "Soledad": "And I, I am no longer of that world"?

No, that too demands a note. That was taken from a teenage drug addict's poem, which was published in a magazine. I don't know who wrote it. I was working on the poem at the time the *New Republic* or *Nation* published it. . . . I think it was an anniversary issue of a magazine, and I read in there this article on drug addiction—during the 1960s, of course . . . and the poem by this one teenage drug addict. And at the time I was getting the book together I had so many other things to do, as usual, that I decided that I just wouldn't spend time on the notes. As a matter of fact, I made some notes, but I decided that I didn't have time to polish them and I would just let it go. Later on, maybe, I'll have a note on it.

I appreciate the puns you use—paronomasia, if you prefer. For example, in "Zeus over Redeye" in terra *is quite effective.*

At the time I didn't think of it as a pun. I was trying to use it as a strange word—you know that. It came out that way. Yes. It's alright if you don't pun too outrageously or too often; I guess you can get by with it.

In "Aunt Jemima of the Ocean Waves" you use an image of "The Sable Venus." *I've seen that picture. Where did you come across it?*

It's an etching that I found in an old book dealing with the slave trade, and I don't know where. Somewhere in Michigan there is a folio volume, and on the frontispiece there is this etching taken from some old book or magazine of this woman standing on a great shell in the sea, "The Black Venus." So that stayed with me after I saw it years and years and years ago. I don't know the book. I don't know where I found it. It stayed with me, and I got it into the poem.

&

And your mother?

Ah, that's Sue Ellen Westerfield. She was Sue Hayden. "The Ballad of Sue Ellen Westerfield" grew out of things that she told about experiencing as a young woman. Now, she didn't fall in love with a man like the one described in the poem, but her first husband had worked on the boats. That's where she met him. He had been, apparently, a very handsome man, and she never forgot him. As a matter of fact, she had three children by him, and she never had any children by William Hayden, and she never loved Pa the way she did her first husband. She talked about it, really, until her dying bed. She always talked about him; she never forgot him. And his name was Jim Barlow. He died young. She and Pa Hayden were together for many, many years, but they were kind of. . . . In their old age they had a kind of miserable life together.

In "Sue Ellen" isn't the person she loves white?

Yes, well, Jim Barlow looked like white. I saw pictures of him. He wasn't, but he looked white.

Isn't there a similarly plotted story in the black folk tradition?

If that's so, then so much the better because I didn't know it at all.

Isn't "Sue Ellen" meant to go with "The burly fading one"?

It does; it's meant to. As a matter of fact, the series of poems I'm working on now, called "Beginnings," will be arranged so that "Sue Ellen Westerfield" and "The burly fading one" will all be a part of that series.

"Burly fading one" is a striking title. Is it your own?

Yes, that's right. Well, I hope it's mine. If I ever find it in somebody else's poem, I'll die. I won't know what to do. But now it's mine. I wanted to suggest, you know, that he's on a photograph. The photograph is fading, and he is a big man. Of course, Pa Hayden wasn't big.

&

Was "The Whipping" like anything that happened in your life?

Yes. Older people did that to children then, and I got a few hidings like that. But my aunt objected strenuously, and I didn't get whipped that way too much. But I was often abused and often hurt physically because they were ignorant people. They didn't know how to handle children, and they were neurotic themselves. My foster mother was just as neurotic as they come; I know that now. I didn't know it then. She had some kind of nervous ailment. They called it neuralgia. She would have dreadful pains in her face, and she even had an operation. They tried to kill the nerves in her face and so on. But nothing helped. I know now that that was psychosomatic because the time came when she didn't have that anymore. The pain was just so terrible, and she would just. . . . Very often it would be brought on by some great angry outburst or something that upset her, and then she would blame me. It was terrible. That part I don't want to get into too much because it was painful; it really hurts me to even think of it. But they were often cruel to me. And, without my knowing it, I guess maybe I was cruel to them. I don't know. But I was a child. I was at their mercy. I really did get abused and hurt and so on. I saw dreadful things. And this has to be told, I mean, because it's there. Our home was a very troubled home. My foster father, Pa Hayden, just despised utterly my foster mother's daughter, whom I called Aunt Roxie, or Auntie, and they would have terrible rows. And then she was something of an alcoholic, and she would come in drunk and turn the house out. Oh God, I mean she would come in and start raving and cursing, and there would be fights and so on. I remember as a child how frightening this was to me. I'd wake up at night, and they would be fighting and shouting at one another. And then, when I was older and in college, I never knew quite what to expect. I mean, I'd go home and there'd be some unpleasantness, and it would erupt into something really dreadful.

In The Night Blooming Cereus *"Smelt Fishing" appears as three haiku almost.*

Yes. They are haiku. That was all kinds of things, and I thought I'd never get that little poem finished. I worked on them and worked on them. I have so many versions of it. It came out of something I heard about when I was in Duluth, Minnesota, for a poetry reading.

I was there in the spring, in the smelt fishing season; and the fishermen were just in a frenzy to get out to the lake and catch those fish as they spawned—millions of them. And the men were just as frenzied as the fish. There was this great rush out to the lake. And they were so involved in catching these fish at night that a young man—he had been showing off or something—fell out of the boat. And there were cries for help, and nobody would do anything. No one stopped fishing long enough to find out who had fallen or to help him. The people who told me about this were scandalized. They said it was a dreadful thing that they would be so intent on catching these fish that this could happen. There were certain implications about the accounts I heard that the young man was showing off his virility. So that there got to be kind of sexual implications in there too: you see, the spawning fish, the virile masculine thing and all that. That's what's behind the poem.

And the "Blank fish-eyes" *apply to both man and fish.*

Yes. They had not found the body when I was there. They had gone out with grappling hooks, but nobody had gone to his aid. . . . When the cries for help came, nobody had gone to help. They had all been intent on catching those fish. I wanted to write a poem about it, and I think I made notes when I was right there in Duluth. But for some reason or other, I couldn't handle the poem in the form that I wished it to take. So it turned into haiku, where you get it all by suggestion and implication.

Referring to "Perseus," *did you feel that sense of power, that desire to destroy, described in the poem?*

No. That's an impersonal poem. At the time it was written, the Rosenbergs were about to be executed, and Betsy (Graves Reyneau)—she read it in manuscript—Betsy said, "That's the Rosenbergs: that's what that is." The idea was that we were all so appalled by the execution of those people . . . in wartime as traitors. The idea being that in your attempts to destroy evil—I've said this in readings I've given—beware that you do not, in the process of destroying evil, yourself become evil. Perseus, destroying this hated truth, himself becomes a destroyer.

Is that image at the end from Keats's urn?

Well, I hope not. But I guess in a way that's alright because that's very Greek. And, sometimes, if it carries you back to somebody like Keats, that's alright because I love Keats, and that doesn't bother me. But if you tell me that I got this from Auden, then I get worried [*laughing*].

ROBERT HAYDEN

A Conversation with A. Poulin, Jr.

I'd like to begin with an obvious question: Under what circumstances did you start writing poetry?

Well, that's a little difficult to answer. I started, really, when I was a child. I read early in my life—before I ever went to school. And, of course, when I was down in the grades, people read to me. When I began to write and was able to read for myself I started trying to write verses, and when I was an adolescent I spent a great deal of time trying to write. I've been at it a long time.

You say you read early and that people read to you; do you recall what you were reading?

Yes. This is going to sound almost too good to be true, but *Uncle Tom's Cabin* was one of my favorites [*laughter*]. Then there was a children's story called "Beautiful Joe, the Story of a Cur," *Robinson Crusoe,* and later on Paul Laurence Dunbar. When I was a little older and began to write poetry, I tried to write dialect verse the way Dunbar did. Of course, I hadn't heard the kind of dialect in which Dunbar wrote his poems.

Much later on, in my adolescence, I read George Eliot's *Romola,* Hawthorne's *The Marble Faun,* and all the Afro-American poets. You know, one doesn't know what to say today—*Negro, Afro-American, Black*—I'm not really used to *Black.* I think I prefer *Afro-American.* Anyhow, in my adolescence I began to read Afro-American poets, besides Dunbar: Langston Hughes, Countee Cullen, and so on. And when I was a little older, I was trying to write very much like those poets.

What was it about those poets that interested you the most?

Hughes and Cullen were especially dear to me because they wrote about themes and subjects, about things, let's say, that I was very

The interview was conducted on 5 March 1975 in the Brockport Writers Forum at the State University of New York–Brockport.

much aware of, that were swirling around me in the old, poor slum section of Detroit where I grew up. And they, especially Langston Hughes, wrote about those matters. I was attracted to them because I wanted to learn how to use that material. I was intrigued by it. There was another thing, too. There was a certain amount of pride I took in knowing that those writers were Afro-American just as I was, and perhaps, if I worked hard enough, I could be like them, I could achieve something, too.

Do you know of any of your own poems that have been specifically influenced by Dunbar or by other Afro-American poets?

No, not now. When I was young, in my teens and early twenties, some of the poems I wrote were very much like Countee Cullen's. I wrote a poem that was very much like Cullen's "Heritage." Mine was about Africa, too, and, you know, it's really a laugh because I was about as far from Africa then as you could get—psychologically and in every other way. But it was a convention that Afro-American poets all seemed to use, and I think I learned something from the experience. Later on, Langston Hughes's poems—using the old blues songs and his poems about ghetto life—taught me how to . . . well, they were poems I learned something from.

But now I don't think there's anything like that in my work. There is a strong element of folklore, a folk motif, in many of my poems because I grew up in a folk milieu; I was used to hearing people talking a certain way and making references to things that were clearly from folk sources.

I sense the kind of experience you're talking about is in a poem called "Those Winter Sundays," which is a very gentle poem arising out of your childhood experience.

That's a favorite poem of mine. It was written for my foster father, who made it possible for me to go to college and all the rest of it. He was a hard-working man—a Baptist. I grew up a Baptist. He cared a great deal for me, and, when the other boys would have to go out in the summers—winters, too, for that matter—and work, why he would help me to stay in school. I owe him a great deal, because, had he been like some of the other fathers in the neighborhood, I might—oh, I might have gotten an education eventually, but he *cared* about my getting an education. He used to say to me, "Get something in your head, and then you won't have to live like this."

What hurts me is that he never lived to know that I cared that much. He didn't know anything about poetry; the people I grew up with didn't, and in a way that was a blessing because they left me alone. Nobody had any prejudice against poetry. When I won the Hopwood Award at the University of Michigan back in the 1930s, my foster father was still alive, and he was delighted; he didn't know what the poems meant, but he thought it was great that the boy had begun to get some recognition and win prizes. So at least he saw that.

I think it was in the 1950s that I wrote this poem, and I can't really tell you what started me to write it. I just had a nostalgic feeling for him and the past and began to work on the poem. I might add that nobody liked it at first, but now it's in many anthologies.

The whole genre of "father poems" seems to have become a favorite one among a number of poets these days.

Well, you know, the search for the father, the search for the spiritual father, and all that . . .

You mentioned a number of Afro-American writers who were significant to you. What about non-Afro-American writers?

Oh, yes, inevitably if you care about poetry. Certainly, as a young person I didn't care who wrote the poems; I mean, if it was good poetry, I read it and loved it. There was a group of us in Detroit at one time who loved John Keats. We were a mixed group, black and white. And we had pretty much decided that we were all going to try to write immortal lyrics and die at the age of twenty-six [*laughter*]. Well, twenty-six has come and gone for me, and I'm really not ready to die yet, because, you know, there are so many things I want to do. But in my early years I think Keats was something of an influence.

Later on, in the 1930s, I discovered Auden, Yeats, Spender, C. Day Lewis, and still later Gerard Manley Hopkins. I also read Hart Crane and Marianne Moore. As a matter of fact, I read everybody I got my hands on; I mean, I *knew* everybody. I sometimes would neglect my schoolwork to read poetry.

I had a marvelous friend at the Detroit Public Library: Alice Hanson. (Alice is now dead; I did dedicate *Words in the Mourning Time,* in part, to her.) There was a poetry room in the Detroit Public Library, which no longer exists, I'm sorry to say, and she would see to it that I got all the new books of poetry because, except for a few off the secondhand tables, I couldn't afford to buy any. As a result, I was reading poetry all the time and was very much aware of what was going on.

There were some poets whom I tried to imitate. I think Hart Crane was one. It wasn't until much later in my life that I really read Yeats and was, and remain, influenced by Yeats—not in terms of my writing so much as in terms of my life, in terms of my thinking. Yeats, you see, was an Irish poet. Or, let me put it the other way around. I think of myself as an Afro-American poet in the same way that Yeats was an Irish poet. I have no desire to ignore my heritage, to ignore my experiences as an Afro-American. I have no desire to turn away from that anymore than Yeats wanted to turn away from being Irish. At the same time, I don't want to be limited to that.

I have wanted to be able to function as a poet who touches on all kinds of things. Betsy Graves Reyneau, a dear friend and a portrait artist (whose work is in the National Gallery now—placed there after her death) made a portrait of Yeats that I keep in my study at home, and I look at it periodically; I look at it every day when I go into the study. Yeats's life is an example to me—in a strange way that I can't. . . . He struggled—an artist who had to come to grips with being Irish, who was disliked by the Irish even, because he did not do what they expected him to do. You know, I feel myself pretty much in the same situation very often. During the 1960s I drew a lot of strength from knowing what Yeats had gone through.

This reference to Yeats leads to some of the statements you make in your introduction to your anthology, Kaleidoscope. *Introducing yourself, for example, you say that you're "opposed to the chauvinistic and the doctrinaire" and that you "see no reason why an Afro-American poet should be limited to 'racial utterance' or to having his writing judged by standards different from those applied to the work of other poets."*

I stand by that statement. I had several things in mind. One thing I had in mind, and still keep in mind, is the fact that very often where the work of an Afro-American writer is concerned, critics approach it as though it were a sociological document or a sociological treatise on what we have to say about our situation as a minority people or as ethnics, as well as what we have to say about the kind of progress that we make when we do write protest poetry. All of those things assume an importance that overrides the work as art or as literature; it allows people to ignore it as literature and think of it as some kind of social statement. And yet, when critics and readers go to the work of some of the poets I've mentioned—or even to your own poetry, for that matter—they aren't going to be concerned first of all with the social implications; they're going to look at it as poetry and judge whether or not it's true to the laws that it sets up for itself. They are going to be concerned with whether or not it's really poetry.

The other point related to this is: I think there is a tradition—I thought it was waning, but it's getting even stronger; maybe *tradition* is not the word I want, but let it go—among Afro-American poets, to emphasize the racial experience, the struggle, rather than other kinds of experience. However, there are some young people who feel pretty much as I do. They don't want to be limited by those racial experiences. I think of Michael Harper, Jay Wright, Alice Walker, and a young poet named Herbert Martin. All those younger poets are doing really vivid and splendid work. Michael Harper sometimes writes about jazz; he writes about Coltrane. One of his books is called *Dear John, Dear Coltrane.* Michael is not interested in setting himself apart from other poets by dealing with some overspecialized kind of experience. He tries to write as a poet who's aware of his racial background. But I can only repeat what I said: he is *not limited by it.*

I want to pursue this just a bit further. In that same introduction you seemingly refused to accept what you called a kind of "literary ghetto," and you implicitly refused to be a spokesman for your race. I wonder if you might expand on that a little.

Well, I can just garble along as I do [*laughter*]. Let me go back to this: when I wrote that introduction—(incidentally, that anthology was intended for high school students and was not to be a trade book)—I didn't think that it was original or earth-shaking; I just tried to make it as good as I could. A good many of the poets who have come along since that book appeared have not become widely known or have not published books.

I feel that we have been in a kind of literary ghetto. Before the 1960s there were a relatively small number of recognized Afro-American poets. If you took a course in American Literature, you might or might not have heard anything about the deaths of those poets. You might or might not have heard anything about Countee Cullen. (I keep mentioning Countee Cullen because I love him so much. I knew Countee, before ... well, I can't say I *knew* him. I met

him and had the chance to tell him how much I cared for his po-
etry. He liked some things of mine, and so on.) Anyway, if you
took a course in American Lit., you might or might not *ever* know
anything at all about Afro-American writers. However, if you took
a course in Negro American Literature—as it would have been
called before the 1960s—you would have had a chance to learn
something about it. Even then, though, you never would have
gotten a clear understanding of the relationship between—oh,
let's take one that you probably don't like—the relationship, say,
between the New Poetry movement (which began in 1912 and
reached its climax in the 1920s) and the Harlem Renaissance. Your
instructor would have given you the Harlem Renaissance as
something almost in a vacuum. Now I thought that that was to
disappear, but I find that it hasn't. Today, if you go into American
Lit. courses, you'll find that, if you really want to know what any
of us have done, you've got to go take a course in Black Lit. I
think this is all wrong.

As far as I'm concerned, there is no such thing as "Black" po-
etry, there is no such thing as "White" poetry in America; there is
just American poetry. I think that it does a lot of harm to keep this
kind of polarization going. I know that some people are capitaliz-
ing on this, are profiting from it. And people who might otherwise
not have any recognition at all can stand up and be called poets be-
cause they're dealing with a particular kind of subject matter.
They're dealing with the liberation of their own people, so they
think. Those are the kinds of things I had in mind.

*One of the things you brought up leads me to play devil's advocate. What
you just expressed might very well result in certain people accusing you of
literary "Uncle Tomism." How would you respond to that?*

I would respond to it by ignoring it [*laughter*]. Because the people
who would say that have never read anything. They don't know the
past. They don't know American literary history; they don't even
know the work of their own people. I would just simply dismiss it
because it is not true. Ralph Ellison is to be judged by the standards
that would be applied to any novelist and not just by some spuri-
ous standards that could be created and applied to a black novelist.
Ellison has been called, as we used to say in folk parlance, every-
thing but "a child of God" [*laughter*]. I guess that's something you
have to be prepared for. But I am not unwilling to stand by those
things I've said.

I think that we are denying something very fundamental. We've been in this country for almost four hundred years; if anybody's got a stake down here, *we have!* I can trace my folks *rather* far back. On my mother's side, the family came from Kentucky, and my father's family came from Virginia. Anybody who tells me I don't have a stake down here is out of his cotton-picking head. What was all that sweating and bleeding and dying about? I had ancestors in the Civil War, and, for all I know, I might have had relatives in the Revolutionary War. I know why people feel alienated, and I know why they feel isolated; but I think that to advocate or to support separatism in any form is to give aid and comfort to the bigots.

I think the "Toms" are the ones who are running around being separate, running around college campuses wanting their own dormitories and their own cafeterias and so on. Those are the Toms. And I feel that this is something that ought not to be. They really are giving aid and comfort to the bigots, who, if they can get rid of us, will push us all over into the corner somewhere. Then nobody will have to bother with us; they won't have to deal with us. If we're in separate dormitories and in separate classrooms, then we don't have to be dealt with. So that's my answer to that.

I want to get on to your own poetry, but I do have one more general question. In the introduction to your anthology you also say that Afro-American poetry has been "shaped over some three centuries by social, moral, and literary forces essentially American." I'd like to know what you understand by essentially American.

I go back again to the Harlem Renaissance and the New Negro Movement. The importance of the Harlem Renaissance is that for the first time Afro-American artists began to get a recognition that they hadn't had before. As they began to work in idioms or modes that they had not worked in before; the novelists became more realistic, and the poets became more experimental. And at the same time that the Harlem Renaissance (which took place in the 1920s and ended roughly in the 1930s) was going on, there was developing in America, in general, more realism in fiction. This was the age of Hemingway, Fitzgerald, and Dreiser. There was a movement from the rural to the urban in literature. The poetry was experimental; the poets were trying to get in as much of so-called reality or as much of the actual world of automobiles and bathtub gin as they could. Well, Afro-American writers were influenced by this, and their work is very similar to the work of other writers in the Jazz Age.

They were reacting to the pressures; they were reacting to the new developments that were occurring in America, just as other writers were. They certainly weren't living in Timbuktu; they were living in New York, Detroit, and Chicago, and they were drawing their material from those sources.

The difference between the writers in the Harlem Renaissance and white writers was that the Harlem Renaissance writers felt that they had a purpose; the racial situation had some influence upon them as it inevitably would. Many of them felt that they were interpreting what was called the "New Negro." They were presenting new images of Negro life in America. Of course, I wasn't a member of the Harlem Renaissance, despite what some people may think; I'm not quite *that* ancient. Afro-American writers were very much influenced by what was happening here. And they did exert some influence on other writers, too. For example, Carl Van Vechten wrote stories about Harlem life. They're sort of artificial and phony, but nevertheless he did it. And Eugene O'Neill's *Emperor Jones* grew out of the interest in the Negro past and the whole emphasis on primitivism.

This reminds me of a funny little story. The Harlem intellectuals sometimes used to put on a great act of being primitive. The people who went up to Harlem slumming and who believed that Afro-Americans lived a very freewheeling and uninhibited life were sometimes taken in by what was nothing more than a kind of in-joke. People used to go up to Harlem thinking, "Oh, they're so primitive!" They were primitive and crazy—like foxes, because they were putting on an act, and they sometimes succeeded in making people pay for it when they'd go into nightclubs to see those "wonderful primitives," who were just as calculating and tough as anybody else could be. I'm sorry about the subject, but I think you see what I mean.

It seems to me that my earlier question regarding your being accused of Uncle Tomism is also answered by your poem "Night, Death, Mississippi"—a strong protest poem that does not engage in propaganda. Would you comment on it?

Yes, of course. That's one of the poems that kept me from being more viciously attacked than I might have been. It was a fact that, when some of the loud-mouthed people who were quick to throw these epithets around finally got around to reading my work, they were surprised.

37

I might say briefly that I wrote this poem as a sort of catharsis for myself. I had read about the young Civil Rights workers who were killed in Mississippi, and I could hardly bear it. I would look at my students—I was teaching at Fisk—and I could imagine that these Civil Rights workers were very much like my students. It was really very painful. I could not rest until I wrote this poem. It took me a long time to bring it off.

I was wondering if you might identify—I know I've done it in my own mind—a poem of yours that you feel is representative of your use of folklore that you spoke about earlier.

There are several, I think. *In Selected Poems* there's one where the folklore is quite obvious; it's called "Electrical Storm." There are several elements of folklore in this poem. The belief that animals draw lightning is not confined to Afro-American people; it is a widespread folk belief. I can remember that during a thunderstorm my folks would shoo the dog away because animals supposedly draw lightning. That's in the poem. I used to hear my aunt say, "God don't love ugly," and then she would say, "and cares . . ."—I won't use the word—"and cares very little for beauty." I guess that was a folk expression that other people must have used also. The word *col-leged*—Langston Hughes and I laughed over that. As a matter of fact, Langston Hughes once said to me, "Boy, you colleged!" I was somebody who had gone to college and had some learning or some education. The whole idea of a thunderstorm being a sign of God's displeasure and the idea that you might get struck by light-ning because God was making you pay for all your sins are in the poem. You know, years and years later, when I was grown and thinking about such things, I used to wonder why God didn't send a thunderstorm and strike down people like Hitler. At the time I described in the poem, it wouldn't have occurred to me to ques-tion that.

The reference to Hitler raises another characteristic of your poetry. You in-clude a variety of nationalities and cultures and draw upon them. You've written a number of poems about Mexico and Mexican culture. You've also written some very powerful poems having to do with the Nazi experience, and, maybe implicitly, you relate it to the Afro-American experience in this country. I think a poem like "Belsen, Day of Liberation" or "From the Corpse Woodpiles, From the Ashes" serves as example.

I would like to say that I don't consciously look around and say, "Let me see if I can get something out of this." I mean, you know *that;* you know what your own process is in writing a poem and how certain subjects just seem to cling to you like burrs. You don't seek them out particularly. I guess what I can say, without sounding like Little Lord Fauntleroy, is that I do believe in the old statement that Terence or somebody—I can never remember who—said that "nothing human is foreign to me."

I have known a variety of people in my life and have had many experiences. I haven't been abroad, except to Mexico. I intend to go to Europe and stay as long as I can. I've known people all over the world, one way or another. Even in Russia they owe me royalties, which I'm sure I'll never get. And, without making too big a thing of it, I guess I have a worldview. I can't help being affected by or (which is the same thing) being concerned about humanity, wherever and however it manifests itself. That's what I had in mind a little while ago when I was talking about the tendency to restrict those of us who happen not to be white, to restrict us and to expect that we're going to be concerned with one particular body of subject matter and not with anything else. A poet could be limited by that.

As an example of what you're saying, one of your poems about the Nazis followed by your poem "Sub Specie Aeternitatis" would suggest your kind of worldview.

"Belsen, Day of Liberation" is dedicated to Rosey Pool, a Dutch woman who died a couple of years ago. A marvelous person, she was interested in Afro-American poetry long before anybody else was. She went to the University of Holland and took her degree, and she wrote her thesis on Afro-American poetry. Later on Rosey came to this country, and she published an anthology called *Beyond the Blues.* I met her, and we became fast friends. She told me a story of a little girl who had been in a concentration camp, and I used this anecdote as the basis of the poem.

The little girl looked out the window and said, "They were so beautiful, and they were not afraid." And you know there is so much that lies behind that statement—what the child must have endured to say that.

Then, there is "Sub Specie Aeternitatis"—"under the aspect of eternity." What prompted this poem was a visit to a Mexican convent in Tehuacán.

It seems to me that poem says something about any kind of cultural, literary, or religious ghetto that eventually deteriorates—but lingers.

Yes. It was often said in Mexico and in books you read about Mexico—I think Octavio Paz and some others have made this point one way or another—that the old Gods, the old Aztec Gods, the old Toltec Gods, are still around; they haven't died. At some of the fiestas, the holy day celebrations, statues of the old gods are out there alongside Christian images. And customs that the Aztecs and Toltecs observed when worshiping Quetzalcóatl are still seen. There's still some of that. I was very much aware of this when I wrote the poem. As a matter of fact, at one point I despaired over this poem; I felt that it was just too obvious and, oh good night! anybody would think that. Maybe it is, but somehow or other people who have read it always like it. I guess it's alright.

There are a number of other poems that I would have liked to ask you to talk about, but it would seem appropriate to end our discussion with "Frederick Douglass" and whatever you might want to say about it.

I wrote this poem a long, long time ago. It appeared in the *Atlantic Monthly* around 1945. Nobody paid much attention to it. I kept revising it and doing things to it. I was attracted to Douglass because he is a kind of universal figure; he fought for Afro-American freedom, yes, and that's certainly important. But for him, where would I be today? He was also concerned with women's suffrage, with temperance, with all the great causes. I think the Bahá'í religion was another thing that attracted me to him. I see a universality in his outlook, some sense of the basic unity, the basic oneness of mankind, which is the cardinal principle of the Bahá'í faith.

ROBERT HAYDEN

Three Book Reviews

A Feel for Irony

Review of *The Delicate Balance,* by Sara Henderson Hay

Reading the best of Miss Hay's lyrics, one is impressed by the poet's moral earnestness, occasional moments of insight, and her feeling for irony and paradox. Restraint, balance, clarity, are often commendable features of her work, yet these poems lack evocative power, partly because they incline toward adroitness rather than intensity and partly because they are, with a few exceptions, conventional in tone, diction, and imagery.

Mallarmé once said that words and not ideas made a poem. Several of Miss Hay's pieces are based on essentially dramatic ideas, but they are not entirely successful because the poet has depended far too much upon the easy word or phrase, the facile image. "Noah" and "The Man Named Legion" are marred in this way. "Sonnet in Modo Antico" is written with a certain urgency and economy, but flat statement ("For I am part of the great body of man") and lackluster phrasing prevent the poem from rising above its rhetoric. The same may be said of the sonnet sequence "Eden," although the concluding sonnet on Cain is perceptive and its language apt. One of Miss Hay's assets is her skillfulness in fusing the serious and the humorous in the same poem, as in "On Suicide" and "The Pitiful Paradox." She has, too, some ability as a gentle satirist.

Strong Plea for Courage in Bleak Age

Review of *The Measure of Man,* by Joseph Wood Krutch

Mr. Krutch's new book is a sort of humanist manifesto that refutes the claims of the determinists and emphasizes the uniqueness and worth of man.

New York Times Book Review, 29 April 1951, 22.

Man, in the author's view, is not to be measured in mechanistic terms and, with all his shortcomings, is of more value than any number of electronic brains.

This book is no effusive outpouring of banalities about man's unconquerable soul or a cliché-ridden diatribe against all science. Neither is it another example of the intellectualized revivalism that many writers are today resorting to in their efforts to point out the road to physical survival.

What we have in this book is a critical examination of assumptions made by mechanistic determinists and a reaffirmation of man based upon ineluctable relationships between metaphysics and the physical sciences.

Scientists like Einstein and Conant have made clear that the space–time continuum theory and the whole matter–energy relationship, far from solving the mysteries of the universe, have brought us to the threshold of new mysteries both physical and philosophical in aspect.

The recognition of these mysteries is central to the author's thesis that man is not merely a "thinking machine" to be conditioned rather than educated by "human engineers" and demagogues.

"It is not necessary," he says, "to solve with absolute finality the metaphysical problem of the freedom of the will any more than it is necessary to solve the paradoxes of time and space in order to live in both. What is necessary is simply to recognize the fact that belief in some sort of autonomy is not incompatible with what is actually known about the behavior of either animate or inanimate matter."

Mr. Krutch makes us aware of the dangers inherent in attempts to condition men and reduce their actions to problems in statistics. These are denials of free will and moral responsibility liable to result in thought control, brainwashing, totalitarianism—evils he feels democracy is not successfully avoiding.

The author has hard words to say about sociologists and psychologists. It is obviously true that these specialists alone can never provide the medication our sick world needs.

It is also equally true that they are not entirely responsible for the misuse to which their discoveries have so often been put.

The Measure of Man is on the whole a book eminently valuable for what it has to say about the basic problems of the Age of Anxiety. It is a brilliant discourse developed with lucidity and admirable logic.

Nashville Tennessean, 11 April 1954, 21C.

Poet Continues Bitter View of Man, Life

Review of *Hungerfield and Other Poems,* by Robinson Jeffers

In "Hungerfield" Robinson Jeffers reiterates the nihilist and anti-human themes of his earlier books.

His has long been the poetry of rejection, and in the present volume his repudiation of life and the human scene appears complete. His work now has about it the finality of a farewell gesture.

For this book, as we gather from the title poem, has been written out of a great sorrow that has left the poet hating life and wholly in love with easeful death.

Written in memory of his wife, the long poem "Hungerfield" is another of Jeffers's narratives of violence and passion that provide tragedy without catharsis.

It tells, briefly, of Hawl Hungerfield's savage fight with the figure of death as it approaches his dying mother's bed and of his momentary triumph over his adversary. Counterpoised against Hungerfield's defiance of death is his mother's hatred of life and her bitter longing for annihilation.

In the end death returns to the Hungerfield home and destroys everyone but the old woman, who lives on for two years longer. Jeffers makes clear to us that his predicament is similar to hers.

Though it contains passages of considerable power, this poem, like others written in the genre Jeffers has made his own, is only partly successful, for its personas are masks of neuroses rather than human types, and their conflicts present little beyond the fascination of disaster.

This volume also contains Jeffers's adaptation of Euripides' "Hippolytus," here titled "The Cretan Woman," a verse play marred by the frequent banality of its diction, the obtrusiveness of its colloquialisms.

The shorter lyrics that complete the book are less distinguished than some Jeffers has written earlier. They repeat his Greco-Calvinist scriptures and his anger at the senseless brutality and wastefulness of modern life—an anger that might be salutary if he identified himself with the human condition.

Nashville Tennessean, 18 April 1954, 15D.

PART TWO *Reviews*

WILLIAM HARRISON

A New Negro Voice

This first volume of poetry represents the emergence of a new and vigorous talent in American letters, with an obviously encouraging prospect of attaining an even higher level of achievement in the future. The reason for this promise—*promising* is often a patronizing term on the lips of a critic, a Pharisaic "assent with civil leer"—is that Mr. Hayden has something to say, and he knows how to say it. There is a true marriage of form and content, a happy fusion of mastery of technique with the rough and raw material of life experience. Among Negro American poets only two challengers to Mr. Hayden come readily to mind: Sterling Brown and Langston Hughes.

Eleven of the poems in this volume won for Mr. Hayden a coveted literary prize, the Jules and Avery Hopwood Award of the University of Michigan, in 1938. The judges deserve to be congratulated for their discernment, as do the editors of *Opportunity,* in whose hospitable pages some of the poems made their debut. The present reviewer became acquainted with Mr. Hayden's work three years ago while in England, and still vivid is his memory of the enthusiastic response given to a reading of "Gabriel," a poem that commemorates the leader of the slave insurrection who is the hero in *Black Thunder,* Arna Bontemps's historical novel.

It is always invidious to quote poetry in truncated form, and some of Mr. Hayden's best poems are longish; "These Are My People," a mass chant, is a case in point. Varied are his moods and language. Like Sterling Brown, he has the exceptional faculty of investing a poem in dialect with tragic dignity, as, for example, "Ole Jim Crow." He has a spontaneity and originality of expression that impart to his verses an intent all their own. Whatever he has learned from English or American literary tradition he has succeeded in integrating in his style, and so, while the reader may recover faint echoes of past and contemporary masters, he will find

---

Review of *Heart-Shape in the Dust,* from *Opportunity* 19, no. 3 (March 1941): 91.

it difficult to identify them with the accuracy that imitation always guarantees.

The address of the Falcon Press is 268 Eliot Street, Detroit, and all lovers of poetry should purchase the volume, which is a distinct contribution to Negro American culture and a bright augury that makes the reader eagerly await other volumes from Mr. Hayden's pen.

GERTRUDE MARTIN

Review of *Heart-Shape in the Dust*

In this first volume of poems Mr. Hayden reveals himself a writer of unquestioned ability. He combines true lyric sense with an intelligence that does not shy away from the problems of the day. In poems like his sonnet to "E." or "The Mountains" or "Leaves in the Wind," to pick at random, his choice of words and figures and his poetic rhythm are those of a seasoned poet. The following short poem, "Old Woman with Violets," shows how apt the author is in transmitting an image with a minimum of words.

> Quiet and alone she stands
> Within the whirling market-place,
> Holding the spring in winter hands
> And April's shadow in her face.

The topical poems and the poems of protest evidence an awareness of the Negro and of the world and some small measure of hope for the future. The mass chant "These Are My People," which has been rendered in Detroit, loses nothing in the reading. The realism of certain of the poems of protest is in marked contrast to the lyric beauty of the other poems.

Mr. Hayden deserves the acclaim and encouragement of readers everywhere, but Detroiters will have a proprietary interest in his success. These first poems have a maturity of conception and a polish of form that make one look forward with interest to Mr. Hayden's artistic development. We hope that, unlike some of the major Negro poets, his career will be one of continued production and improvement.

Review of *Heart-Shape in the Dust,* from the *Michigan Chronicle,* 4 January 1941, editorial page.

JAMES W. IVY

Concerning a Poet and a Critic

The first title is a collection of poems by Robert E. Hayden. The second is a critical examination of the writings of Paul Laurence Dunbar. Mr. Hayden is a young Negro poet, a native of Detroit, who has already published many of his poems in the periodicals and who while a student at the University of Michigan won the Hopwood Award for his verse. . . .

   Mr. Hayden has lyrical ability, and his poems are readable, though many of them are banal and lacking in real poetic fire. Probably the best piece in the book is the initial "Autumnal." It sings itself into the soul of the reader. "To a Young Negro Poet," though imitiative in theme, is good too. The poems that especially appealed to me were "Gabriel," "Speech," "Shine, Mister?" and "These Are My People," a mass chant. Mr. Hayden does not write as a Negro poet oversensitive of the wrongs of his race but as a sensitive singer poetically aware of the ineffable beauties of nature and love and life. Social, economic, and racial themes are handled with a deft ironic touch hesitatingly suggestive of the tragedy that lies beneath the oft-glittering surface. Most of the poems are short lyrics. Mr. Hayden is a poet worth watching.

Review of *Heart-Shape in the Dust,* from the *Crisis* (April 1941): 128.

SELDEN RODMAN

Negro Poets

It is possible that this modest pamphlet, containing thirteen short poems by two young Negro poets, may come to be regarded as the entering wedge in the "emancipation" of Negro poetry in America. Perhaps because writing poetry demands a greater degree of self-consciousness, perhaps because verse by Negroes has hitherto tended to lean heavily and uneasily on the inimitable folk art of spirituals and blues, there has been nothing in the contemporary field to compare with, say, the painting of Horace Pippin or Jacob Lawrence. The recent books by Margaret Walker and Gwendolyn Brooks were steps in the direction of independence from a limited minstrel quaintness, but they lacked the experimental vigor of these poems.

One feels instantly behind the work of both of these very gifted poets not a persecution complex or a nostalgia for the past or for a hot piano but the whole weight of modern poetry at the service of a tragic human situation. They have learned the value of restraint. Hayden opens thus:

> Snow alters and elaborates perspectives,
> confuses South with North and would deceive
> me into that egregious error
> but for these trees that keep their summer-green
> and like a certain hue of speech mean South.

And [Myron] O'Higgins thus concludes his very moving poem on the death of Gandhi:

> Now they have taken your death to their rooms
> And here in this far city a false Spring
> Founders in the ruins of your quiet flesh
> And deep in your marvelous wounds
> The sun burns down
> And the seas return to their imagined homes.

Review of *The Lion and the Archer,* from the *New York Times Book Review,* 10 October 1949, 27.

CEDRIC DOVER

All for a Dollar

yes really it is like that and like this so you can see it is original and l'art and worth a dollar because whenever something is printed in 12 point without capitals you know because it has been known for forty years that it is original and full of dazzleclustered trees and jokes of nacre and ormolu and poltergeists in imperials and of course worth a dollar for a swooney evening on the leopard skin exploring the navel with candybar joy.

indeed all for a dollar you can join robert hayden's heart when it escapes from the mended ferris wheel and the clawfoot sarabande in its dance among

> metaphorical doors, decors of illusion
> coffeecups floating poised hysterias;
> now among mazurka dolls offering
> death-heads of peppermint roses and real violets.

now ain't that somepin and dont it prove that *counterpoise* is right in the icecream battle of azure awareness that experimentation is an "absolute necessity in keeping the arts vital and significant in contemporary life."

yes really it is like that and more like that than like this and maybe just maybe someday somewhen mr hayden will get right into selden rodman's anthology instead of *the negro caravan* (dear mr editor dont worry because you can minuscule the word when it's art) which will prove the oneness of mankind and the vision of being "violently opposed" to the wickedness of thinking that while there is sociology and politics the poet is the first sociologist and the vanguard politician.

but before you spend your dollar because it really is like that the sad truth has to be faced that in myron o'higgins the cerebral landscape's full of good brown earth and that it looks like he will scoop

Review of *The Lion and the Archer*, from the *Crisis* (August 1948): 252.

it up and sift it and mold it if he isn't "ambushed under the vines" because like a few million others in the gloryland he knows days when "the rain came down in ragged jets / and made a grave along my street."

in fact it's got to be said that o'higgins in spite of the *o* has more poise than counterpoise and that he is a Negro (with a capital) poet in the sense that every good poet who is a Negro is also a Negro poet and that only a eunuch in utopia can be a poet period and no adjective.

finally this o'higgins has roots and enough selfcriticism to know that words alone dont make a poem nor posturings a genius and believe me the young poet who can write about the young poet is no longer young

> Somebody,
> Cut his hair
> And send him out to play

also the suggestion has an attractive air of blasphemy about it on the last page of *counterpoise* but I may be wrong and you can only find out by spending a dollar with no extra charge for the 2 autographs for which one way or the other you'll surely have a dollar worth of fun.

RALPH J. MILLS, JR.

from "Four Voices in Recent American Poetry"

Robert Hayden's *A Ballad of Remembrance* is the first volume in a projected series undertaken by a small London publisher and dedicated to making available the "poetry of the North American Negro." The venture is an extremely courageous one and deserves widespread applause and support. Mr. Hayden is a poet who often takes a good many chances with his language and whose musical sense is varied and insistent. Much of his best work results, in part at least, from his obvious love of words in combination with the careful exercise of rhythmic and musical powers.

Mr. Hayden's poetry has grown out of his experience as an American Negro. Though he would certainly be entitled to open expressions of rage and denunciation, he is, instead, an objective, controlled artist who achieves durable effects. In many poems he reaches his desired accomplishment through quiet understatement and dispassionate observation. Let us select, as an example of this manner, "Tour 5," which recounts an automobile trip through the South: [quotes "Tour 5"]. With the various stages of the journey the tension of the poem increases, moving toward the climactic closing line. But only in the last few words [*harsh as bloodstained swords*] does the author release the tight reins he has kept on his emotions, and then he does so with an overwhelming force that is yet shrewdly directed through the same thematic channels as the rest of the poem.

"Tour 5" illustrates one facet of Mr. Hayden's art, for he has not limited himself to restrained accounts of his experience. In a poem like "O Daedalus, Fly Away Home" he tries, I think more successfully in some stanzas than in others, for a rich music that will carry the reader on its movements, its urge toward the dance:

Review of *A Ballad of Remembrance*, from the *Christian Scholar* 46 (Winter 1963); 337–40.

Drifting night in the Georgia pines,
coonskin drum and jubilee banjo.
   Pretty Malinda, dance with me.

Night is juba, night is conjo,
   Pretty Malinda, dance with me.

The folk element is strong in a poem of this sort, and it is very hard to maintain that element without falling into sentimentality or decorativeness. I believe that Mr. Hayden goes further with the talents mentioned previously when he employs them to render more intractable material. The title poem of his collection is a case in point. As I recall the story told me of the origins of "A Ballad of Remembrance," the author of the poem and the poet-critic Mark Van Doren were turned away because of Mr. Hayden's race from a New Orleans hotel where they wished to dine. Apparently, this occasion provided the source in the poet's own life for the poem, though it is merely touched on by way of homage to Van Doren in the last stanza. As for the rest of the poem, it uncovers a nightmare world, a shrill and terrifying carnival of death. The figures who come and go, now in shadow, now in a raw exposure of light, convey strikingly the impression of violence and corruption:

Quadroon mermaids, afro angels, black saints
balanced upon the switchblades of that air
and sang. Tight streets unfolding to the eye
like fans of corrosion and elegiac lace
crackled with their singing: Shadow of time.
Shadow of blood.

Shadow, echoed the Zulu king, dangling
from a cluster of balloons. Blood,
whined the gunmental princess, floating
over the courtyard where dead men diced.

What will you have? she inquired, the sallow vendeuse
of prepared tarnishes and jokes of nacre and ormolu,
what but those gleamings, oldrose graces,
manners like scented gloves? Contrived ghosts
rapped to metronome clack of lavalieres.

In this passage we should find it nearly impossible to trace a rational pattern of thought that operates as a control for the emotional pressures at work. But what is sacrificed—and no doubt something is—on the side of reason and logic is compensated for by the expansion of feeling and suggestion. We might say that there ought to be a balance of the two, but the hallucination that is essential to the poem is enhanced by the seeming absence of rationality. On the other hand, I do not wish to be misunderstood; my point is not that Mr. Hayden has written without plan or thought but that he has allowed the poem to be guided forward in general by the dictation of his emotions. And there can be little doubt that such a theme as he has chosen, as well as the immediate circumstance from which he has drawn details, does not lend itself very readily to detached treatment. Yet Mr. Hayden never loses the grip on his art or permits his moral vision, which is a just and compassionate one, to deteriorate into the whims of momentary feeling. We must recognize that the qualities of "A Ballad of Remembrance" are selected and achieved—the result of craft and intelligence as well as imagination.

These same qualities are evident in "Middle Passage," the most ambitious and, in that respect, fully realized poem in the book. Based on historical incident—the mutiny of Negro slaves aboard the *Amistad* in 1839—it is an intricate and moving poem of several voices, each of which adds to the total significance of the action from a different point of view. Interwoven with the chronicle of events the theme of Christian love and charity supplies ironic commentary on the supposed religiousness of the white slavers, who are hunted down by disease, fear, and finally an open rebellion by the slaves that destroys all but two of them; these men are spared in order to bring the ship to land. Through navigational miscalculation they come to America:

> voyage through death
> > to life upon these shores.

The literary devices of this poem owe something, I should think, to Browning, to Eliot's "Gerontion" and Pound's *Cantos,* though they are in no sense just imitations. Through the several perspectives and the alternating passages of irony, lyricism, dramatic tension, and genuine religious emotion the poem progresses toward the hope and human possibility implicit in its conclusion. To give some idea of the full-bodied poetic statement Mr. Hayden can muster, I will quote a part of the lengthy speech of one of the two survivors. The lines are rich and also ironical; they exhibit the desperate energy of life at the extreme: "But for the storm that flung up barriers" [and next twenty-five lines].

These lines represent Mr. Hayden at his best, I believe, and a reading of the whole poem should be sufficient to demonstrate this writer's capacity for capturing the subtleties of human motive and activity in dramatic fashion and with remarkable objectivity. This mode, over and above the more reflective one of "Tour 5," gives the poet a firm base from which he can look to further successes. There is no question but that they are forthcoming.

from Books Noted

We need the poet who "lives in life," mixes with mud, rolls in rot, claws the scoundrels, bleeds and bloodies, and, gasping in the field, writes right there, his wounds like faucets above his page, at once besmutching and ennobling it. We need, also, the poet who finds life always interesting, sometimes appalling, sometimes appealing, but consistently amenable to a clarifying enchantment via the powers of Art. His reverence for the word *Art* is what chiefly distinguishes him from Poet I. Poet II, moreover, may postpone composition until he is off the field, rid of the fray's insignia, and has had a bath.

Poet II is Robert Hayden, one of a growing group of Negro poets believing that matter is not enough, believing that there should be a marriage between matter and manner. Robert Hayden, for at least thirty years, has busied himself with a very active and earnest subscription to his faith in spite of occasional light heckling from the bare-fight-boys, the snarls of whom, indeed, have been at least half-affectionate because few are quicker than they to sense authentic quality in the work of the "enemy" and to salute it.

To young poets fascinated by the problems of technique Robert Hayden is a little school. He reaches richly, then molds and resolves with confidence and precision. And life is right there, in the finished piece. It has not been lost in the refining process. Read "The Whipping," in which a used woman, after cruelty to her child,

> . . . leans muttering against
> a tree, exhausted. purged—
> avenged in part for life-long hidings
> she has had to bear.

Read the long and powerful "Middle Passage":

Review of *Selected Poems*, from *Negro Digest* (February 1966): 51–52.

"That there was hardly room 'tween-decks for half
the sweltering cattle stowed spoon-fashion there;
that some went mad of thirst and tore their flesh
and sucked the blood . . . "

Read "The Ballad of Nat Turner":

And, purified, I rose and prayed
and returned after a time
to the blazing fields, to the humbleness.
And bided my time.

Read the well-made and passionate "Runagate Runagate":

Come ride-a my train
Mean mean mean to be free.

Listen to "Those Winter Sundays":

Sundays too my father got up early
and put his clothes on in the blueblack cold,
then with cracked hands that ached
from labor in the weekday weather made
banked fires blaze. No one ever thanked him.

I'd wake and hear the cold splintering, breaking.
When the rooms were warm, he'd call,
and slowly I would rise and dress,
fearing the chronic angers of that house,

Speaking indifferently to him,
who had driven out the cold
and polished my good shoes as well.
What did I know, what did I know
of love's austere and lonely offices?

In that straightforward but achieved simplicity we are given a
household, a race, a world.

Important, too, are the bits of languorous lyricism, which have
as much right to live as have roses (with or without compendium,
chant, or regress).

Robert Hayden is brother to many things—dolora, premise,

apprehension, sublimity, homage, terror, origin; other relatives are love and a dedication to the highest of which he himself is capable.

The jacket of *Selected Poems* is disfigured with this legend: "Writing, of course, out of his experience as an American Negro, his lines are *NEVERTHELESS* carefully controlled and disciplined." The furious capitalization and italics are mine.

DAVID GALLER

from "Three Recent Volumes"

If war presents a growing problem for poetry, being an American
Negro presents a worse one. The subject matter is inescapable—
and, if one is a Negro, he will not wish to escape it. The subject
matter is explosive and elemental; hard stuff for poets, it pro-
vides a discouraging paradox: the more you face it, the more
you are driven to one of two extremes—sentimentality or hyper-
erudition. Hughes or McKay would illustrate the former, Tolson
the latter. Hayden is saddled with both. He oscillates from semi-
dialect blues and corrupted ballads to Poundian notation; pre-
dictably, he resorts to the former for portraits of his childhood,
family, and friends and to the latter for "historical evidence" poems
describing the white man's burden. Predictably, too, with a subject
so fearfully basic and seemingly insoluble, Hayden is capable of
high eclecticism when dealing with salvation (on the theological
plane); witness his poems concerned with the Bahá'í faith, a
prominent nineteenth-century Persian sect whose leader was mar-
tyred. Might not the example of Jesus have sufficed? For the white
man, probably.

Hayden is as gifted a poet as most we have; his problem is not
one of talent but frame of reference. It is fascinating, moving, and
finally devastating that the finest verse in his book (the speech on
pages 69–70) is spoken by a Spanish sailor, a witness of the *Amistad*
mutiny, who describes the slaughter of their captors by "murderous
Africans." This speech the sailor delivers to American officials, say-
ing at one point:

> . . . We find it paradoxical indeed
> that you whose wealth, whose tree of liberty
> are rooted in the labor of your slaves
> should suffer the august John Quincy Adams

Review of *Selected Poems*, from *Poetry* 110 (1967): 267–69. Copyright © 1967 by
the Modern Poetry Association and reprinted with permission of the editor of
Poetry.

> to speak with so much passion of the right
> of chattel slaves to kill their lawful masters . . .

Hayden is a superb ironist in this passage. The crime of it is he has not chosen his forte; it has chosen him.

JAMES A. EMANUEL

On *Selected Poems*

Most of the best poems in this first volume of Hayden's to appear in the United States (*A Ballad of Remembrance* was published in a limited edition by Paul Breman in 1962 in London) reflect, sometimes in diction but mostly in content, his experiences as a Negro. Miscegenation subtly begins, then poignantly overspreads, "The Ballad of Sue Ellen Westerfield." The fantastic images of "Ballad of Remembrance" employ a hoodoo dance to explore "the down-South arcane city with death / in its jaws." The restrained hatred faced by Negro travelers in the South gives a tense atmosphere to "Tour 5." The extravagant charlatan of "Witch Doctor" develops an archetype solid and vivid in Negro satire. In "Night, Death, Mississippi" the strange coexistence of nostalgic beauty and bestial cruelty flares up from a languorous domestic scene. Two of Hayden's best-known poems, "Middle Passage" and "Runagate Runagate," dramatize, respectively, the revolting deprivations that caused the *Amistad* slave mutiny and the escape of slaves on Harriet Tubman's underground railway. The dramatic appeal of "Witch Doctor," "Runagate Runagate," and "Frederick Douglass"—a forceful, flowing tribute—was soundly demonstrated in the late 1966 Broadway presentation of Negro poetry, "A Hand Is on the Gate."

Hayden's power, though movingly authentic in his racial matter, is variously proved in his craftsmanship. The absolute economy and spare shapeliness of "The Diver," the opening line of "Belsen, Day of Liberation" ("Her parents and her dolls destroyed"), and the final stanza of "La Corrida" exemplify technical, emotional, and philosophical richness. His unsentimentality balances his occasional penchant for words like *androgynous, quondam,* and *ensorcelled.* His perfect descriptions ("the bickering spray," "kindling porches," and "leashed-back / mica'd / fall of the sea") cancel out obvious wordplay ("My candles held no power"); the quiet humor in "Mourning Poem for the Queen of Sunday" vies with the

Review of *Selected Poems,* from *Books Abroad* 41, no. 4 (Autumn 1967): 470.

grimness appropriate to "Idol (Coatlicue Aztec goddess)." Literary allusions (to Donne, Keats, Frost, Conrad, Elizabeth Stuart Phelps), counterpoint, synesthesia—these and other attractions await the reader who has not discovered this serious, able poet.

JULIUS LESTER

Words in the Mourning Time

The recent publication of Robert Hayden's new book of poems, *Words in the Mourning Time,* once again brings us the work of one of the most underrated and unrecognized poets in America. Until the publication of *Selected Poems* in 1966, Hayden was unrepresented by a book of his own poems, except for two small, privately printed books and a volume published in England. Now fifty-seven years old, he has had to wait too long for the recognition that his work has merited for twenty years. But that is primarily because he is black.

If there was scarcely a market for black writers before the 1960s, black poets must have been regarded as something odd indeed, particularly a poet who refused to be pressed into anyone's preconceived mold of what a black poet should be. Yet Hayden persevered—teaching, writing, publishing where he could and giving occasional readings.

When I entered Fisk University in the fall of 1956, he had already been there ten years in that miasma of black bourgeois gentility. On the campus he was regarded as just another instructor in the English department, teaching fifteen hours of classes a week, from two sections of freshman English to American literature to creative writing. No one at Fisk has the vaguest notion of what a poet's function was, not that they gave it any thought. Yet, somehow, Hayden continued to believe—in himself and poetry—though no one except his wife and a few students and friends in New York ever cared.

Within these circumstances being a poet could bring him no joy. Despite his pain and loneliness, he always made it clear to those of us who were foolish enough to think that we wanted to write that perhaps our experiences would be different. In creative writing classes he tried to teach us that words were our principal tool,

Review of *Words in the Mourning Time,* from the *New York Times Book Review,* 24 January 1971, 4–5, 22.

and, no matter how important we considered our "message" to be, it was the words that expressed it. Assuming that we had something to say, the importance of saying it as well as our ability allowed us could never be underestimated.

When I read his poetry, I know that I am in the presence of a man who honors language. His images give the reader a new experience of the world. In his *Selected Poems* are found such lines as: "Graveblack vultures encircle afternoon"; "palmleaf knives of sunlight"; "autumn hills / in blazonry of farewell scarlet." And in *Words in the Mourning Time* these lines appear: "His injured childhood bullied him"; "God's brooms had swept / the mist away." He chooses words with the care of a sculptor chipping into marble, and in his poem "El-Hajj Malik El-Shabazz," from *Words in the Mourning Time,* a vivid historical portrait of Malcolm X is presented in six short lines:

> He X'd his name, became his people's anger,
> exhorted them to vengeance for their past;
> rebuked, admonished them,
>
> their scourger who
> would shame them, drive them from
> the lush ice gardens of their servitude.

Such a simple phrase—"He X'd his name"—but it sets up reverberations that extend back to August 1619.

I left Nashville in 1961, and, though I saw Mr. Hayden a few times afterwards, our relationship slowly diminished. I, his "son," had to find my own way, and he found new sons in succeeding classes. The last time I saw him was in May 1966. I was working for the Student Non-Violent Coordinating Committee and had just come from the meeting in which Stokely Carmichael had been elected chairman. Black power was just a few weeks away, but Mr. Hayden had already felt the heat of its approaching flames. At a writers' conference held at Fisk a few weeks before, he had been severely attacked as an "Uncle Tom" by the students and other writers. When I walked into his house, his first words to me were a tirade against the "nationalists."

He had also just been awarded the Grand Prize for Poetry at the First World Festival of Negro Arts at Dakar, Senegal. That honor was not enough, however, to offset being rejected and attacked by black students and black writers. He had always insisted on being known as a poet, not a black poet, and he could be belligerent about it. I listened to him again as he angrily maintained that there was "no such thing as black literature. There's good literature and there's bad. And that's all!" I couldn't wholly agree then (and I'm still not sure), nor could I understand why he was so vociferous in denying that he was a black poet. After all, he was the man who had written "Middle Passage," "Frederick Douglass," and "Runagate Runagate," three of the finest poems about the black experience in the English language. Why couldn't he admit that he was a black poet?

To be a black artist has always been difficult. The mere fact that he is black means that he is associated with a "cause." It is his birthright, whether he wants it to be or not. Yet, while no one expects Philip Roth, for example, to be a spokesman for Jews, it is the black writer's fate to have his work judged more on the basis of racial content than artistic merit. This is because whites only grant the right of individuality to whites. A black is not an individual; he is the representative of a "cause." Unfortunately, blacks concur in this evaluation. They see each other as "causes" and have little, if any, use for a black writer who does not concern himself with the "cause." Both races think the black writer is a priest, offering absolution to whites or leading blacks to the holy wars.

The prevailing black aesthetic was summarized succinctly by Ron Karenga when he said, "All art must reflect and support the Black Revolution and any art that does not discuss and contribute to the revolution is invalid. Black art must expose the enemy, praise the people and support the revolution." In other words, art should be the voice of political ideology, and the black artist must comply or find himself with an indifferent white audience and no black one.

To a black artist, like Mr. Hayden, who was not conceived or reborn in the womb of black power, such thinking is not only repugnant; it is a direct assault upon art itself. By its very nature art is revolutionary, because it seeks to change the consciousness, perceptions, and very beings of those who open themselves to it. Its revolutionary nature, however, can only be mortally wounded if it must meet political prescriptions. That, however, is now being demanded of the black artist.

Robert Hayden refuses to be defined by anything other than the demands of his craft. He does not want to be restricted solely to the black experience or have his work judged on the basis of its relevance to the black political struggle. First and foremost, he is not a pawn in some kind of neo-medieval morality play. His task is, in his words, merely that which has always been the poet's task: "to reflect and illuminate the truth of human experience."

Now, I know that his desire to be regarded as nothing more or less than a poet was not a denial of his blackness but the only way he knew of saying that blackness was not big enough to contain him. He wanted to live in the universe.

In the ninth part of the title poem of *Words in the Mourning Time* he writes:

> We must not be frightened nor cajoled
> into accepting evil as deliverance from evil.
> We must go on struggling to be human,
> though monsters of abstraction
> police and threaten us.
>
> Reclaim now, now renew the vision of
> a human world where godliness
> is possible and man
> is neither gook nigger honkey wop nor kike
>
> but man
>   permitted to be man.

If we ever reach that time when man is permitted to be man, one of the reasons will be men and women like this poet, Robert Hayden, who, when pressed into the most terrifying corners of loneliness, refused to capitulate to those who, in the screaming agony of their own pain and loneliness, could do nothing but return evil for evil.

ANGELA JACKSON

"The Night-Blooming Cereus"

The Night-Blooming Cereus, by Robert Hayden, is a wisp of a book. What is here to hold onto?

Most of these poems are more practiced memory of deliberate dream than memory hung in the center of life; never at the center of Black/activity in this world; it dwells along the periphery, coreless.

There are moments of spiritual hush and whimsy that tag the dry movement: the title poem and this brief enchantment, "Dance the Orange":

> And dance this
> boneharp tree
>
> and dance this
> boneflower tree
>
> tree in the
> snowlight
>
> miming a dancer
> dancing a tree

I keep thinking of a silhouette of a spiny and muscular African ballet or boogaloo. Maybe Hayden has some other folk/dances in mind? In "Smelt Fishing" Hayden tells a three-part story in haiku; the result is not stunning or acute. There is a pinpoint of illumination at the ending. This is trick-or-treat for the intellect.

The most definite joy of this volume is "The Night-Blooming Cereus." It is lithe and sure, a dancing whisper to "celebrate the blossom" and the original miracle of life. I will remember the encroaching hush of this last stanza:

Review of *The Night-Blooming Cereus,* from *Black World* 24, no. 11 (September 1975): 87–88.

> We spoke
> in whispers when
> we spoke
> at all.

That is the way of this volume at its best. At its least it is artificial and artistically conventized. Intellectually circumscribed. That is how "The Ballad of the True Beast" is remembered, along with "The Peacock Room" and the few remaining moments in this book. The tone and diction of the bulk of the volume are frankly studied. I can hear the sculptor's chisel sound in the center of a sentence.

Even in this voice of sterile and omitted memory and vision Hayden knows best the words for this night:

> a world
> abstract as memories of earth
> the traveling dead take home

There is a faint pulse, but I still do not hear a heart.

WILLIAM LOGAN

Language against Fear

Offered the chance that all selections offer, to expunge, silently, the errors and excesses of early work, Robert Hayden has retained all but two of the poems that formed his 1966 *Selected Poems*. This is a poet secure about the past, and the past work. That work, continued here by eight new poems and the bulk of two interim volumes, has shifted its emphasis, gradually, from narrative to symbolism. The earlier poems, heavily dependent on story, have broken down now entirely into words, some of rich personal association: "Plowdens, Finns, / Sheffeys, Haydens, / Westerfields. // Pennsylvania gothic, / Kentucky home-spun, / Virginia baroque." The new poems have a spareness that resists first reading but which eventually rewards with the radiance of hard-earned, hard-edged memory. Of a night-blooming cereus:

> Lunar presence,
> foredoomed, already dying,
> it charged the room
> with plangency
>
> older than human
> cries, ancient as prayers
> invoking Osiris, Krishna,
> Tezcátlipóca.

Hayden exploits the classics and the contemporary, historical anecdote and personal encounter to demonstrate that what grants history poignancy—that it cannot be altered—also gives pathos to the personal. His explorations of black history appear in choice of subject matter and a slight widening of technique to include occasional swatches of song and dialect, rather than as impenetrable

---

Review of *Angle of Ascent*, from *Poetry* 130 (July 1977): 267–69. Copyright © 1977 by the Modern Poetry Association and reprinted by permission of the editor of *Poetry*.

anger or voguish posture. He produces homages to both Mark Van Doren and Malcolm X; his poems conjure up a variety of lives caught in the desperation of poverty or that of decadence. His most extreme emotions, and successes, reserved for the era that began with the arrival of slaves in America and ended with the Civil War and Reconstruction, produce a number of serious, haunted poems, including "The Dream," "The Ballad of Sue Ellen Westerfield," and the stunning "Middle Passage."

"Middle Passage" is a deceptive piece, a perfectly modulated pastiche of voices contained in diary, deposition, and reminiscence, which has for its subject the slave trade between Africa and America. The poem exhibits a toughness of language and a variety of method, including prose, parody, and prayer, that create effects of horror and anger in service of a passage through history, the "voyage through death / to life upon these shores."

> Sails flashing to the wind like weapons,
> sharks following the moans the fever and the dying;
> horror the corposant and compass rose.

> *Deep in the festering hold thy father lies,*
> *of his bones New England pews are made,*
> *those are altar lights that were his eyes.*

>   A plague among
> our blacks—Ophthalmia: blindness—& we
> have jettisoned the blind to no avail.
> It spreads, the terrifying sickness spreads.
> Its claws have scratched sight from the Capt.'s eyes
> & there is blindness in the fo'c'sle.

As "Shuttles in the rocking loom of history, / the dark ships move, the dark ships move"; woven from the mingling of many tales, many terrors, is a display of the mortal blindness at slavery's heart, of self-interest that destroys the self and breaks men like twigs. "Middle Passage" is the best contemporary poem I have read on slavery. It is a singular performance, one that Hayden's later poems have not matched, in part because it is a poem whose special construction does not invite imitation.

Hayden has not discovered other methods rich enough to encompass public or private history so well. The defects that mar his poetry include compositional tics (repetition, for example: "the name he never can he never can repeat") and, especially in the newer poems, occasional opaqueness. Some recent poems are contrived from feelings so momentary that only a fleeting satisfaction is achieved. At worst, in the new work the phrases break up, the words fly apart, and the associative structure holds no meaning. The poems may shatter into component images, individually attractive but fragmentary. There are few first-rate metaphors; the poems that remain in the mind persuade by narrative, not image. As one moves through the book, it is disconcerting to find the older poems last. Such an ordering places the newer poems, whose methods are smaller, and which should be seen as the product of development, at a disadvantage; as the older poems drape themselves in description and narration, the newer work seems insubstantial.

MICHAEL S. HARPER

Angle of Ascent

This is Robert Hayden's sixth book of poems, its appearance auspiciously occurring almost simultaneously with his election as the 1975 Fellow of the Academy of American Poets for "distinguished poetic achievement," an award that has been a long time in coming. Hayden was born and raised in Detroit and grew up as one who feared "those who feared the riot-squad of statistics." A Spanish major in college, he studied with Auden at the University of Michigan, where Hayden has taught since 1969. There he won the Hopwood prize for a sequence of poems tentatively entitled "The Black Spear." In those poems are the seeds of his bicentennial classic, "Middle Passage," and other highlights like the rhythmically accented sonnet that ends *Angle of Ascent*, "Frederick Douglass":

> Oh, not with statues' rhetoric,
> not with legends and poems and wreaths of bronze alone,
> but with the lives grown out of his life, the lives
> fleshing his dream of the beautiful, needful thing.

Hayden has always been a symbolist poet struggling with historical fact, his rigorous portraits of people and places providing the synaptic leap into the interior landscape of the soul, where prayers for illumination and perfection are focused on the oneness of mankind. Having committed himself to the improvement of language, he has sometimes been falsely accused of timidity of commitment to the black struggle because of his refusal to "politicize" his work for expedient and transient goals. But it is Hayden's poetry that best captures the Afro-American tradition of the black hero, from the slave narratives and the testimonials of Douglass, Harriet Tubman, Sojourner Truth, to musicians and jazz singers

Review of *Angle of Ascent* from the *New York Times Book Review* 22 February 1976
34 35.

such as Bessie Smith, Billie Holiday, Miles Davis. Hayden is the
master conversationalist and handler of idiom; his perfect pitch is
always pointed toward heroic action and his central images are
almost always an embracing of kin. He has never abandoned his
people. One might find them on St. Antoine Street, where Hayden
lived as a boy with his foster parents, making visits to local stores,
seeing synagogues become black churches ("But the synagogue be-
came / New Calvary"), or just catching glimpses:

> then Elks parades and big splendiferous
> Jack Johnson in his diamond limousine
> set the ghetto burgeoning
> with fantasies
> of Ethiopia spreading her gorgeous wings.

Though Hayden has not written about his mother directly, it is
her voice that informs his love of detail and spice; he alludes to her
passing in "Approximations" ("In dead of winter / wept beside
your open grave. / Falling snow"), an approximate haiku fused with
his own experience. He has been critical of his own slow pace in
turning out poems, of what he has summarized as "slim offerings
over four decades." But his own assessments should include the
teachableness of this volume to an increasing public audience. From
Detroit's Paradise Valley—

> The sporting people
> along St. Antoine—
> that scufflers'
> paradise of ironies—
> bet salty money
> on his righteous
> hook and jab

—to the composite persona parceled from asides he got from his
mother—

> A shotgun on his shoulder,
> his woman big with child and
> shrieking curses after him,
>
> Joe Finn came down from
> Allegheny wilderness
> to join Abe Lincoln's men.

> Goddamning it survives the
> slaughter at the Crater.
> Disappears into his name.

—Hayden is the poet of perfect pitch.

His living in the South for twenty-two years while at Fisk University accounts in part for his small output:

> Here symbol houses
> where the brutal dream lives out its lengthy
> dying. Here the past, adored and
> unforgiven. Here the past—
> soulscape, Old Testament battleground
> of warring shades whose weapons kill.

Hayden could not accommodate or adjust himself to the "Locus" of segregation, the nightmare landscape ever present in our history.

His experiments with the ballad form have produced singular achievements—ballads in spirit in the language, with dramatic tension and economy that adapt to his personal view of history:

> And purified, I rose and prayed
> and returned after a time
> to the blazing fields, to the humbleness.
> And bided my time.

Hayden's "Ballad of Nat Turner," written before the Turner controversy of the late 1960s,* demonstrates how he does this, dwelling on the high points of the mysterious and archaic roots of black folk rhythms.

His search for kinfolk is the permanent condition of his poetry and his personality:

> And when he gets to where the voices were—
> Don't cry, his dollbaby wife implores;
> I know where they are, don't cry.
> We'll go and find them, we'll go
> and ask them for your name again.

---

*Editors' Note: William Styron's novel of 1967, *The Confessions of Nat Turner,* prompted widespread debate because of Styron's interpretation of Turner's motives for leading a slave rebellion in Virginia in 1831.

Or in "Belsen, Day of Liberation":

> Her parents and her dolls destroyed,
>   her childhood foreclosed,
> she watched the foreign soldiers from
>   the sunlit windows whose black bars
>
> Were crooked crosses inked upon
>   her pallid face. "Liebchen,
> Liebchen, you should be in bed."
>   But she felt ill no longer.

Hayden memorializes the experiences of Rosey Pool, who at Fisk told a black convocation how people in concentration camps wanted to pray but could not agree on what prayers; "they sang Negro spirituals and poems by Negro poets," she told them.

Angle of Ascent is a book that is told. The title comes from the poem "For a Young Artist," which grew out of a conversation with a young musician set upon "astral projection," the attempt to live and create on the highest spiritual plane. Hayden's answer is to find transcendence living among the living. In "Stars" Sojourner Truth "Comes walking barefoot / out of slavery / ancestress / childless mother / following the stars / her mind a star," giving testimony to Hayden's living "angle of ascent / achieved."

RICHMOND LATTIMORE

from "Poetry Chronicle"

The new volume by Robert Hayden includes, with three earlier books, a valued handful of new poems. Hayden writes mostly as a black man and mostly in exquisitely pure English (colloquial only when appropriate). The record of wrong, past and present, is inevitably there. "Middle Passage," a six-page poem about the early slave trade, spares nothing, though it can pause to note the names of slave ships—*Jesús, Estrella, Esperanza, Mercy, Desire, Adventure, Tarter, Ann,* and *Bella J*—as "the dark ships move, / their bright ironical names / like jests of kindness on a murderer's mouth." And there are the terrifying lynch memories of "Night, Death, Mississippi" and the runaways of the Civil War (and the black soldier, too) on down to the black man of today ("Tour 5"), who stops to "buy gas and ask directions of a rawboned man / whose eyes revile us as the enemy." These not surprising themes never degenerate into hysteria or propaganda. The poet who pursued them comes through as a temperate warm wise and cultured man and above all as a poet well skilled in language and line. His matter is varied and by no means exclusively black; or sometimes, if so, in subtle and sophisticated ways. "The Peacock Room" is simply a lovely poem. Or consider "Butterfly Piece":

> Brazilian butterflies, static and perfect as
>   enamelwork by Fabergé. Jewel corpses fixed
> in glass. Black opal flowerskin banded
>   neargold yellow; sea-agate striped berylgreen;
>
> Colors so intense I imagine them heavy enough
>   to have broken the live wings—as human
> colors in our inhuman world burden, break.

Review of *Angle of Ascent* from Hudson Review 2, no. 1 (Spring 1976): 163–20.

There is something universal about that short poem. Or consider "A Plague of Starlings." On Fisk campus the workmen have been shooting the swarming birds. The poem ends:

> And if not careful
> I shall tread
> upon carcasses
> carcasses when I
> go mornings now
> to lecture on
> what Socrates,
> the hemlock hour nigh,
> told sorrowing
> Phaedo and the rest
> about the migratory
> habits of the soul.

Starlings are blackish, and the survivors had returned "like choice-less poor / to a dangerous / dwelling place." True. But the irony and the compassion belong only to a master poet moved by such feelings.

EDWARD HIRSCH

Mean to Be Free

In "[American Journal]," the last poem in this collection, Robert
Hayden—who once said that "nothing human is foreign to me"—
wryly assumes the voice of an extraterrestrial observer reporting on
a "baffling / multi people," a country of charming and enlightened
savages, "brash newcomers lately sprung up in our galaxy." The en-
gaged yet alienated observer was a fitting persona for a man who
always identified with the figure of the outsider and who often re-
ferred to himself as an "alien at home." I once saw a documentary
on Hayden that showed him moving through his old neighbor-
hood on Detroit's east side, talking about his past and pointing out
the familiar landmarks of his childhood. The trouble was that few
of those landmarks remained. A warehouse had replaced the house
where he was born, and, across the street, a parking lot and power
plant stood in place of the house where he was raised. As Hayden
paused there—gentle, nearsighted, bundled up against the bleak
January afternoon—it was easy to understand why displacement
was a central poetic subject of his. Because no single place was
home for him, every place was home.

   And yet it is also revealing that Hayden's alien stand-in observes
and contemplates not the entire earth but only the portion of it
called America, a place that is, as he says, "as much a problem in
metaphysics as / it is a nation." For Hayden America represented "a
kind of microcosm," a heterogeneous new world working out an
emblematic destiny. He was repelled by our "strangering" racial dis-
tinctions but intensely attracted to our ideal of freedom, and, like
his alien ethnographer, he spent much of his intellectual energy
trying to penetrate and name some American "essence" or "quid-
dity." However internationalist he was in outlook, his life's work
makes clear that he was an American poet, deeply engaged by the
topography of American myth in his efforts to illuminate the
American black experience. He read American history as a long,

Review of *Collected Poems*, from the *Nation*, 21 December 1985, 685–86.

tortuous struggle in psychic evolution, an exercise in humanity. An alien at home, he nonetheless contended with America as the place where "we must go on struggling to be human." His *Collected Poems* should become one of our exemplary poetic texts.

Scrupulously and unobtrusively edited by Frederick Glaysher, Hayden's *Collected Poems* brings together work from nine books written over more than forty years. His first volume, *Heart-Shape in the Dust,* published in 1940, and his two pamphlets, *The Lion and the Archer* (1948) and *Figure of Time: Poems* (1955), are poorly represented here because he came to feel they poorly represented him. He considered his early poems "'prentice pieces" and only a limited number survived for publication in his first mature volumes, *A Ballad of Remembrance* (1962) and *Selected Poems* (1966). Hayden's early work dutifully followed the themes and forms of the Harlem Renaissance and relied heavily on his experience as a folklore researcher for the Detroit branch of the Federal Writers' Project in the late 1930s. As his work progressed, he began to shed his first poetic models: Edna St. Vincent Millay, Carl Sandburg, Langston Hughes, and, most important, Countee Cullen. Slowly he developed a consciously modernist style, a type of tersely written symbolic lyric, often with an Afro-American inflection that was all his own.

By the time of *A Ballad of Remembrance,* which starts off the *Collected Poems,* Hayden had already developed his characteristic style: "meditative, ironic, richly human," as he wrote of Mark Van Doren. He was a "romantic realist," a formal lyricist with a feeling for the baroque, a symbolist poet who distrusted external reality but nonetheless felt compelled to grapple with history. Like his mentor Auden, with whom he studied, Hayden's work is a little anthology of poetic forms, though in general he favored two types over others: the spare, well-chiseled, "objective" lyric and the long, fragmentary, collage-like history poem. Hayden was never prolific, and his *Collected Poems* is not a long book—in addition to *A Ballad of Remembrance,* it consists of *Words in the Mourning Time, The Night-Blooming Cereus, Angle of Ascent,* and *American Journal.* And yet it has a profound and passionate scope. Every one of its poems is meticulously crafted.

At the time of his death, in 1980, Hayden, who was a professor of English at the University of Michigan and the first black consultant in poetry to the Library of Congress, had finally begun to receive the recognition he deserved. But most of his writing life was spent in relative obscurity. As Michael S. Harper recalls in a recent special issue of *Obsidian,* Hayden often thought of himself as the "best *unknown* American poet in the country" and used to add: "I'm in trouble with the Afro-Americans *also.*" He meant by this that during the 1960s, when he was teaching at Fisk University, he was frequently attacked for not being "black" enough, for writing in traditional Western forms and for privileging poetry over race. Hayden followed the lead of Countee Cullen and insisted, sometimes at considerable personal cost, that the Afro-American poet ought to be considered and judged first of all as a poet. He thought of Afro-American poetry as part of American literature, and he believed the poet was an individual maker, bound by his own conscience, and not a sociologist. All of Hayden's poems are alive with the experience of a black American, but he was determined to bridge the wide chasm of race.

Freedom is the great subject of Hayden's work, his poetic touchstone. He considered the need for freedom a constant beyond history—"the deep immortal human wish, / the timeless will," as he said in "Middle Passage"—but understood that the struggle for freedom takes place inside history. In a number of long poems dealing with nineteenth-century America (which he once planned as a unified series to be called "The Black Spear"), Hayden rediscovered and celebrated a group of individual heroes, primarily blacks, who ferociously opposed slavery: Sojourner Truth, who "comes walking barefoot / out of slavery"; Cinquez, who led the successful slave rebellion on the *Amistad;* Harriet Tubman, who escaped from slavery and then became one of the most spectacular agents of the Underground Railroad, continually making the hard journey from "Can't to Can"; Nat Turner; John Brown; and, of course, Frederick Douglass. Hayden's characteristic method in these poems is the collage, a form that works by the ironic juxtaposition of different voices. In "Middle Passage," for example, he mixes his own descriptive commentary with the voices of slave traders, hymn singers, and even the dead. So, too, he splices together and adapts descriptions from journal entries, ships' logs, depositions, and the eyewitness accounts of traders. These formal innovations give his history poems an uncanny ethnographic basis, a profound sense of the human suffering caused by slavery.

Like Harriet Tubman, all Hayden's heroes "Mean mean mean to be free" and lead others to freedom. Their legacy is the lives their lives insure: the nameless slaves escaping to freedom in "Runagate

Runagate," the "many lives" transfigured in "Middle Passage." This idea is resoundingly expressed in Hayden's sonnet to Frederick Douglass, which begins,

> When it is finally ours, this freedom, this liberty, this beautiful
> and terrible thing, needful to man as air,
> usable as earth.

and concludes by affirming that Douglass will be remembered

> not with statues' rhetoric,
> not with legends and poems and wreaths of bronze alone,
> but with the lives grown out of his life, the lives
> fleshing his dream of the beautiful, needful thing.

Hayden's fine rhetorical poem, reminiscent of Hopkins's sonnet "That Nature Is a Heraclitean Fire," asserts that what matters is not freedom for the self alone but the communal realization of the dream. In this sense he is a utopian poet.

Hayden's historical and public poems are counterbalanced by personal lyrics like "Homage to the Empress of the Blues," "Mourning Poem for the Queen of Sunday," "'Summertime and the Living . . .,'" "The Rabbi," and, my personal favorites, "The Whipping" and "Those Winter Sundays." Written at various times during his life, these poems rely on childhood experiences in a Detroit slum ironically known as Paradise Valley. Hayden refused to sentimentalize his past—as a child growing up, his primary desire was to escape the world that surrounded him, and he also determined to remember it accurately. He was born Asa Sheffey but raised as Robert Hayden (a duality that haunted him), and he knew both his natural and foster parents. He was bound to his childhood as the foster son of poor, working-class people and remained committed to what he liked to call "folk" people: poor, uneducated, dignified, all those who quietly fulfilled "love's austere and lonely offices."

There is a certain detachment even in Hayden's most personal lyrics, a slight distancing of what he calls "the long warfare with self / with God." He once said that "reticence has its esthetic values, too," and his typical method was to exteriorize and objectify the past by speaking about it in the third person or by using the disguise of a persona. In a sense he was like the diver in the opening lyric of the *Collected Poems:* a man who needed to keep control as he moved down into the oceanic depths, who longed to fling aside his mask and be done forever with the "vain complexity" of the self but continually managed to pull himself away from the silenced wreck and recommence "the measured rise." There is a muted but powerful longing for transcendence in Hayden's work, and the diver is close kin to the figure of the old man with bloodstained wings in "For a Young Artist," who begins sprawled out in a pigsty but ends by somehow managing to fly again, "the angle of ascent / achieved." Both the diver and the old man are figures of the triumphant artist.

PART THREE *General Essays*

Robert Hayden Remembered

A few years ago, when I read Arna Bontemps's introduction to *The Harlem Renaissance Remembered* (1984), I complained privately that he evoked the Renaissance with the whispers of memory and nostalgia, not with the stentorian voice of analysis and scholarly research—a voice that I would have preferred to hear. As I prepared for this presentation, however, I found myself succumbing to the temptation to imitate Bontemps. No matter how hard I tried to focus on facts to demonstrate the achievement of Robert Hayden, I could not resist recalling how three incidents have shaped my thoughts about him as a poet. Finally, I surrendered to a procedure against which I advise my students. Rather than controlling my thoughts, forcing them to carry me to my analytical destination, I allowed them to range freely. Eventually, we reached an end—not with the promised "The Achievement of Robert Hayden" but with a presentation more aptly entitled "Robert Hayden Remembered."

I

The first incident occurred in 1968. By this time Hayden had published five volumes of poetry: *Heart-Shape in the Dust* (1940), *The Lion and the Archer* (with Myron O'Higgins, 1949), *Figure of Time* (1955), *A Ballad of Remembrance* (1962), and *Selected Poems* (1966). I wanted to include his poetry in an anthology that I was editing, but the permissions fee far exceeded the amount that I could pay from the modest budget that my publisher had approved. When I called Hayden's publisher to negotiate a lower fee, the permissions officer told me curtly: "We've got to get as much as we can out of him now. We haven't made any money from him before." The episode

---

Keynote Address at the Robert Hayden Memorial Conference, University of Michigan, 22 February 1990.

ended more pleasantly. I called Hayden, who, although he scarcely knew me, was sufficiently kind to lower the fee.

As I prepared this essay, memory of the permissions officer's brutally candid conclusion caused me to wonder why the author of five volumes of poetry would remain relatively unknown and underappreciated, not only during the 1950s and 1960s but even during the late 1960s. The officer's response caused me to wonder why Hayden had been undervalued even by his colleagues at Fisk, where, as John Hatcher has pointed out, the administration required him to teach a load of fifteen or more hours per week;[1] and why he would be undervalued in his early years at Michigan, where—as Hayden told me years after the fact—his department head refused to grant him leave when he was first invited to be a Consultant in Poetry at the Library of Congress, even though he would have been the first Black to be so honored. Why did his light shine so faintly?

First, neither literary agents nor publishers expect to buy palaces from the proceeds of poets,[2] but the plight of a Black poet of the 1950s and early 1960s was even more severe than that of others. Neither white publishers nor white scholars considered Black poets marketable. During the years before the 1960s a reader of the most widely circulated American anthologies—those used in classrooms—would have seen scant work from African-American poets. Perhaps there would be a dialect poem or two from Paul Laurence Dunbar, one of America's three most popular poets at the turn of the century—a poet highly praised by the eminent William Dean Howells; a writer who, in ten years, published more books of original fiction and poetry than any other Black writer, from Phillis Wheatley in 1773 until Langston Hughes finally matched him in the late 1950s after three decades of publications. Perhaps there would be a poem or two from Countee Cullen, who benefited from the high praise of George Lyman Kittredge, a famous literary scholar at Harvard University. Perhaps a poem by Langston Hughes. And, during the 1950s, perhaps a poem by Gwendolyn Brooks, who had won a Pulitzer Prize for poetry in 1950—the first African-American to receive a Pulitzer for literature. What room was left for the poetry of a Black teacher of English at a small Black college in the South? He could find a place in an all-Black anthology, such as the Hughes-Bontemps *The Poetry of the Negro* (1949). But all-Black anthologies were few. The result for most Black poets can be summarized by the experience of Frank Marshall Davis, an

African-American poet of the 1930s and 1940s. In 1971 Davis told me that his poetry had appeared in more anthologies during the three years between 1968 and 1971 than during the twenty-five years preceding.

A second reason for the relative invisibility of Robert Hayden is that, during the decades of the 1940s through the 1960s, his literary light seemed faint when compared with the sparkling rays of fellow African Americans. In 1940, when the twenty-seven-year-old Hayden published his first book of poetry, Richard Wright's *Native Son* stunned American readers and sounded a tone of social protest for Black literature of the decade. Wright so dominated the African-American literary scene that some critics—simplistically, I believe—have applied the label of the "Richard Wright School" to most Black writers who published their first novels in the late 1940s: Chester Himes, *If He Hollers Let Him Go* (1945); Ann Petry, *The Street* (1947); Willard Motley, *Knock on Any Door* (1947); William Gardner Smith, *The Last of the Conquerors* (1948); and even Frank Yerby, who followed the protest tradition in an early short story, "Health Card" (1944).

Although most readers familiar only with his later poetry would be astonished to consider him identified with the protest tradition, Hayden, in his first book, denounced economic oppression, racism, and lynching. Nevertheless, his blunt opposition to oppression in this work does not reveal Hayden's artistic genius. For example, in "The Negro to America," an anti-lynching poem, the persona of the poem challenges America:

> You are not free
> So long as there's
> A mortgage on
> My liberty;
> So long as I die
> On the Klansman's tree,
> You are not
> Democracy.

Twenty-six years later, in "Night, Death, Mississippi," Hayden explored the subject of lynching with an artistic restraint that conjures a horrifying reality missing from the earlier poem.

Even though Hayden's talent and temperament did not assert themselves best in the overt protest for which Black literature of the 1940s is remembered, he fit comfortably into African-American literature of the 1950s. By 1950 America, in the five years since the end of World War II, seemed to have improved conditions for Black Americans. The postwar economy and the GI Bill enriched Blacks economically and opened doors to higher education that might increase their economic opportunities even further. In 1948 President Harry Truman established a Fair Employment Practices Commission and integrated units of the Armed Services. He was reelected later that year despite opposition not only from the Republican Party but also from the Dixiecrat Party—Southern rebels from the Democratic Party who disapproved of his "liberal" positions. His victory seemed to guarantee that America would improve civil rights and economic opportunities for African Americans. In the late 1940s also, the moguls of Hollywood were forced to agree to substitute more favorable images of Blacks for the derogatory caricatures that previously had shuffled across motion picture screens. And a few judgments by the Supreme Court increased the access of Blacks to higher education—colleges, universities, professional schools.

The decade of the 1950s produced even more significant stepping stones by which Blacks hoped to journey "from Can't to Can." The most notable of these were the 1954 Supreme Court decision in *Brown v. the Board of Education,* which provided an opportunity for Black children to enter previously all-white public schools, and the Montgomery Bus Boycott, which gave birth to Martin Luther King, Jr. In a decade that spawned optimism many African-American writers forsook overt social protest in favor of work exploring the culture and, above all, the humanness of Black Americans. By examining the lives and natures of individualized Blacks rather than presenting prototypical representatives of the race, the writers revealed how closely their protagonists—despite some cultural differences, despite differences of hair texture, despite more sun-tanned skins—resembled the best white Americans in the important characteristics of virtues and hopes. A list of only a few works will reveal this theme: Gwendolyn Brooks's *Annie Allen* (1949), Ralph Ellison's *Invisible Man* (1952), James Baldwin's *Go Tell It on the Mountain* (1953), Louis Peterson's drama *Take a Giant Step* (1953), Paule Marshall's *Brown Girl, Brownstones* (1959), and Lorraine Hansberry's *Raisin in the Sun* (1959).

This was an African-American literary environment in which Robert Hayden, thirty-eight years old in 1951, should have flourished, for, as Pontheolla T. Williams has stated in her excellent analysis of Hayden's poetry, Hayden delineated "the black experience as it applies to every man."[3] But, as has often been said, the myopic American literary establishment seems capable of seeing only one or two Black writers at a time. In the 1950s Richard Wright was still the focus of critical attention in fiction; Gwendolyn Brooks was the Pulitzer poet; Langston Hughes still produced prolifically; and, at the end of the decade, Lorraine Hansberry won a Drama Critics Circle Award. Even Ellison and Baldwin did not shine in the limelight during the 1950s. *Invisible Man* was not fully honored, not even by Black scholars, until a poll of critics and writers during the 1960s proclaimed it to be the most distinguished American novel since World War II; and, despite the artistic merit of the essays in *Notes of a Native Son* (1955), Baldwin did not receive popular national acclaim until he published the more angry *Nobody Knows My Name* (1961). In the restricted gallery provided by the American literary establishment of the 1950s, there was still scant place for the poet teaching English at Fisk University.

Black literature of the 1960s seemed to contrast dramatically with that of the 1950s. The civil rights demonstrations blaring from the television sets at dinner time startled many white Americans, who turned to autobiographies and essays by Blacks to learn who "these people" were and what they wanted. Baldwin's *The Fire Next Time* (1963), King's *Why We Can't Wait* (1964), Malcolm X's *Autobiography* (1965)—these were the books that white Americans wanted to read. On the other side, many young African Americans desired works that would "tell it like it is."[4] By the end of the decade the new literary heroes for these young Blacks were young writers, some of whom had not published a book—young writers who proposed to use their poetry and drama as political weapons: LeRoi Jones (soon to call himself Amiri Baraka), Don L. Lee (today Haki R. Madhubuti), Nikki Giovanni (a student at Fisk while Hayden—and John O. Killens—taught there), Sonia Sanchez, Etheridge Knight, and others. Fiery, sometimes profane, often seeming to value message above art, these writers sold slim volumes of poetry in numbers that still baffle many English teachers, who ask, "How can any poet be considered a revolutionary for the masses when everyone knows that only a few, select people read poetry?"

Midway through this decade Hayden stumbled into a controversy about Black Art. The battle began on his own campus but spread so far that, as John Hatcher has observed, "for the next several years, hardly an anthology or discussion which included Hayden did not mention the controversy regarding his stand."[5] At the very moment at which Africans celebrated Hayden in the motherland, he had become a pariah among some young African Americans, who charged that he was not sufficiently "Black."

Because Hayden had not benefited from the visibility that he deserved during the 1940s, 1950s, and 1960s, it is perhaps no wonder that the publisher in 1968 greedily wished to recover the maximum cost from anyone who would print Hayden's work.

II

The Black Arts controversy is the point at which to introduce the second incident that shaped my thoughts about Hayden as I prepared this essay. In the academic year 1970–71, while I taught at the University of Michigan, the Center for African and Afro-American Studies sponsored a festival that included a reading by Hayden, who by then had returned to the University of Michigan from Fisk. While discussing possible topics for the paper that he was required to write in my class, a young Black student informed me that he planned to boycott Hayden's presentation. Although he had never read a poem written by Hayden, the student thought that he had heard enough about the controversy to know that no right-thinking Black should waste his time listening to Hayden. With malice in mind, I promptly encouraged the student to write his paper about Hayden; then I sent the student upstairs to Hayden's office in Haven Hall to arrange an appointment. By the time the student completed the paper, he had become genuinely converted to belief in Hayden, had read all of Hayden's books of poetry, and now praised him as ardently as he previously had denounced him.[6] What the militant, nationalistic student had expected to find in Hayden's office was an "oreo"—to use the term that was popular at that time: a person who was black on the outside, white on the inside. What the student found, instead, was a Black human being who needed no slogans or signboards to assert his Blackness.

As Hatcher insists, the controversy has been discussed too long. Summarized simply, the situation was this. At a conference of Black writers at Fisk University in 1966 the writers were asked whether they were, first, Negroes or artists. Whereas other writers proclaimed the primacy of their negritude, Hayden responded that he was a poet. Attacked by other writers, Hayden stubbornly fought back for the very right that Black cultural nationalists were demanding for Black people: the right to define himself and to resist any definition thrust upon him by others.

Hayden was not the only African-American writer of the times to be wounded similarly by poisoned words from members of their race. Envenomed pens also probed the hearts of such writers as Ralph Ellison and James McPherson, who subsequently became the first Black American to win a Pulitzer Prize for fiction (*Elbow Room,* 1977). The times proved false the childhood rhyme "Sticks and stones may break my bones, but words can never hurt me." The rhyme was false, for the words challenged the lives and souls of mature African Americans who had struggled against racist oppression for more years than their young assailants had lived. I recall the great scholar Saunders Redding muttering furiously that, if young *Negroes* thought that they were experiencing difficulty in white colleges during the 1960s, they should have been around when he attended one during the 1930s. Redding needed no new racial name to affirm his identity; he had labored to bring dignity and pride to the word *Negro.* Therefore, when he and Arthur Davis published their anthology of African-American literature, he defiantly threw down the gauntlet by calling it *Cavalcade, Negro American Writers from 1760 to the Present* at a time when *Black* had been adopted by white publishers, who were willing to permit "those people" to call themselves anything that would sell books.

I did not and do not take sides in the controversy on a personal or ideological level. On a personal level I hope that I have enjoyed the respect and friendship of Madhubuti and of Hayden, who, at times, stood at the front as the champions of the warring camps of poets.

In ideology the clash, simply or simplistically stated, seemed to be this: Black Arts writers and critics—such as Baraka, Larry Neal, Ron Karenga, Madhubuti, John Killens, and Addison Gayle—insisted that Black writers should write about Black subjects, for Black people, to educate them to their need for liberation. Moreover, Black writers should use only styles derived from Black tradition, should write according to a Black Aesthetic, and should accept criticism only from those who respected their purposes. By 1966 Robert Hayden would have responded that a Black writer should be permitted to write on any subject, for any audience, for any purpose, with any style, and with any aesthetic. Even though I believe that many of the attacks on Hayden, Ellison, and McPherson were ill advised, I respect the integrity of the Black writers and critics who, knowing that African Americans must muster a unified front against America's racism, wished to persuade all Blacks to join them in what they believed to be the only plan that would insure survival and success. But I defend with equal vigor the right of Robert Hayden, like Jean Toomer and Countee Cullen a generation before him, to define himself and his identity as a writer. (Ironically, Toomer and Cullen had fought against the efforts of white critics to define Black writers, whereas Hayden battled against his own race.) In short, I insist that any description of the canon of Black American literature must include both Baraka and Madhubuti and their entourage and Hayden and his. They all are ours, and we are theirs.

Except for the deep wounds that it left, I would call the Hayden–Black Arts controversy as exaggerated as that of Booker T. Washington and W. E. B. Du Bois. In both instances uninformed adherents identified only polar differences and failed to note the similarities. If Washington argued for a trade education for Blacks and seemed to surrender political rights, he nonetheless sent his son to a Black university (Fisk) that offered a classical education, and he campaigned secretly for political rights. If Du Bois, at Fisk or Harvard or Atlanta, seemed the symbol of classical education, he nonetheless proposed education in the trades for some Blacks. Just so, in the arts controversy of the 1960s the opposing camps were more closely allied than many camp followers knew. While proclaiming that Black writers should use only Black heritage as a source, Baraka echoed Franz Kafka's novel *The Trial* (1937) in his drama *Great Goodness of Life* (1970), just as he earlier had identified *The System of Dante's Hell* (1965), his only novel, with the "Inferno" section of Dante's *Divine Comedy*. Similarly, Ed Bullins, spokesman for political street drama, utilized dramatic technique and thought comparable to that from Alice Gerstenberg's drama *Overtones* (1921) and from the European drama of Albert Camus, *The Just Assassins*. Moreover, despite his identification as the archetypal opponent of Hayden, Madhubuti has insisted that the strongest line in Black poetry is the conclusion to Hayden's "Runagate Runagate":

> Mean
>
>> Mean
>
>>> Mean to be free.

On the other side, although Hayden, in 1966, proclaimed his right to be whatever kind of poet he wanted to be, a generation earlier—before some of the Black Arts writers were born—he had blazed a trail similar to the one that they would trace. In "The Poet and His Art" Hayden wrote:

I was in college, of course, during the thirties, . . . and the motivating force behind poetry, behind most writing of this period, in fact, was social consciousness. Most of the young writers I knew were terribly earnest about politics, about the class struggle. . . . We believed that our poems had to have a social message, had to preach, had to offer a solution. These were the passwords into the literary cliques of the times—*message, solution, the masses.* The Zeitgeist favored poetry that was documentary, realistic, propagandistic. As young poets, we were encouraged to take as our masters revolutionary poets like Funaroff, Lola Ridge . . . Sandburg, Langston Hughes. We imitated their styles, their themes. As a fledgling poet in Detroit, I heard almost nothing of Wallace Stevens, Frost, Marianne Moore, Hart Crane. None of my friends talked of them, or if these poets were discussed, they were likely to be dismissed as bourgeois, as ivory-tower writers with no special message, as escapist.[7]

By 1948 Hayden had even published his manifesto, just as Black Arts writers would issue theirs. In "Counterpoise" he had written:

we are unalterably opposed to the chauvinistic, the cultish, to special pleading, to all that seeks to limit and restrict creative expression

we believe experimentation to be an absolute necessity in keeping the arts vital and significant in contemporary life; therefore we support and encourage the experimental and the unconventional in writing, music, and the graphic arts, though we do not consider our own work avant-garde in the accepted sense of the term

as writers who belong to a so-called minority we are violently opposed to having our work viewed, as the custom is, entirely in the light of sociology and politics

to having it overpraised on the one hand by those with an
axe to grind or with a conscience to salve

to having it misinterpreted on the other hand by coterie ed-
itors, reviewers, anthologists who refuse us encouragement or
critical guidance because we deal with realities we find it nei-
ther possible nor desirable to ignore

છે

we believe in the oneness of mankind and the importance of
the arts in the struggle for peace and unity.[8]

By 1966, therefore, Hayden, like Saunders Redding, saw no need
to seek an identity. Hayden, in fact, had anticipated some of the
Black Arts writers' presumptions, but he had adopted these prac-
tices from choice rather than command. That is, even though he
endorsed Countee Cullen's dictum that a Black poet had as much
right as William Shakespeare to go excursioning, to write about
any subject and any people, as long as the poet entertained the
reader—even though he endorsed this dictum, Hayden focused a
significant percentage of his poetry throughout his career on Black
subjects. Moreover, Hayden drew style and substance from the
wellspring of the African-American heritage—not only by em-
ploying the Blues but also by using the oral tradition, Black folk
speech, Black folklore, and Black myth.

Let me briefly illustrate my comments about Hayden's subject
matter and use of African-American heritage. As long as no one re-
quired him to write only about Black subjects, Hayden frequently
turned to them. In *Selected Poems* (1966) more than one-third of the
poems center on Black subjects; and the book concludes with five
of his strongest poems about Blacks: "Middle Passage," "O
Daedalus, Fly Away Home," "The Ballad of Nat Turner," "Runa-
gate Runagate," and "Frederick Douglass." In *Words in the Mourn-
ing Time* (1970), his first volume of poetry after his public insistence
that he not be restricted, six of twenty poems focus on Blacks, and
four others have strong reference to Blacks. In the nine new poems
included in *Angle of Ascent* (1975) four concentrate on Blacks, and
a fifth includes a strong section on Sojourner Truth. In his last
book, *American Journal* (1982), six of the twenty-three poems, plus
the eight in "Elegies for Paradise Valley," focus directly on Blacks

Other poems celebrate the poor and oppressed, who might be Black. In short, regardless of his public proclamations, Robert Hayden frequently wrote about Black subjects.

Because Hayden was Hayden, he did not restrict his Black portraiture to the renowned. An anonymous African-American man in "'Summertime and the Living . . .'" recalls the barrenness of the land, the death, the religious diatribes, that readers must contrast with Ira Gershwin's lyric delusion that living is easy for Blacks in the summertime. Anonymous African-American men are lynched in "Night, Death, Mississippi." "The Dream" recreates both a Black slave who fights in the Union Army and the woman he left behind. In "Unidentified Flying Object" Will tells a skeptical audience how his Mattie Lee departed on a spaceship, whose light transformed her into "every teasing brown he's ever wanted, never had."

But, if he often wrote about unknown, anonymous Blacks, Hayden also commemorated Black heroes and heroines of the Black heritage. In the careless inexactitude of classrooms I have said that Robert Hayden probably wrote more poems about African-American heroes, heroines, and history than any other African-American poet. Listen to the roll call: Joseph Cinquez, Phillis Wheatley, Crispus Attucks, Nat Turner, Gabriel Prosser, Harriet Tubman, Frederick Douglass, Sojourner Truth, Bessie Smith, Paul Robeson, Malcolm X, and Martin Luther King, Jr., to name only some of the more notable. He did not limit himself to honoring artists and intellectuals; he also commemorated African-American heroes and heroines identified as physically strong and virile revolutionaries.

Hayden also used Black folk myth, folk speech, and folklore. Decades before Toni Morrison, in *Song of Solomon* (1978), revived the Georgia Sea Island myth of the flying African, Hayden, in "O, Daedalus, Fly Away Home," wrote of such an African:

> My gran, he flew back to Africa,
> just spread his arms and
> flew away home.

Moreover, Hayden did not use folkways, speech, and traditions ostentatiously. He worked them into artistic Modernist poetry. For example, in "Electrical Storm" he naturally and simply incorporated folk sayings, folk speech, and the folk belief that dogs attract lightning:

God's angry with the world again,
the grey neglected ones would say;
He don't like ugly.
Have mercy, Lord, they prayed,
seeing the lightning's
Mene Mene Tekel,
hearing the preaching thunder's deep
Upharsin.
They hunched up, contracting in corners
away from windows and the dog;
huddled under Jehovah's oldtime wrath,
trusting, afraid.

Finally, even though he was a Modernist poet, Hayden emphasized the oral tradition in his poetry. By creating poetry intended to be read aloud, to be performed, Black Arts poets presumed that they were not only continuing the oral tradition from which Black American literature was derived but were also rejecting Modernist poetry, which asks to be deciphered by readers who, in quiet rooms, study the poetry with reference books and thesauruses at hand.[9] Despite his use of multiple voices, I would have identified Hayden as a poet to be scrutinized in a study—until I heard him read orally at the University of Michigan. As he began to read one poem, he faltered, then stopped and insisted that he be permitted to begin again so that he could create the rhythm that he considered essential to the art of the poem. One year later Hayden would publish an illuminating statement: "I hear my lines as I write them. I'm almost as concerned with the way my poems sound as I am with what they say. I think of the two elements interacting."[10] When I heard him at Michigan, however, I did not know his sentiment. I knew only that I must examine more closely the oral quality of his poetry, particularly his use of multiple voices.

Scholars who have analyzed Hayden's poetry have pointed to poets such as Edna St. Vincent Millay, Countee Cullen, Mark Van Doren, W. B. Yeats, and Langston Hughes, who influenced Hayden's development; but, as far as I know, no scholar has identified an authorial source for Hayden's frequently employed technique of developing a poem through several speakers or voices rather than through the one voice—the one persona—that most readers expect in a poem. Hatcher suggests that this technique emerged naturally from Hayden's early experience reading his poetry aloud to union workers in Detroit. Others might surmise that Hayden's interest in drama caused him to create a poetry dependent upon several voices. Regardless of the cause, the fact is that Hayden not only wrote many poems in which the narrator or persona strives for space with other voices, but Hayden even required the reader to identify the different speakers as one might while listening to a drama on radio. The reader must distinguish the voices by the subject, the diction, the language, or the tone. Four voices speak in "Night, Death, Mississippi." In "Aunt Jemima of the Ocean Waves" the narrator records a Black woman's monologue as he comments on his encounter with her. In "Runagate Runagate" Hayden gives voices to a persona-narrator, a slave owner, a slave who escaped, and Harriet Tubman. In "Middle Passage" Hayden speaks through a persona-narrator, a slave ship captain, a sailor writing in a diary, a sailor giving a deposition, a slave trader with twenty years in the business, and a Spanish member of the crew of the *Amistad*.

Hayden derived subject, thought, and style from Black American culture and experience. He even agreed with the Black Arts poets about a purpose for poetry. In 1978 he wrote:

Poetry *does* make something happen for it changes sensibility. . . . Academicians and purists to the contrary notwithstanding, great poets of the past as well as the present have often been spokesmen for a cause, have been politically involved. . . . To be a poet, it seems to me, is to care passionately about justice and one's fellow beings. . . . [M]uch political or protest or socially conscious poetry is bad, not because of the poet's loyalties or affiliations but owing to a lack of talent.

What Hayden would not accept was the failure of writers to comprehend that poetry is an art requiring "craftsmanship, form, style" and "*saying what cannot be said or at least not said so effectively in any other form.*"[11] What Hayden also would not accept was any restriction on his subject, style, or thought. He could not, would not, accept ideology that would require him to reject his Bahá'í belief "in the fundamental oneness of all races, the essential oneness of mankind, . . . the vision of world unity."[12]

III

Hayden's faith recalls the third incident that directed my thoughts as I planned this address. In 1974 I invited Robert Hayden to speak and to read his poetry at the University of Iowa's annual summer institute on Afro-American culture and experience. Because the topic of that year's institute was "Slave Narratives," most participants were as eager as I to greet the author of "Middle Passage," "Runagate Runagate," and "The Ballad of Nat Turner." At the reception following his presentation one participant stood at the fringe of the crowd clustered around Hayden, her eyes wide with adoration, her posture reverential. He was, she had told me, her hero, her favorite Black author. After a while, however, she left the Hayden circle, wandered over to where I stood, and muttered in disgust, "Just because someone asked him about the Bahá'í Faith, he started preaching."

I remembered with amusement an experience one decade earlier. In Gary, Indiana, I had given a lecture as part of a program that included a score of contestants in a beauty pageant as well as the young Cassius Clay, who had already signed a contract for his title fight with heavyweight boxing champion Sonny Liston. At the reception afterwards, I was neither surprised nor annoyed that the beauty pageant contestants crowded around the handsome, articulate, famous, charismatic Clay. Gradually, however, the young women drifted, one by one, to the vacant chairs at my table. Since I knew that my charisma had not risen during the preceding hour, I asked what was happening. One young woman informed me that Clay, soon to become Muhammad Ali, had spent the entire time at dinner trying to convert an Episcopalian minister to Nation of Islam belief and now had started explaining to the contestants how they must change themselves in order to become proper Black Muslim wives. At least Hayden had waited until someone asked him about his faith before he began to attempt to convert his listeners.

Lacking knowledge of the principles of the Bahá'í Faith, I will not speculate about the specific ways in which Hayden's faith influenced his writing. John Hatcher can provide that analysis far more effectively than I. Doubtless a detailed knowledge of those principles helps explicate particular passages of Hayden's poetry. But even one who lacks such detailed knowledge cannot fail to discern that the poetry reflects love and compassion, not only for human beings regardless of race or creed but for all God's creatures, large and small. The poem "Words in the Mourning Time" is often cited as evidence of his love and compassion. But many other poems might serve as well. Hayden heard the unvoiced pleas of prisoners:

> Believe us human
> like yourselves, who but for Grace. . .
> ("The Prisoners")

He perceived the kinship that joined his persona and Aunt Jemima, once "the Sepia High Stepper" of the European tour, to Kokimo The Dixie Dancing Fool, to The Spider Girl, to The Snake-skinned Man, and to other inhabitants of the "freak" show ("Aunt Jemima of the Ocean Waves"). The slaughter of cattle to increase the price of beef reminded him not only of "the starving / whom their dying will not save" but also of

> men women children
> forced like superfluous animals
> into a pit and less than cattle
> in warcrazed eyes like crazed cattle slaughtered.
> ("Killing the Calves")

This is the Robert Hayden I remember: an underappreciated poet who, consequently, may have enjoyed even more the honors that came so relatively late; a craftsman who knew that poetry is art and knew that he was African-American and fused these facts into a literature that recognized no boundaries; a compassionate human being who joined with other "partisans of freedom and justice" and "keepers of a nation's conscience."[13]

I must close with an admission. I prepared this address about Robert Hayden out of respect for Hayden and for Robert Chrisman, who invited me. It became a Herculean task; for, even though I enjoy reading poetry and have enjoyed writing it, I do not like to teach poetry or to write about poetry. The reasons are two. First, I believe that a poet deserves to be recalled in elevated, artistic language, not in the pedestrian prose that frequently characterizes scholarship. But, when I strive to create the artistic language a poet deserves—especially one whose work I admire profoundly—I hear the dreaded demons of deadlines pursuing me; and I turn aside to subjects that I can comfortably address in a more prosaic style. Even more, when I view poetry I do not want to imitate the surgeon coldly dissecting the body to uncover the conjurer's heart. Instead, I wish to imitate the child who, gazing at a fireworks display, points to the pyrotechnic wonders dazzling his skies and murmurs, "There. There! Isn't it beautiful!" For these reasons, had I been left to my own choices, I probably would have written little more about Hayden than I stated at the beginning of a speech that I presented twenty years ago as part of the Distinguished Lecture Series of the National Council of Teachers of English:

> Today, I should not need to spend time justifying the teaching of literature by Afro-American writers. But, for the sake of those in this audience who continue to doubt the value of such literature, let me read the following poem by Robert Hayden, a Black writer. [*Reads "Frederick Douglass."*]
>
> That poem explains the value of Afro-American literature as effectively as anything I might say. The poem encourages the black child to think with pride about a member of his race. It educates the white student to awareness of a Black American hero. . . . [The] work reminds the teacher of an oversight in traditional practice. We frequently insist that we encourage students to read literature of diverse cultures so that they will improve their understanding of those different peoples. Yet, we have restricted the search generally to the literature which describes the people and cultures of Great Britain and Europe—Northern Europe at that. Most important of all, when judged according to any aesthetic criterion a teacher may use, "Frederick Douglass" is a good poem.[14]

I told those audiences twenty years ago that I could only *talk* about Black literature whereas the poem "Frederick Douglass" *showed* them Black literature. Just so, I tell you today, remember the poem: That is the Robert Hayden who lives.

NOTES

1. John Hatcher, *From the Auroral Darkness: The Life and Poetry of Robert Hayden* (Oxford: George Ronald, 1984), 20.
2. I knew that the Liveright Publishing Company was in trouble when the permissions editor informed me that the company was trying to keep itself afloat on reprint fees for Hart Crane and Jean Toomer.

3. Pontheolla T. Williams, *Robert Hayden: A Critical Analysis of His Poetry* (Urbana: University of Illinois Press, 1987), 108.

4. If necessary, they were willing to read according to their vision rather than that of the author. Thus, they ignored the fact that, in such works as *Another Country* (1962) and *Blues for Mr. Charlie* (1964), Baldwin, a former minister, continued to create sermons based on the text of the New Testament: Love thy neighbor as thyself. Instead, many young Blacks read these as fiery denunciations of "The Man."

5. Hatcher, *From the Auroral Darkness*, 85.

6. Although credit for the conversion belongs to Hayden rather than to me, I was as proud as I had been a few years earlier when a Black student-poet entered my class determined to be another Beat poet and left worshiping at the altar of the seventeenth-century English metaphysical poets.

7. *Collected Prose: Robert Hayden,* ed. Frederick Glaysher (Ann Arbor: University of Michigan Press, 1984), 133–34.

8. Ibid., 41–42.

9. I do not want to belabor this generalization; for Gwendolyn Brooks's oral reading of her Modernist poetry dramatizes the manner in which an author's intonations, pauses, and timing can reveal nuances that would not be suspected by a person who examines only the printed words.

10. *Collected Prose,* 145.

11. Ibid., 11–12.

12. Ibid., 200.

13. Ibid., 16.

14. Darwin T. Turner, "The Teaching of Literature by Afro-American Writers," *The Promise of English* (Champaign, Ill.: National Council of Teachers of English, 1970), 75–76.

MICHAEL S. HARPER

Every Shut-Eye Aint Asleep / Every Good-bye Aint Gone

Robert Hayden (1913–1980)

> How shall the mind keep warm
> save at spectral
> fires—how thrive but by the light
> of paradox?
> —"Stars"

I met Robert Hayden at the University of Michigan at a poetry reading I was giving, one of several in the area as part of a circuit; I had spotted him seated toward the rear, near the exit, and when I concluded I walked up to him and said: "Mr. Hayden, it's a great honor to meet you, to have you come to my reading. You're a great poet—would you sign *Words in the Mourning Time* for me?" Taking his *Words* in hand, and smiling, he said, "I was all prepared not to like you."

A decade later I'd published the limited edition of *American Journal*. Hayden and I had become close friends; his charm, vulnerability, and poetic rigor, his *humaneness*, was often couched in a subtle humor. Images of recall come back haphazardly: Hayden was very much a character operating in a lunar landscape—he always loved what he called "the folk idiom, the folk person"; he was erudite, a true ancient and modern, and futuristic; he loved the arts, people, philosophy. Here are some anecdotes and some lessons, what I like to think is a Hayden catechism. When Hayden was invited to the Carter White House, early January 1980, for a program honoring America's poets, where he, along with others, was to read, we talked on the telephone just before the new year; I asked him if he had a book to give to the presidential library—he hadn't, he'd given all his copies away. I sent a copy each, one to Hayden, one to his wife, Erma, express mail. In line, in front of the White House, on a cold

From *Obsidian / Black Literature in Review* 8, no. 1 (spring 1981): 9–15.

wintry day, Hayden had no identification to get through the Secret Service; Erma Hayden had the presence of mind to point to Hayden's photograph on the cover of his book, and they gained entrance. He read "The Night-Blooming Cereus" and "Frederick Douglass" in the East Room. I remember Hayden's ambivalence about the cover design of *American Journal,* which Lawrence Sykes, the photographer, had created; the globe, which Hayden as poet-remembrancer ventured over, his many lunar landscapes, reminded him of a naked eyeball and no doubt his poor eyesight. Finally, after I quoted the lines from his poem "Astronauts"

> What is it we wish them
> to find for us, as
> we watch them on our
> screens? They loom there
> heroic antiheroes,
> smaller than myth and
> poignantly human.
> Why are we troubled?
> What do we ask of these men?
> What do we ask of ourselves?

he agreed to let the globe/eyeball remain.

In a "Voice of America" program taped at the Library of Congress in 1976 during Negro History Month and rebroadcast all over Africa and Eastern Europe, he said he wanted to bring people (poets) together. "[American Journal]," his bicentennial poem, was the Phi Beta Kappa poem at the University of Michigan; he was unsure of the version he had and many others he'd written. "Poets work for what they get," he often quipped—"Imagine this a found manuscript, or an interior monologue inside the mind of a Being from elsewhere; the Being's forgotten his travel kit of words *and he aint sorry.*"

Hayden wanted to collect all the poems from his old neighborhood, Paradise Valley, where he'd grown up, into a special collection to give to his friends—not only "Elegies for Paradise Valley," which he continued to expand, but "Free Fantasia: Tiger Flowers," "Homage to the Empress of the Blues," "The Rabbi," "'Summertime and the Living. . . .'" ("the only really good song in *Porgy and Bess*"), "The Whipping," "Those Winter Sundays"—the poem he'd written for Pa Hayden, his stepfather:

> What did I know, what did I know
> of love's austere and lonely offices?

the final lines of "an adapted sonnet" with the Yeatsian rhetorical question.

I'm reminded of what James Wright, the American poet born into poverty in Martins Ferry, Ohio, had to say about Hayden's poem:

> The word "offices" is the great word here. *Office,* they say in French. It is a religious service after dark. Its formality, its combination of distance and immediacy, is appropriate. In my experience uneducated people and people who are driven by brute circumstance to work terribly hard for a living, the living of their families, are very big on formality.

Hayden thought of himself as a formal poet; he said he needed "pattern" to write freely, but he never thought of himself as traditional, and he "loathed the middle class" and their stale, prescriptive attitudes.

When he was Consultant in Poetry at the Library of Congress, Hayden insisted on being a producing poet, one who continued to write. He was invited to Los Angeles for a television program, "At One With," for NBC, with Keith Berwick moderating, a half-hour program. He said he didn't get paid because he had to join the actor's union. "Did you get a copy of the tape," I asked him, "as partial payment?" "I never thought of that," he said. The tape was soon erased. He thought this apt, erasure; he never found a play he'd written about Harriet Tubman, "the Moses of her people," when he was on the Federal Writers Project. His poems were often dramatic; he loved the scene, the hidden narrator, the elevated tone, the baroque style, exotic words, the metaphor under "extreme control."

When he visited our family as houseguest, he ate lox and bagels, lounged in his blue pajamas, and tantalized the children with "Mother Goose" rhymes, his holdovers from childhood. He always elongated the deadline, waiting for visitations that would "let me complete the poem." One came to him while he was vacationing in the Virgin Islands. "More than cane / was crushed"—Phillis Wheatley demanding he finish the poem about her. Hayden's "stranger" appeared in many poems about art and religion. Charles T. Davis once told me that he would focus on Hayden as a religious poet, even more clearly than Hayden's "Uses of History" poetics, should he have time to write another essay. We were in the Calhoun College Master's living room at Yale in New Haven; Larry Neal was teaching there—he'd asked for Hayden's "Middle Passage," "so many students wanted to hear it," then we could talk about *life upon these shores*. Hayden knew the Yale campus better than many; he often came for Bahá'í meetings or discussions of his editing of *World Order*, the Bahá'í journal or reading in unpublicized seminars in the various colleges. He often thought of himself as the "best *unknown* American poet in the country." "I'm in trouble with the Afro-Americans *also*." He meant the decade of the 1960s, an attack in *Black World (Negro Digest)*; once a spectator, during a question and answer period at the Library of Congress, called Hayden an "Uncle Tom"; Hayden was sharing the program with Derek Walcott. Soon after Hayden left Fisk to teach at Michigan, he was offered the consultantship in poetry at the Library of Congress but had to turn it down because he could not get a leave of absence from Michigan—he'd just arrived!

In 1976 I sent him a postcard with Auden's picture (from London); he'd studied with Auden in the early 1940s in Ann Arbor. That instruction helped him with the schematic of "Middle Passage," a poem Hayden read the background for over several years, at the Schomburg, the New York Public Library, trying to control the "voices of complicity" in the transatlantic slave trade. He sent it to Du Bois for publication; it was soon anthologized. Hayden felt, at his death, he had a few minor changes to make, the ending he thought was weak. He was very pleased with his appointment at the Library of Congress; May Miller, daughter of Kelly Miller, gave the Haydens a splendid introduction to Washington—celebrities came. Later, when Henry Kissinger had an office on the same floor as his, in the Library, Hayden spoke of security (thoughts of terrorism came to mind), the men's room, the elevator, and him "barely able to see his way out." His concern had the bemused tone of ironical twists he was again witness to. He had invitations to go abroad to read; he had no birth certificate and worried about ever getting whatever documents he needed for travel abroad. I told him that any man who'd been invited to read to The Senate had no worry about passports and wrote to Ed Brooke, the senator from Massachusetts, for assistance; Brooke was happy to assist, but Hayden, his notions about "identity" a psychograph for his own poetic development, decided to leave well enough alone, at least for the moment. He was Asa Sheffey at birth, Robert Hayden all his life; the contradiction was to haunt him until the grave. He knew his seminal and adopted parents, both.

Hayden's concern for *adaptation* as a method of composition, with the formalist idiom as a critical approach, was sometimes a means of coming to the delicate balance of autobiography and imaginative form. His stories came from his experience, the poems were always transformed. Blake's phrase, "the self is not a genie in a bottle," was something Hayden considered as a practicing artist. A visitation from Phillis Wheatley was a poetic enterprise; the framing of the poem, epistolary, connects mode of speech with mode of literary expression; Blake's "chimney sweep" is the private persona of commisseration, as much as the free black woman, Obour Tanner, in Boston. London is the site; the Declaration is the rhetorical model, as sacred document; private aspirations are sometimes subliminal genius: Phillis is a patriot in the sense of the highborn—"(I thought of Pocahontas)—." Hayden's adapted ballad in the fifth elegy ("Elegies for Paradise Valley") gives voice to the nobility of the lowborn; Hayden's ballads also extend the tradition to include selections of emphasis—a revaluation of the "tragic mulatto" stereotype in "The Ballad of Sue Ellen Westerfield" or the gothic mysticism of the Old Testament visionary persona in "The Ballad of Nat Turner."

Hayden's approach to form is a skillful indicator of the mode of innovation, an apparent improvised form that echoes the imprint of the classical; his mode is inclusive (see "A Ballad of Remembrance") of race, human personality, and what Hayden called the "needful *heart transplant,*" a conceit he tried to capture in an unpublished poem. He is a poet of spiritual transformation, but he often begins with the dross.

As poets, we shared "Shields Green," who accompanied John Brown at Harpers Ferry; Hayden said he was jealous when I published a poem on subject matter he'd begun during the Writers Project years. He wanted to extend and people the territory of *John Brown's Body,* offered by Benét. Once he insisted we call Muriel Rukeyser, then recovering from a stroke—her biography *Willard Gibbs* included a chapter on the *Amistad* that Hayden read when researching "Middle Passage"—from a phone booth in New York, a cheerful word-reminder that she was not forgotten, even from the provinces: Ann Arbor and Providence.

He loved words: *subluxations* was one he laughed about, insisted

I use. He loved to send flowers to friends, roses usually; he loved fantasy and science fiction. He opened his reading as Consultant in Poetry at the Library of Congress with two birthday poems, one by President Senghor of Senegal, who writes in French, "Two Flutes," in an English translation; the other ceremonial birthday poem was his own "October" for his daughter, Maia, a poem that describes the colors of autumn without mentioning colors:

(ii)

I wept for your mother
in her pain, wept in
my joy when you were
born,
      Maia,
that October morning.
We named you
for a star a star-like
poem sang.
        I write this
for your birthday
and say I love you
and say October
like the phoenix sings you.

(iv)

Rockweight
of surprising snow

crushed
the October trees,

broke
branches that

crashing set
the snow on fire.

He ended the reading with an encore, "Unidentified Flying Object," about a woman living near Nashville who "clean disappeared"; he once thought of calling a collection of his "Po' Wayfaring Stranger," because he was not at home in the world. Once, when he read "For a Young Artist," his title poem from *Angle of Ascent,* he told of talking with a young man who thought "astral projection" would solve man's problems in the world. Hayden thought it began in the pit, where effort provided piecemeal wings that finally resulted in transcendence. When he was holding court, at the end, right after a tribute at Michigan in his honor, he spoke to me of his first order of business, as soon as he recovered enough to go out: his haircut was too short, he looked like a kid, he was going to "cut loose" his barber, whom he'd had for years. He loved art, as invocations from paintings, introduced into his poems, clearly announce; he loved the lost (and the found) and did not believe in innocence as protection from the dross. He'd done time, as a youth, in the red-light district; he'd done time in the Baptist church, where so many folk people lived. He'd seen Jack Johnson and Joe Louis and Robeson in Cadillac Square. Langston Hughes praised his poems, and helped in the Dakar prize; Richard Wright he never met, though they had a correspondence. He remembered home and brought it to light, the librarian who saved him books, *Your Heritage House,* Bessie Smith and Leontyne Price. He sent me a draft of his poem for his grandson, "The Year of the Child," which he wanted me to comment on. Did I object to being named in the poem, "after all both had the same name"; what improvements could I offer, *"knowing our need / of unearned increments / of grace"* (my italics)?

> May Huck and Jim
> attend you. May you walk
> with beauty before you,
> beauty behind you, all
> around you, and
> The Most Great Beauty keep
> you His concern.

Hayden knew we were our best selves in poetry. He left high-water marks all around him, as a teacher, as a poet and friend, as a human being. He appreciated complexity, outsiders, the journey—"The Dream," a dialogue in vernacular about one who stays behind in slavery, one who participates, as soldier, in his own liberation. He believed in literature and in technique and in the highest vision, which we'll call the spiritual or the imagination or the intuitional gift of cosmic/personal exchange in the lowest of the low: human existence. He left unfinished business: poems for Josephine Baker, the complete Matthew Henson, codiscoverer of the Pole, other "portraits of our oneness."

The barbershop awaits us, and the haircut.

DENNIS GENDRON

On *Heart-Shape in the Dust*

Inextricably woven into the fabric of Robert Hayden's personal and family life is a sense of time and place: the facts of the poet's youth and his search for identity do not take place in a vacuum but in Detroit in the 1920s and 1930s. The history of that city and the conditions of its Paradise Valley slum, are pervasively present in Hayden's poetry—especially in his first volume, *Heart-Shape in the Dust*.

Besides spending the first twenty-five years of his life in Detroit, Hayden was from 1936 to 1938 involved in the Federal Writers Project (FWP) of the Works Progress Administration (WPA) and, in addition to publishing "Autumnal" in the FWP anthology *American Stuff*, worked at collecting Negro folklore and Detroit history. In fact, "black history" constitutes a large part of the history of Detroit and proved particularly evocative to the sensitive, socially conscious young poet. An English census made in 1773 (seventy-two years after the founding of the city) counted ninety-six slaves among the population.[1] Later, the Ordinance of 1787 made slavery illegal in the American Northwest Territory, and by 1830 the city—just a river away from Canada and freedom—had become a major stop on the Underground Railroad. This period of Negro pre–Civil War history is the subject of Hayden's play *Go Down, Moses* and of his poem "Runagate Runagate." In 1833, however, a riot occurred that established the ambivalent attitude of the city toward its black citizens. Defying fugitive slave laws, a mob composed of people of both races demonstrated and freed Thornton Blackburn and his wife, who were being held for return to the master from whom they had escaped. After the riot authorities jailed every black on the streets, and blacks identified as participants in the riot were sentenced to work, chained, in the city streets.

From "Robert Hayden: A View of His Life and Development as a Poet" (Ph.D. diss., University of North Carolina at Chapel Hill, 1975).

Detroit continued as a hotbed of controversy surrounding slavery until the Civil War and on 12 March 1859 was the site of one of the seminal meetings of antislavery forces. At William Webb's Congress Street home, John Brown met with black and white abolitionists (including Frederick Douglass) to reveal plans for his Harpers Ferry raid. The two central participants in the meeting, Brown and Douglass, figure significantly in the poetry of Robert Hayden. Directly, Douglass is one of Hayden's heroes and the subject of his often-anthologized quasi-sonnet "Frederick Douglass." Indirectly, interest in Brown led Hayden to Stephen Vincent Benét's *John Brown's Body,* which is a principal influence on Hayden's poetic style. The multiple points of view in "Middle Passage," for example, are a variation of Benét's technique, and descriptive scenes of Nat Turner's vision in Hayden's "The Ballad of Nat Turner" are free adaptations of Brown's in the Benét poem.

Despite the very visible activities of Detroit's abolitionists, however, the city was no secure haven for its black population either in the Civil War era or after. The draft riots that were a national phenomenon in 1863 hit Detroit in great force. Frightened by the carnage of the war and by the prospect of becoming a part of that carnage, whites attacked the black symbols of the war's cause and forced many of the city's Negroes to flee for their lives. The mob became murderous when a black man, William Faulkner, was arrested for allegedly sexually assaulting a white child, a charge proved false after Faulkner had spent seven years in prison. The usually liberal *Detroit Free Press* echoed the general feeling of whites concerning the riot when it commented: "We regret the mob. If our voice could have controlled it, it never should have occurred; but what could Democrats do when the Abolition press were raising heaven and earth to chain the rights of white men to the experiment of nigger liberty?"[2] Such incidents of racial violence became more commonplace and, at times, even organized, as the city rapidly expanded and attracted increasing numbers of blacks: the ninety-six Negroes counted in 1773 grew to 1,400 in 1860; 4,111 in 1900; 5,000 in 1910 (still only 1 percent of the population); 40,000 in 1920; and 120,000 in 1930.[3] Moreover, the influx of immigrants from Europe and whites from the American South, correlated with the limited number of available jobs, further exacerbated racial tension in the city.

Detroit began publicly drawing attention to its racial attitudes in the mayoralty campaign of 1924. Charles Bowles, the Ku Klux Klan write-in candidate, received over 123,000 votes—some 7,000 votes more than his closest opponent—but lost the election when influential Catholics had 17,000 votes invalidated. However, John W. Smith, the eventual winner, who had Negro support, recognized KKK power and announced: "I must say that I deprecate most strongly the moving of Negroes or other persons into districts in which they know their presence may cause riot or bloodshed."[4] Thus, although direct control of city government was denied it, the KKK nevertheless wielded considerable influence and pervasively propounded its views at such mass meetings as the one in June 1923, when over a thousand KKK neophytes were initiated and the Klan burned a cross at the City Hall,[5] or the one that drew over ten thousand Klansmen, on 11 July 1925,[6] and through "neighborhood improvement associations." On 9 September 1925 just such an improvement association (in this case the Waterworks Park Improvement Association), with the tacit approval of Detroit police, attacked the home of Dr. Ossian H. Sweet, a Negro gynecologist who had dared with his family to invade a white residential area. A white "observer" of the scene, Leon Breiner, was killed by a bullet from the Sweet home, and the eleven occupants—including Sweet's wife—were arrested and tried for first-degree murder. Clarence Darrow, the National Association for the Advancement of Colored People (NAACP), a staff of local Negro lawyers, and the facts of the Sweet incident faced the public prosecutors, an all-white jury, and an officially concocted version of the affair. With the glare of national publicity on him, Darrow trapped and confused prosecution witnesses, boldly challenged the jury, and won the case. Mrs. Sweet's physical and emotional health was broken, Sweet's brother Henry—who admitted killing Breiner and faced a second trial, at which he was acquitted—contracted tuberculosis in jail, and Sweet himself subsequently committed suicide.

Sweet, a Dr. Fred Turner, and an undertaker named V. A. Bristol—all of whom tried to cross Detroit's residential color line—are only three black men who ran afoul of Mayor Smith's and Detroit's "Negro policy," which touched every black in the city. Capturing the attitude of racial injustice and frustration in Detroit, Robert Hayden prays in "Litany" for change:

> Give us, give us
> heart-shaped syllables
> to call the outcast home.

Give us, give us
love bright and hard as metal
and tensile to our straitest need.

Give us, give us
heroes whose valor
living, not dying, must define.

Give us, give us
courage to deny
no man his meaning.

"The Departure," the poem immediately after this supplication in *Heart-Shape,* prophesies the violence that must follow if the poet's litany is not answered:

Prophecies hang black flags
of smoke in the wind.
. . . .
Violence, an interval suspended,
waits to fall.

Unfortunately, the "Litany" was not answered, but the prophecies of "The Departure" were. The 1920s and 1930s saw the proliferation of KKK-like organizations in Detroit: the National Workers' League, the Black Guards, the Roseville Riflemen's Association, the Bullet Club, the Modern Patriots, and a particularly violent organization called the Black Legion. In "Coleman" Robert Hayden focuses on one Negro victim of the Black Legion in the "Season of violence," which has succeeded the "interval suspended" of "The Departure." A precursor of his character poems, "Coleman" is also an experiment in Hayden's technique of objectifying a subject that moves him deeply. Hence, the actual violence done the Negro veteran is barely touched upon. Instead, the poem centers on Coleman's significance to other blacks:

(Coleman, our days are full of such journeys,
and roads we knew grow treacherous, strange)

to all men:

(Through one they strike at the heart of our world)

and to the future:

> tell us the blood seeps down
> to give rich suck unto the roots
> of yet another season.

The tone of "Coleman" is restrained and finally hopeful. More typical of *Heart-Shape,* however, is "Essay on Beauty," a poem also ostensibly motivated by Klan- and Legion-type violence against Negroes. Although the poem does treat the "urgent fact of T.B.-riddled slums" and "justice klansman-eyed," its focus is diffused by the poet's attempt to include too many high and low moments of black history. Again, the fulfilled prophecy of "The Departure"—another "murderous season"—establishes the Detroit and national climate toward Negroes; next, we are reminded of "slaves at Valley Forge fighting for liberty" and of "Toussaint's freedom-dream, the Douglass memory"; and the poem concludes with a general lament for the condition of black people:

> There is no beauty that can cry to me
> More loudly than my people's misery,
> No beauty that can bind my heart and they not free.

Searching for a cause of urban violence, an explanation for the many violences done Negroes in the city, Kenneth Clark theorizes that ghettoes such as Detroit's Paradise Valley "are in fact social, po-litical, educational, and, above all, economic colonies. Those con-fined within the ghetto walls are subject peoples."[7] If other large cities are "economic colonies," Detroit—dominated by the auto-mobile companies—is especially so. Indeed, the influence of the automobile industry infiltrated every corner of black life, including the church, and, like housing problems and the violent outlaw or-ganizations already discussed, this aspect of his home also became the subject of Robert Hayden's "social" poems in *Heart-Shape.*

In the four years between 1899 and 1903 four automobile com-panies established factories in Detroit—Oldsmobile, Cadillac, Packard, and Ford—but, with European immigration at the flood tide, they employed only 569 Negroes in a work force of 105,159.[8] The war virtually eliminated the immigrant worker pool. Hence, Ford's 1914 promise of five dollars per day, as it was designed to do, attracted thousands of blacks and poor whites to Detroit from the South, bringing with them violent racial attitudes and the possibility of the company's pitting one racial group against another economically for a limited number of jobs. In fact, even two years after Ford's promise,

> 30 percent of the company's payroll [consisted of workers who] were getting less than five dollars a day. Probationers got only $2.72 per day, and thousands of workers . . . were hired, kept on for six months' probation, and then fired, to be replaced with other $2.72-a-day workers. Most women workers were not eligible for the five dollars a day pay. Nor were unmarried men under twenty-two. Married men involved in divorces were not eligible, nor was any worker who lived "unworthily."[9]

As a result of this probationer policy, the turnover rate in the automobile plants "was as high as 40% annually."[10]

The unemployment and racial problems in Detroit were further aggravated by the Depression and unionism, and both phenomena caused blacks to be used in an intrinsically antagonistic fashion. The former saw Negro competition for a limited number of jobs driving wages down. The latter saw Negroes used as strikebreakers against white unionists. From both developments racial hatred and violence resulted. Whites achieved a victory of sorts in the Depression as they assumed previously Negro-held low-paying jobs. Of the approximately thirty thousand black families in Detroit in 1931, twenty-two thousand were on relief rolls.[11] Referring to this mass Negro unemployment, Robert Hayden's "Shine, Mister?" links the frustration of Detroit's Paradise Valley residents with a blues rhythm to create an effective "period" poem:

> Ford ain't hirin—
> *Shine em up,*
> *Shine, mister?*
> Briggs is firin.
>
> Man at Cadillac
> Said: Gwan back home.
> Went an played me a number
> But it wouldn't come.

Asked for a shovel
On the W.P.A.,
Man said: Uncle Sam
Ain't handin out today.

Shine em up,
Shine, mister, shine?

Got in a crap-game,
Luck was ridin high—
Oh, rent-money, eatin-money!—
When the cops come by.

They throw me in jail,
Put me on the show-up line,
Slap me in the mouth
And make me pay a fine.

Standing on the corner
With these no-job blues;
Leave this hard-luck town
If I had some walkin-shoes.

Standing on the corner
Tryin to make a dime—
Lawd, a po workin man
Has a helluva time.

Shine em up, mister,
Shine?

Hayden's ironically titled "Bacchanale" develops the picture of
black frustration further as the persona asks,

What the hell's the use'n
Miseryin on?

and then resigns in despair: "Gonna git high."

If whites fared better than blacks in the Depression, both races
achieved some kind of reconciliation and a degree of success in the
union movement. Although the Negro got off to a poor start in the
movement and had to live down the memory of 1919, when blacks
were used effectively to break the Detroit strikes, radical union or-

ganizers eventually realized that any successful union movement would have to include all workers and so cooperated with influential members of the Paradise Valley community to present a united labor front. In this period, from the middle to the late 1930s, Robert Hayden became involved with radical socialism and the labor movement and, giving poetry readings throughout the city, became known as "The People's Poet" of Detroit—a title he now views with some amusement.

Although unionism in Detroit began in fragmentation and failure, the common experience of the depression, worsening working conditions on the assembly lines, and the "democratic" antiunion policies of Ford Service Department intimidators made concerted action by black and white workers a necessity. Communists organized marches in 1930 and 1932, which drew thousands of demonstrators, surprising city officials as well as the Communists themselves. Workers protesting arbitrary wage cuts successfully struck Briggs and Motor Products plants early in 1933. Later in the same year blacks organized their own Federation of Negro Labor. However, a giant step toward worker unity occurred in 1934 when the Communist Party decided to work within the broad labor movement rather than to establish strictly Communist unions. Continuing the spirit of unity, various automobile union delegates met in 1935 to initiate a four-point program democratizing and organizing industry unionism: "They forced William Green, president of the AFL, to call a convention of AFL auto delegates in Detroit in August 1935. At that convention the structure of a national union was created."[12]

Still, as a national union, the AFL continued a policy of segregation. The CIO, however, filled the void and became the only large American union organized without segregation. By 1939 events proved that auto industry strikebreaking days were over. In November of that year Chrysler hired sixty black workers to cross picket lines at its Dodge plant. Instead of leading to violence, their action brought a call for united action from Louis Martin, editor of the Negro *Michigan Chronicle,* and from other black leaders.[13] When more Negro workers were brought in, persuasion was still the only weapon used to achieve unanimous action. At least within the structure of unionism, the old cry, "Black and white, unite and fight!" finally became a reality. Robert Hayden's was one of the voices urging black-white unity. "The People's Poet" was quite naturally concerned with the activity to organize and integrate unions, and,

considerably influenced by radical socialist thought; he reflects his
concern and the cry for unity in "Speech":

> Hear me, white brothers,
> Black brothers, hear me:
>
> I have seen the hand
> Holding the blowtorch
> To the dark, anguish-twisted body;
> I have seen the hand
> Giving the high-sign
> To fire on the white pickets;
> And it was the same hand,
> Brothers, listen to me,
> It was the same hand.
>
> Hear me, black brothers,
> White brothers, hear me:
>
> I have heard the words
> They set like barbed-wire fences
> To divide you,
> I have heard the words—
> **Dirty nigger, poor white trash—**
> And the same voice spoke them;
> Brothers, listen well to me,
> The same voice spoke them.

Quite apart from his poems as "The People's Poet" and poems
relating to specific events in Detroit history, Hayden's *Heart-Shape
in the Dust* consists of poems on black life generally, antiwar poems,
and hazy poems of what he calls "youthful *angst.*" The entire vol-
ume, in fact, is simply what would be expected from a sensitive
young black man with poetic potential but with limited experi-
ence. It is what Hayden himself called "a trial flight" and is, there-
fore, heavy with "'prentice pieces"—experimental and almost-
successful poems.[14] For example, the diversity of the subjects in
Heart-Shape manifests Hayden's search for topics and themes sym-
pathetic with his poetic spirit. The fact that he never again deals
with many of the subjects comprising this volume suggests that it
is an early work and that he matures beyond its youthful concerns.
Similarly, Hayden experiments with rhythms and points of view in

Heart-Shape; his mature use of blues and folk rhythms and his characteristic objectivity are present here embryonically.

"To a Young Negro Poet" and "Dedication" establish the poetic credo of Robert Hayden, which expands in meaning as he matures. In *Heart-Shape,* however, this credo is severely limited by the environment in which Hayden places these two poems, preceded by works about black life and immediately followed by "Southern Moonlight," a rather common and superficial treatment of a black-white love affair. Thus, the selection and arrangement of poems in *Heart-Shape* present us with a "dark singer" primarily concerned with black life, with its social problems, and with the poet's own emotional involvement in both. "'We Have Not Forgotten'" is typical of Hayden's approach to black life during this early poetic period. The persona, a young Negro, reacts emotionally to every cliché associated with the history of "black fathers" and "black mothers"; "cabin-gloom," "cottonfields," "shackled limbs," and "anguish" are all invoked. The moral enunciated from this roll call of history is as familiar as the clichés:

> And if we keep
> Our love for this American earth, black fathers,
> O black mothers,
> . . . it is because your spirits walk
> Beside us as we plough. . . .

Influenced by the Harlem Renaissance and himself part of what Wallace Thurman fraternally referred to as the American "niggerati," Robert Hayden also worked within an established Negro literary tradition in this early period and quite naturally imitated his more successful contemporaries in many of the *Heart-Shape* poems. "Ole Jim Crow," a vernacular poem on a subject that has attracted countless black poets, is notable chiefly for its use of a distancing persona. "Southern Moonlight," mentioned earlier, also treats a stock subject and bears a resemblance to Albert A. Whitman's "An Idyl of the South." The ironically titled "Diana" describes the murder of a Negro man for happening upon a naked white woman who wickedly entices him. Obviously influenced by Langston Hughes's "Silhouette" and James Weldon Johnson's "White Witch," "Diana" has a tone of violence ("Flay, rend, burn, / BURN!") antithetical to the later Hayden. "Poem for a Negro Dancer," besides borrowing its subject from Claude McKay's "Harlem Dancer" and its tropical descriptions from his "Tropics in New York," markedly parallels Waring Cuney's "No Images." Hayden's first four lines are:

> You should live naked,
> Naked and free
> Under the leaves
> Of the mango tree.

As such, they are remarkably similar to Cuney's second stanza:

> If she could dance
> Naked,
> Under palm trees
> And see her image in the river
> She would know.

Again mining from Claude McKay, Hayden's "We Are the Hunted" with its "lantern-eyed hounds" is inspired by "If We Must Die" with its "hunted" blacks and its "mad and hungry dogs." Langston Hughes, one of the guiding forces of the Harlem Renaissance, guided young Robert Hayden as well. Hayden's eight-page "These Are My People," in its plea for America to be a home for Negroes, recalls Hughes's "Let America Be America Again," and its repeated references to "great, dark, myriad hands," "black hands, black hands idle in the sun," recalls Wright's "I Have Seen Black Hands." More comparisons can be made between poems by Hayden and poems by other black poets; however, the object of showing that Hayden has been influenced by others is not to reveal him as a derivative poet but to focus on him as a young poet in search of subjects and in search of a voice suited to those subjects and to his own temperament. Twenty-four of the forty-two poems in *Heart-Shape* are clearly about black subjects, and another half-dozen are open to a "black" interpretation. Many of these twenty-four poems are angry—some even violent in tone—but they are so unlike Robert Hayden today that he usually laughs them off and asks that they be forgotten.

Achieving some measure of effectiveness, three of Hayden's poems in *Heart-Shape* point to his later style in handling Negro themes. "Sunflowers: Beaubien Street" avoids the poet's personal emotional involvement with his subject by focusing on the images of sunflowers grown by ghetto residents and on their music, letting these images carry the burden of producing feeling. The first stanza describes the link between the sunflowers and Detroit's Beaubien Street Negroes:

> The Negroes here, dark votaries of the sun,
> Have planted sunflowers round door and wall,
> Hot-smelling, vivid as an August noon.
> Thickets of yellow fire, they hold in thrall
> The cruel, sweet remembrance of Down Home.

After references to the juba and the folksong "Ezekiel Saw a Wheel," the last stanza provides a hopeful conclusion through Negroes' release in the blues:

> Here phonographs of poverty repeat
> An endless blues-chorale of torsioning despair—
> And yet these dark ones find mere living sweet
> And set this solid brightness on the bitter air.

A second poem, "Gabriel," focuses on the slave revolt and hanging of Gabriel Prosser and, like "Sunflowers," also treats the subject with objectivity. In "Gabriel," though, the objectivity is achieved (as in the later "Ballad of Nat Turner") by allowing the title character to speak in his own voice. This device enables the poet to maintain his emotional distance from his subject and avoids blatant sentimentality in the handling of an essentially emotion-charged situation. Finally, perhaps the best poem in *Heart-Shape* is the haiku-like "Old Woman with Violets":

> Quiet and alone she stands
> Within the whirling market-place,
> Holding the spring in winter hands
> And April's shadow in her face.

Most characteristic of his mature style, "Old Woman," although inspired by a Negro flower vendor, never mentions the race of its central figure. Instead, her humanity, her standing alone like a pillar against time, is framed in a sharp and moving image. As he develops poetically, Hayden increasingly emphasizes the humanity of his black subjects, presents them objectively (either through their own voices or through a distancing persona), and trusts to the drama of their own situations to affect the reader, thus using techniques haltingly and sporadically attempted with varying degrees of success in *Heart-Shape.*

Hayden's first volume is not restricted to poems on black themes, however. A second category of subjects is war. Part of the generation that took Bertrand Russell's pledge for peace, Hayden was horrified by European events in the late 1930s, and his poems reflect this horror and the fear that war was imminent for America.[15] Referring to a news article that predicted "a big offensive in the spring," "Words This Spring" echoes Henry Reed's ironic pun on the word *spring* and continues to picture war through a gruesome application of Herrick's poem:

> And when a-maying fair Corinna goes,
> She picks her way among the dead—
> Finds instead
> Of posies in the grass, a stark death's head.
> She wears a gas-mask, fair Corinna does,
> And thinks of spring's first air-raid while
> seeking spring's first rose.

This poem manifests Hayden's characteristic ironic stance and succeeds at least in portraying a grim reality of war. Others of his antiwar poems have neither a sense of irony nor an air of reality but are marked by a romantic and generally hazy *Weltschmerz*. For example, "Words This Spring," part 3, painfully asks:

> Can there be spring for us again?
> Can there be joy again for us
> In plum-trees standing nebulous
> In crystal afterglow of rain? . . .

The only way to spring again is, of course, to "Make April talismans to bring us peace." The very next poem in *Heart-Shape,* "Poem in Time of War," is similarly romantic, as the young poet apostrophizes:

> O poets, lovers, eager-lipped young men,
> Say with me now that life is worthy—O give
> It affirmation. . . .

Hayden's antiwar poems and his poems on Negro and Detroit life are consistent in their flaws. Either the poet is too emotionally involved with his subject to present it fairly and effectively, or he attempts to present the breadth of a large subject—for example, social injustice toward blacks or the inhumanity of war—in too restricted a format and is doomed by the very vastness of the subject to convey only blurred general impressions. William Faulkner addressed these very problems when, in a series of lectures at the University of Virginia in 1957, he offered an observation on what he considered the principal obstacle facing black writers:

> There's no reason at all why the Negro shouldn't produce good writers. He has got to have—he's got to be freed of the curse of his color. He's got to have equality in terms that he can get used to it and forget that he is a Negro while he's writing, just like the white man hasn't got time to remember whether he's a Gentile or a Catholic while he's writing, and the Negro has got to reach that stage.... But you can't write sympathetically about a condition when it's constant outrage to you, you see. You've got to be objective about it.[16]

Of course, Faulkner's criticism applies to war or to any "condition when it's constant outrage to you," not simply to Negroes or Negro life. And to Hayden's credit he achieves this objectivity in some poems even in the experimental *Heart-Shape in the Dust,* in "Sunflowers" and "Old Woman with Violets," for example. "The Wind, the Weathercock and the Warrior's Ghost," an antiwar poem, also achieves a measure of objectivity—and success—by utilizing the frame of allegory. "Book Two" of Stephen Vincent Benét's *John Brown's Body* provides the weathercock image and the thematic question that Hayden attempts to answer: "And yet—what happened to men in war? / Why were they all going out to war?"

For Hayden the wind, "with eight-column streamers / alternating salvation with death, mingling soldier with savior," announces the call for war. The weathercock with "tin eyes" points the way of duty for young men. The warrior's ghost, mangled, "an iron sword buried / to the hilt in his heart," provides a warning from past reality; but "the wind blew dust and leaves / into the mouth of the frustrate ghost." Ironically, only the reader sees what happens to men in war, and not even he really knows why they go.

The final class of subjects dealt with in *Heart-Shape* is the vague poetry of what Hayden calls his period of youthful angst, poetry about painful love and the agony of being a poet:

Youthful *angst*—I was full of it. As if I didn't suffer enough as a young person, I sometimes wanted to bear some wonderful agony, you know. I wanted to be madly in love: I wanted to suffer for love and be all noble and magnificent [*laughing*]. I had many moods of sorrow and despair that were rather enjoyable. As I say . . . as if I hadn't had enough to go through, I still wanted something romantic and marvelous. I wanted some sort of picturesque agony, to endure just that—some picturesque agony. To suffer. Let it be known that I was capable of tremendous suffering and great sensitivity.[17]

"Primaveral" illustrates the poet's general world sorrow, as he makes his way through life with

> No song of welcome on my lips for spring
> Who cannot ease my heart of sorrow's tread.

But the closest we come to seeing what motivates that sorrow is the middle stanza of the poem:

> Although I walk by spring's new loveliness befriended,
> The road my feet must take is hard and lone.
> Although I sink to rest by April hosts attended,
> I lie beneath these blossomed boughs on stone.

"Poem" clarifies somewhat the springs of a poet's pain, for he is doomed to write what once "was music and lighted windows and armoring flame" in "the drifting snow":

> Write it in prismed syllables of dew, and let the sun
> Drink up its lustre—Oh, let it go,
> A word whose meaning is forgotten, a loveliness gone
> Like dew, like snow.

The "word," of course, is the poem itself; and, although it is ephemeral and therefore painful, that is its nature—"We shall not mind." The young Hayden, in love with poetry of the ideal and with the Romantics he studied in school and read on his own, was almost constitutionally drawn to Shelley, and several Shelley-like pieces are included in *Heart-Shape*. Representative of this Shelley strain of angst poems, *He Is Foredoomed* portrays the poet as similar to the dreamer of "Alastor." Like Shelley's dreamer, Hayden's persona has "known / An angel's too-bright mouth," and a female angel-emanation

> Shall lie with him at night and seal his eyes
> With crystal kisses cooler than white rain;
> Enchanted, lonely, fearful, he shall rise
> At dawn with splendors aching in his brain.

Hayden also sees the consequences of the persona's other-world fascination as a kind of delicious death:

> And longing for that angel turned to ghost,
> By cold caresses bruised to the bone,
> He shall lay siege to heaven and be lost
> To earth, who will not know him for her own.

Repeated in many of his early poems, this desire not to be known to earth as "her own" is in striking contrast with Hayden's desire in other poems to be a poet of the people, but it is thoroughly consistent with Hayden's youthful enthusiasm in his approach to whatever subject. If his subject is love or loneliness, he is tormented. If it is injustice, he is outraged.

This final group of poems completes the portrait of the Robert Hayden who wrote *Heart-Shape in the Dust*. The twenty-seven-year-old poet was immersed in the exciting play of ideas in graduate school, was confronted with such socially urgent problems as trade unionism, racial injustice, and socialism, and was forced for the first time to review his early life and background from a new, enlarged perspective. As a consequence of Hayden's active and immediate involvement in these issues, his first volume is intense, frequently emotional, and even propagandistic, seldom objective. His models sometimes show embarrassingly, like a woman's slip hanging slightly below her skirt; and the pressing tone of his socially centered poems now seems dated. However, *Heart-Shape* is also a declaration of strength and promise. It is the "trial flight" of a poet in love with humanity, a poet whose search for his own identity makes him sensitive to the problems of all of us in the same predicament. And its experiments with personae, with verse forms and rhythms, and with subject matter are evidence of a developing talent.

NOTES

1. Arna Bontemps and Jack Conroy, *Anyplace But Here* (New York: Hill and Wang, 1966), 287.

2. Quoted in James M. McPherson, (Preface), *Anti-Negro Riots in the North, 1863* (New York: Arno Press, 1969), iv.

3. Ray C. Rist, *The Quest for Autonomy.* Center for Afro-American Studies Monograph No. 4 (Los Angeles: University of California C.A.A.S., 1972), 8.

4. Quoted in Bontemps and Conroy, 4.

5. Sidney Glazer, *Detroit: A Study in Urban Development* (New York: Bookman Associates, 1965), 341.

6. B. J. Widick, *Detroit* (Chicago: Quadrangle Books, 1972), 9.

7. Kenneth Clark, *Dark Ghetto* (New York: Harper and Row, 1965), 10–11.

8. Widick, 291.

9. Ibid., 33.

10. Allan Nevins and Frank Ernest Hill, *Ford: Expansion and Challenge: 1915–1933* (New York: Charles Scribner's Sons, 1957), 518.

11. Bontemps and Conroy, 296.

12. Widick, 65.

13. Prior to the publication of *Heart-Shape,* Hayden "was a drama and music critic" for the *Michigan Chronicle.* "Also, I was a rewrite man and I wrote headlines." Louis Martin became interested in Hayden as a poet and was Hayden's first publisher. "He set up a press purposely to publish *Heart-Shape in the Dust.*" Interview in Connecticut.

14. *How I Write / I,* ed. Paul McCluskey (New York: Harcourt Brace Jovanovich, 1972), 143.

15. Hayden still remembers the Oxford Oath and quoted it in our interview.

16. *Faulkner in the University,* ed. Frederick L. Gwynn and Joseph L. Blotner (Charlottesville: University of Virginia Press, 1959), 53–54.

17. Interview in Connecticut.

ROBERT CHRISMAN

Robert Hayden: The Transition Years, 1946–1948

Nineteen hundred and forty six was a year of transition for Robert Hayden both as a person and as an artist. The year, the acknowledged starting date of the Cold War, inaugurated significant postwar changes in U.S. politics and culture, which were important contexts for the transition of Hayden to a new poetics. After receiving his M.A. degree in English from the University of Michigan in 1944 and working there as a teaching assistant for two years, in 1946 Hayden secured a position as assistant professor in English at Fisk University, in Nashville, Tennessee. Having been reared in Detroit and having participated in its multiracial struggles for integration in housing and employment, Hayden found it difficult to adjust to Jim Crow segregation in the South.[1] The following passage from "Letter from the South," written in 1946, reveals his frame of mind:

> wherever I turn, wherever,
> there are divisions and amputations
> and masks that leer and lour and grin and evade and dissemble
> and try to be human faces.
> Wherever I turn, wherever I turn, I see the deformed and the
> injured, distortions of double-exposure,
> pathetic processions hobbling, faltering on stumps of feet, on
> burnt-matchstick legs, getting nowhere.[2]

With powerful invective "Letter from the South" directs its anger against the system of segregation, its perpetrators and, implicitly, its victims, "the deformed and the injured." In their critical biographies Pontheolla T. Williams and John Hatcher comment upon Hayden's frustration with his treatment and working conditions at Fisk. The Hayden family lived within the shelter of Fisk's academic community, but, in contrast to their experiences in Detroit and New York,

Fisk life was barren and sterile. Segregation further limited basic cultural experiences. Hayden refused to see films in Nashville because of its segregated seating:

> There was a time, for example, when I never went to the movies in the South, because in order to go to the movie you had to enter the theater through an alley and then go up and sit in what we used to call the buzzard's roost, a Jim Crow balcony.[3]

However, by 1948, the Haydens had fostered a community of artists and intellectuals that often gathered at their home for music, conversation, and poetry. According to Williams:

> He became the guiding spirit of a group of young writers including William Demby, a World War II veteran and a student in Hayden's writing class; Myron O'Higgins, a visiting research consultant at the university; and Ben Johnson, also a veteran and one of his creative writing students.[4]

In 1947 Hayden received a Creative Writing Fellowship from the Julius Rosenwald Foundation. Hayden, Demby, and O'Higgins, another Rosenwald fellow, founded Counterpoise, an editing, publishing, and ideological group committed to new, nonsectarian explorations and expressions in art and culture. Its first project was a volume of poems, *The Lion and the Archer* (1948), which contained six poems by Hayden and six by O'Higgins. It was accompanied by a manifesto, the Counterpoise Statement:

> We are unalterably opposed to the chauvinistic, the cultish, to special pleading, to all that seeks to limit and restrict creative expression. We believe experimentation to be an absolute necessity in keeping the arts vital and significant in contemporary life.

Further, the authors argued:

> As writers who belong to a so-called minority, we are violently opposed to having our work viewed, as the custom is, entirely in the light of sociology and politics, to having it overpraised on the one hand by those with an axe to grind or with a conscience to salve, to having it misinterpreted on the other hand by coterie editors, reviewers, anthologists who refuse us encouragement or

critical guidance because we deal with realities we find it neither possible nor desirable to ignore.

Counterpoise concluded by asserting, "We believe in the oneness of mankind and the importance of the arts in the struggle for peace and unity."[5]

This wide-ranging statement would remain Hayden's credo for the rest of his life. What is most striking about Hayden's transition years is his reformulation of his aesthetic from Left populism to modernism. The poetry of *The Lion and the Archer* marked a new direction, with rich imagery, complex rhythms, and a highly connotative symbolism, all of which combined to celebrate the play of imagination rather than explicit social statement. Some familiar with Hayden's previous writing and social activism could interpret the Counterpoise Statement as a fundamental retreat from the values of his earlier poems in *Heart-Shape in the Dust* (1940), which explicitly protest war, social injustice, racism, and intolerance. Hayden did distance himself from these earlier efforts, not for their values but from a dedication to aesthetic excellence and imaginative range that at times went to excess. In this final stanza from "Speech," a poem he dropped from his canon, Hayden expresses his belief in brotherhood:

> I have heard the words
> They set like barbed-wire fences
> To divide you,
> I have heard the words—
> **Dirty nigger, poor white trash—**
> And the same voice spoke them;
> Brothers, listen well to me,
> The same voice spoke them.[6]

Hayden's objection was not to its sentiments but to the expression of them in a generalized language that lacks the transforming power of individual voice and metaphor. Hayden stated his case with trenchant vigor in the introduction to his anthology, *Kaleidoscope: Poems by American Negro Poets:*

> Protest has been a recurring element in the writing of American Negroes, a fact hardly to be wondered at, given the social conditions under which they have been forced to live. And the

Negro poet's devotion to the cause of freedom is not in any way reprehensible, for throughout history poets have often been champions of human liberty. But bad poetry is another matter, and there is no denying that a great deal of "race poetry" is poor, because its content seems ready-made and art is displaced by argument.[7]

Hayden's criterion here is usually interpreted as applying only to protest poetry of the 1960s and 1970s, but Hayden applied these standards to the protest poetry of the 1930s as well, even as that poetry included his own. The key motif in the Counterpoise Statement is the insistence upon freedom from dogmatism, from the "minotaurs of edict," whatever their source, that Hayden would delineate in these lines from the 1948 version of "A Ballad of Remembrance":

> my heart
> rested, released, from the hoodoo of that dance,
> where it spoke with my human voice again and saw
> the minotaurs of edict dwindle feckless, foolish.

Such freedom, argues Counterpoise, provides the artist fullest opportunity to flourish.

Other factors were involved in this period of transition. The Left populist movement of the 1930s, which had nurtured Hayden during his apprentice years, was exhausted. Poets such as W. H. Auden became disaffected with the project of activist literature, writing in "September 1939," "for poetry makes nothing happen." With the beginning of World War II, Left activists suspended class struggle to fight fascism and, in this process, obviated the basis for the Left aesthetic. In a further irony the catastrophic events of World War II solved the pressing problems of the Depression: war mobilization relieved the problem of unemployment and the theme of unity to defeat fascism effected a temporary reconciliation of class and ethnic antagonisms burgeoning in the United States in the 1930s.

The advent of the Cold War between the Soviet Union and the United States had as a domestic correlative the reemergence of strong anticommunist sentiment in the U.S. social, political, and cultural spheres. Major black leaders and artists in the United States, such as W. E. B. Du Bois, Paul Robeson, Richard Wright, and Langston Hughes, who often affiliated themselves with Left and liberal causes, were especially vulnerable to McCarthyism.

Although Hayden had been a member of Detroit's John Reed Club, he had not joined the Communist Party. However, the concluding verse of "Letter from the South" indicates his keen perception of the dangers of the segregationist South; in its concluding trope he likens the region to a deadly bedlam:

> This is no feverchart territory, no shifting cinematic acre
> Of the mad, certainly,
> but as tentacular, as non sequitur, as phosphorescent
> With imageries of guilt;
> as savage in its threats of death by claustrophobia, death by
> Castration, death by division. Death.

Doubtless, the McCarthyism of the period also had a chilling effect upon the explicit statement of social criticism, and it was also a factor in the cloaking of protest in symbol. Such was the context for Robert Hayden, as he launched his writing and teaching career at Fisk University in 1946, at the age of thirty-three.

In the early 1940s the main focus of Hayden's Left populist aesthetic was his unpublished project, "The Black Spear," a modernist poetic sequence written in response to Stephen Vincent Benét's long poem *John Brown's Body.* Hayden had two objectives: to answer Benét's call for "the black spear" to recount the saga of blacks in the Civil War—"Oh, blackskinned epic, epic with the black spear, / I cannot sing you, having too white a heart, / And yet, some day, a poet will rise to sing you"—and to "correct the misconceptions and to destroy some of the stereotypes and clichés which surrounded Negro history."[8]

Although the collection "The Black Spear" was never published in its entirety, significant portions appeared in periodicals after Hayden received the 1942 Hopwood Award for the work in manuscript. The poems "The Black Spear," "Spiritual," "Vigil Strange I Kept on the Field One Night," and "Prologue" appeared in the *Michigan Alumnus Quarterly Review.* "O Daedalus, Fly Away Home" was published in *Poetry* in 1943 and retained in all of Hayden's subsequent collections. Five sonnets from the collection "The Black Spear" were published in Louis B. Martin's short-lived monthly, *Headlines and Pictures,* in May 1945.

The publication of the sonnets, titled "Five Americans: A Sequence from *The Black Spear,*" has several historically significant features. These sonnets to abolitionist leaders William Lloyd Garrison,

Abraham Lincoln, Harriet Beecher Stowe, Sojourner Truth, and Frederick Douglass are written for the most part in the explicit, value-oriented, hortatory style of his social poetry. It marks the only time the title *The Black Spear* appears in print to designate its poems. It also carries Hayden's dedication, "(For my mother, G. Ruth Scott)," his biological mother, Ruth Sheffey. But, perhaps of most significance, the sonnet sequence contains the earliest published version of "Frederick Douglass." In Hayden's words "'Douglass' was to be the culminating, the climactic poem in the series," but "the sonnet on Douglass was the only one I liked, and so in time I discarded the others."[9]

"Five Americans" also provides an opportunity to see Hayden in transition, reworking this material into a more modern mode. The sonnets to Garrison, Stowe, and Lincoln are reminiscent of the lofty sonnets of the Romantic era, such as Wordsworth's on Milton, and suffer stylistically. But "Sojourner Truth" is a creditable sonnet. With its terse verbs and sparse decoration, it anticipates the rhetorical strategy of "Runagate Runagate," in which Harriet Tubman is the focal figure:

II. SOJOURNER TRUTH

Comes walking barefoot out of slavery,
ancestress, turbaned and gaunt and biblical,
face rich in pentecostal shadow. Wanders
the violent landscape, tall in spiraling wind.

I have been dead and now am summoned from
the dead; nameless, and my christening
has come; a mourner and a longtime seeker,
no more a mourner but a seeker still.

Affirms, accuses, prophesies—
woman of earth and pythoness whose speech
is bright as eyes with love or anger lit,
lambent, piercing as the spike of Jael.

Journeys toward the future, liberty
her calling, and her credentials truth.

The elision of narrative sequence through multiple voices, the incantatory quality of Truth's speech in the second quatrain, the precipitant verbs that open the lines, the sense of inevitable forward movement, the biblical aura, and terse epiphany of Truth in the sestet—"Affirms, accuses, prophesies—woman of earth . . ."—foreshadow the methods of "Runagate Runagate," even to the use of the epithet *woman of earth* and the verb *summon,* which appear in verse 2 of "Runagate Runagate": "Harriet Tubman, / woman of earth, whipscarred, / a summoning, a shining."

By 1947 Hayden had achieved what was essentially the final form of "Frederick Douglass," and it was printed in the *Atlantic Monthly.* Of the "Frederick Douglass" of "Five Americans" only its title and rhetorical strategy survived. What follows is the earliest version, from 1945:

III. FREDERICK DOUGLASS

Such men are timeless, and their lives are levers
that lift the crushing dark away like boulders.
Death cannot silence them, nor history,
suborned or purchased like the harlot's crass
endearments, expatriate them. Like negatives
held to the light, their weaknesses reveal
our possible strength. Their power proves us godly,
and by their stripes are we made whole in purpose.

Douglass, O colossus of our wish
and allegory of us all, one thinks
of you as shipwrecked voyagers think of
an island. Breasting waters mined with doubt
and error, we struggle toward your dream of man
unchained, of man permitted to be man.

The final version in the *Collected Poems* retains the architectonic qualities of what I'll call Douglass 1945. It links metaphors for a cumulative effect; it speaks in hyperbole, and it expresses a millenarian ideal of fully achieved freedom and self, but with a great deal more power and sophistication.

The poetic distance is quite different in the two versions. As in the other sonnets from "Five Americans," in Douglass 1945 the poet and the reader are extrinsic to the processes of the poem; the semiotics of statues, tableau, and picture, often found in *Heart-Shape in the Dust* and "'The Black Spear," are present, even in the images "negatives / held to the light" and "colossus of our wish." There is no immediate engagement. Because in Douglass 1945 Hayden intends to instruct and reveal (as he frequently does in his mythohistoric poems), this combination of poetic distance and didactic motive produced a rhetoric of declamation. In Douglass 1945 the octave valorizes Douglass as the hero who has fully achieved his mission of freedom. Douglass is "timeless," his life a lever "that lift[s] the crushing dark away." He cannot be silenced by death or corrupted by the "crass endearments" of history. Even his weaknesses "reveal our possible strength." His power "proves us godly. / and by [his] stripes are we made whole in purpose." He is in fact a Messiah, as indicated in the trope "that lift the crushing dark away like boulders," a reference to Jesus' resurrection from the tomb, and in the last trope of the octave, "Their power proves us godly. / and by their stripes," which suggests Calvary. In the sestet Douglass's legacy and example are presented as "wish and allegory of us all." Hayden phrases the injunction to achieve his ideal in the familiar language of faith: "Breasting waters mined with doubt / and error, we struggle toward your dream of man / unchained, of man permitted to be man."

In the final version Hayden reverses his emphasis: the poem opens with immediacy and engagement. Poet and reader are brought at once into the poem through the first-person plural pronoun and the ongoing struggle for freedom, "When it is finally ours, this freedom, this liberty, this beautiful / and terrible thing." Also, Hayden reverses emphasis in presenting the relationship between Douglass and freedom: freedom gets primary emphasis, but the quest is still conditional. The cumulative effect of clauses in the opening unit commencing with *when* emphasize the conditional quality of an unachieved freedom and create suspense within the reader: "When it is finally ours," "when it belongs at last to all," "when it is truly instinct," "when it is finally won," "when it is more than the gaudy mumbo jumbo of politicians." These conditional clauses are prelude to the introduction of Douglass in line 7, "this man, this Douglass," which is followed by a series of parallel appositives embellishing him. When Douglass appears, he is not the invincible figure of Douglass 1945 but a vulnerable man:

> this man, this Douglass, this former slave, this Negro
> beaten to his knees, exiled, visioning a world
> where none is lonely, none hunted, alien,
> this man, superb in love and logic, this man
> shall be remembered.

Here Douglass is fully human and the stark passion of his lonely experience suggests a subterranean self-referencing of Hayden as well. This is not the triumphant Christ risen from the tomb but the Jesus who stumbled under the Cross at Calvary. The vulnerability of Douglass outlined in the later version—in contrast to the triumphalist rendering of him in Douglass 1945—further sustains the suspense of the poem until his climactic apotheosis:

> Oh, not with statues' rhetoric,
> not with legends and poems and wreaths of bronze alone,
> but with the lives grown out of his life, the lives
> fleshing his dream of the beautiful, needful thing.

Hayden shifted from conventional iambic pentameter in the first version to an accentual verse, modeled after Hopkins's sprung rhythm in the revised version. The freer line offered new rhetorical possibilities for him. According to Hayden, "[Hopkins] altered the sonnet form, pushed it beyond conventional limits, made it freer than it had been before." Hayden continues:

> Well, when I was working on my own sonnets I was also studying Hopkins, and under his influence I decided to experiment with stressed verse. I thought this would make for the kind of intensity I was after. I succeeded, more or less, in adapting Hopkins's technique to my own purposes, though I don't feel I imitated him any more than Dylan Thomas or Auden did when they too employed aspects of his technique in their own poems.[10]

But, besides the liberty afforded by accentual verse, the cumulative effect of powerful, subordinate clauses that climax in the final lines imparts a Shakespearean structure to the sonnet.

Composed of two periodic sentences augmented by extensive parallel constructions and resolved with a concluding antithesis, the finished "Frederick Douglass" is a remarkable piece of rhetorical design. Hayden's fusion of the experimental and traditional resources of the English language is impressive.

Hayden's perfectionism has mitigated against a full appreciation and understanding of his poetic development. He omitted from his oeuvre poems and entire volumes that did not satisfy the criteria he set for himself as a mature poet. Although Hayden began writing in 1931, very few poems he wrote before 1946 were included in his *Collected Poems*—only "O Daedalus, Fly Away Home" and

"Middle Passage." Of the six poems published in *The Lion and the Archer* only three were included in *Collected Poems*. Hayden's next volume, *Figure of Time* (1955), consisted of twelve poems: four were dropped from his canon, and two were heavily rewritten. As a result of this severe editing, one does not readily see the organic development of Hayden's style, from Left populism on to the modernism of his maturity.

Few of Hayden's writings, letters, or journals are available until the late 1940s. One notebook is available from 1938–39, when Hayden was attending the University of Michigan. References in that journal indicate that Hayden was reading Yeats, Lorca, Bertolt Brecht, and Herbert Read. However, Hayden maintained several substantial working notebooks from 1946 through 1949, which provide a valuable resource for tracing his poetic development during his transition years.

In reading the notebook titled "1946" and labeled as folder 24 from box 29 of the Hayden archive, one is struck immediately by Hayden's diligent study of the image. Begun in July at Brooklyn, Michigan, folder 24 opens with dense notes on haiku, succinctly defined by Hayden as "a small arc for which the reader supplies the rest of circle." Basho's great haiku "The ancient pond sleeps. / Suddenly—that sound of water? / A frog leaps" is copied out and followed on the next page by Hayden's own effort, "Cordilleras of clouds / At night the frogs sound like / flat notes on a plucked string." The technique is transferred to his more immediate concerns: "She moved through darkest night with no more noise than a root makes growing deeper in the earth (for Harriet Tubman)." At other times the exercises are mannered, as in this entry of 12 July 1946:

> the moon seen first through the two long flamingo-tinted clouds, the moon very white and full: the clouds slowly passed over the face of the moon, diffused themselves into the softly roseate hues of the sky, and left it clear and solitary and brilliant as a polished precious stone; the full moon reflected in the water of the dam nearby. I thought of Lorca's poems on the moon— his description of it as a thing of delight, as a swan, and as a *dramatis persona*.

Besides references to Lorca and Marc Chagall, Hayden copies out several well-wrought passages from Virginia Woolf, such as the following:

Then suddenly the smooth narrative parts asunder, arch opens beyond arch, the vision of something for ever flying, for ever escaping, is revealed, and time stands still. ("De Quincey's Autobiography," *The Second Common Reader*.)

Hayden notes of this entry, "A beautifully cadenced sentence; imaginative power. Its imagery recalls Surrealist and Seventeenth Century perspectives." He also copied passages from Woolf's *Orlando*.

Hayden's entry for 10 August indicates how these elements began to coalesce in his imagination to produce new poetry:

Poem on New Orleans now in progress is to be a baroque poem of impressions [*things*—crossed out] etc. of the city—of its tragic [*interracial*—crossed out] biracial life, etc. [space] Completed August 21. Not what it started out to be, however.

Hayden's entry for 2 September reads, "'A Ballad of Remembrance'—my New Orleans baroque poem—accepted for publication in the British Poetry Quarterly's 'Selection of Recent American Poetry.'"

Hayden's fundamental strategy during this period was to isolate and emphasize the image as the essence of the poem. This effort would eventually culminate in the rich language of *The Lion and the Archer,* a style that Hayden characterized as "baroque." A number of critics have regarded use of this term as a whimsy of Hayden's, but Hayden used his literary terms with precision. Throughout the seventeenth century European art was baroque: sensuous in detail, extravagant in concept, robust in structure, repetitive and expansive. English poetry had its great baroque poets—John Donne, George Herbert, Henry Vaughn, Richard Crashaw, John Milton—but the majority of critics and scholars have adhered to Samuel Johnson's term *metaphysical poets* to describe them, a term that was set in stone by T. S. Eliot's essay "The Metaphysical Poets" and by his separation of Milton from that tradition with his essay "Milton." Milton is thus seen as an isolated figure, rather than as the culmination of an imaginative, sensual, and intellectual style that began with Donne. The consequence of this separation has been to put both the metaphysical poets and Milton in free-fall. Of particular importance in Hayden's use of the term is the great Spanish Baroque poet Luis Góngora, who was celebrated by Federico García Lorca in an important speech delivered in Granada in 1932 on the tercentenary of Góngora's death, "The Poetic Image in Luis Góngora."[11] Lorca found in Góngora's strategy of metaphor an extravagance of imagination, a linguistic creativity, a quest for the essence of things that was compatible with his own surrealism.

Reading Lorca, André Breton, Aimé Césaire, Pablo Neruda, and studying painters of the German Expressionist and French Surrealist schools, Hayden began to develop a new approach to metaphor that freed him from the single-author narrative strategies of Romantic and populist poetry. Hayden had taken a B.A. degree in Spanish from Wayne College (now Wayne State University), which familiarized him with Spanish literature and its aesthetics. By 1940, four years after Lorca's death, the majority of his texts had been gathered.[12] Lorca was available to Hayden in English and in Spanish. His influence was such that Hayden lists a poem on García Lorca that he wrote in 1940, although the text is lost. It is likely that Hayden based his "baroque" poetics upon combined influences of Lorca and, indirectly, Góngora. Replacing narrative with dream and valuing the "logic of metaphor" over the logic of exposition, surrealism also provided Hayden with new ways of viewing and valuing the demotic and collective experience of black people. In "Surrealism and the Romantic Principle" (originally the introduction to Surrealism [1936] by André Breton and others) Herbert Read argued for the revolutionary function of art:

> By the dialectical method we can explain the development of art in the past and justify a revolutionary art at the present time. In dialectical terms we claim that there is a continual state of opposition and interaction between the world of objective fact—the sensational and social world of active and economic existence—and the world of subjective fantasy. This opposition creates a state of disquietude, a lack of spiritual equilibrium, which it is the business of the artist to resolve. He resolves the contradiction by creating a synthesis, a work of art . . . which for the moment gives us a qualitatively new experience.[13]

In the First Surrealist Manifesto, Breton would observe:

> The Image is a pure creation of the mind.
> It cannot grow out of a comparison but only out of a union of two more or less distant realities.
> The more distant and true the connection between the two

realities which are being united, the stronger will be the image and the more emotional power and poetic truth it will have.[14]

Besides this radical body of theory, Surrealist artists had a practical history of social protest and activism, among them, Neruda, Lorca, and Césaire. Hayden's study of surrealism, then, provided him with new resources for his development as a poet and Left humanist.

The Lion and the Archer was the culmination of Hayden's renovation of his style in the mid-1940s.[15] In addition to demonstrating a modernist aesthetic, the six poems in *The Lion and the Archer* establish themes, methods, and interior tableaux that would characterize Hayden's mature poetry. Meditative poems about art and the nature of reality ("Magnolias in the Snow," "Invisible Circus," "The Lion and the Archer"), chronicles of popular black life ("Homage to the Empress of the Blues"), surrealist portraiture ("A Ballad of Remembrance"), and issues of persecution of minorities and outsiders, in this instance, Jews ("Eine Kleine Nachtmusik"), manifest the concerns and the palette of Hayden's new style.

"A Ballad of Remembrance" remains one of Hayden's most enduring and defining poems, and has been reprinted with few revisions in Hayden's subsequent volumes. The only significant changes between the 1948 version and the final version are the omission of the lines "and saw / the minotaurs of edict dwindle feckless, foolish," in the eighth stanza, which then concludes with "my human voice again" and the change of the line "for Bernice and Grady, for Mentor, for George and Oscar" to "for the troubled generous friends" in the concluding stanza.

Artifice is central to baroque expression. In accord with this principle Hayden's poems in *The Lion and the Archer* are predicated upon artifice and popular artifacts: a Mardi Gras parade, a blues performance, tropes of the circus or a night serenade, a mosaic of flowers and snow. In the case of "A Ballad" there are multiple layers of artifice that, combined with the poet's feverish imagery, convey the powerful sense of derangement that Hayden experienced: the Mardi Gras parade, the black figures wearing blackface and bizarre costumes reflecting the racism and brutality of slavery.

The theme of bizarre antithesis is established in the opening phrase of the first stanza, *Quadroon mermaids,* in which the mixed-race female has her hybridity compounded by a fetishist, mixed-species mermaid costume, emphasizing the special sexual attraction octoroons and quadroons held for white men in the South. "Afro angels, saints / blackgilt" continue this willful parade of racist fetishes, in which divine effigies in blackface sing and perilously negotiate the violent potential of the parade, "the switchblades of that air."

Because the agon of "A Ballad" is the derangement of the protagonist by a flood of degrading images from his Afro-American past and its language reflects that derangement, exact paraphrase is not possible nor completely necessary. However, it is clear that after the first stanza Hayden offers a host of characters from this particular parade, which was called *zulu*. Zulu, according to cultural critic Kalamu ya Salaam, "had a tradition of kicking off Mardi Gras with a parade that began at sunrise and meandered from bar to bar throughout the black neighborhoods until sunset. . . . Zulu always—and still does—paraded in blackface and threw coconuts." Until 1966 the parading tradition was segregated, and all the major parades were white except the "zulu" parade.[16]

The power of this spectacle is such that the protagonist becomes disoriented:

> masked Negroes wearing chameleon
> satins gaudy now as an undertaker's dream
> of disaster, lighted the crazy flopping dance
> of my heart, dance of love and hate among joys, rejections
> and caught up in its false ideologies.

The three major groupings established in "A Ballad"—the zulu king, the gunmetal priestess, and the saints, angels, and mermaids—each represent a different black orientation. "Throned like a copper toad," the zulu king advises accommodation; love is recommended by the fetish images of saints, angels, and mermaids. Wearing the iron collar of a recaptured slave, the gunmetal priestess speaks:

> Hate, shrieked the gunmetal priestess
> from her spiked bellcollar curved like a fleur-de-lys:
>
> As well have a talon as a finger, a muzzle
> as a mouth. As well have a hollow as a heart.

Still disoriented, the protagonist suffers a racial incident at a coffeehouse, "coffeecups floating poised hysterias." He regains stability with the company of Mark Van Doren.

Then you arrived, meditative, ironic,
richly human. And your presence was shore where my heart
rested, released from the hoodoo of that dance,
where I spoke with my human voice again and saw
the minotaurs of edict dwindle feckless, foolish.

His crisis resolved, "released from the hoodoo of that dance, /
where I spoke with my human voice again," the protagonist can see
the pageant for what it is: an offering of dehumanizing values, atti-
tudes, and choices deriving from a brutalizing past suffered by
blacks and whites, "minotaurs of edict" that finally "dwindle feck-
less, foolish."[17]

The hysteria of the parade subsides and Hayden's concluding
stanza is written in a measured language, without surrealist tension.

In his reading of "A Ballad," "Witch Doctor," and "The Diver" and
their "nonreferential language" Charles Lynch perceives influence
from Hart Crane's aesthetic, "the logic of metaphor," in which, in
Crane's words, "the motivation of the poem must be derived from
the implicit emotional dynamics of the materials used, and the
terms of expression employed are often selected less for their logi-
cal (literal) significance than for their associational meanings."[18]
While noting that "A Ballad" is structured on the voyage motif,
Lynch does not pursue its structural affinity to a later work, "The
Diver." In each poem Hayden's protagonist is immersed in a hallu-
cinatory environment in which he becomes deranged and drawn
into a nearly fatal embrace of a compelling life that is buried in
sunken memory; in "The Diver":

> I yearned to
> find those hidden
> ones, to fling aside
> the mask and call to them,
> yield to rapturous
> whisperings, have
> done with self and
> every dinning
> vain complexity.

The surrealist nature of Hayden's poetics also permitted him a
"conceptual surrealism." With "A Ballad" Hayden also adds to his
repertoire the poem that deals with bizarre and anomalous, yet

defining, elements of human experience. Among such poems are "Aunt Jemima of the Ocean Waves," "Unidentified Flying Object," "Smelt Fishing," and "The Tattooed Man." After a dense two-page exegesis of criticism on Marc Chagall in his 1946 journal, Hayden establishes the conceptual framework for these poems: "The grouping of disparate elements of actuality in such a way that they become metaphorical is often characteristic of the best symbolic poems." This passage is immediately followed by another entry, the first harbinger of "'Summertime and the Living . . .'": "Flowers and anxieties / magenta [*unclear*] and ancient pieties / Sunflower steeples and riotous sobrieties," which constellates the key images of piety, drunkenness, flowers, and flamboyance, which organize that poem published nine years later in *Figure of Time.*

Hayden's journals from this transitional period also document his cultivation of the painterly quality in his poems. His mature poetry contains images of great visual acuity, due in part to his intensive work with haiku. There are also images that derive from painters such as Monet, Whistler, and Rousseau as well as from Egyptian masks and circus posters. The genesis and development of the pictorial poem "Invisible Circus," abandoned after its publication in *The Lion and the Archer,* is well documented in the journal "1946." These entries also provide additional information on other of Hayden's future poems, such as "'Summertime and the Living . . .'" and "Elegies for Paradise Valley" and reveal some of the submerged personal tensions of his childhood that they would explore:

INVISIBLE CIRCUS

Peacock's feather of a boy,
piebald giraffe (obscurantist creature)
on which he displays himself
with sprigged-with-sorrow-joy:

Oh they could show us jingling marvels
but pelting us with subtleties
make us create our own
comiques and flying devils:

From their gemglitter stance we must infer
the clocked and tilting frivols
of Maximo the Merry
on his filament floor.

Reefer whimsey of a conniving
beast: nocturnal oddment of
a boy—so nothing but
themselves: jewel in setting,

Eye in socket. Yet a part
of the living statuary
of the three-ring heart.

The poem first appears as a journal entry:

Idea for a poem—Boy and Blue Giraffe (after a surrealist painting)
A very suggestive fantasy by Karl Prielie, "The Piebald Giraffe."
—might be used as title for a book or group of poems.
[In the left-hand margin Hayden has written, "A first complete
draft finished Dec. 24, '46 tentative title—'Invisible Circus.'"]

A draft then follows after this entry:

Boy and Blue Giraffe
Quite possibly he of the [*with his* crossed out] sequined
    and plum gold skin,
Ready to cavort and caper,
    ethereal jitterbug,
[*Celestial dancer of the Charleston* crossed out]
Quite possibly, he is nothing
    but a nocturnal mood
Or a reefer whimsy or a projection
    of your own desire
for something, something, God knows what really,
[*by but something, anything, but this sameness* . . . crossed out]

The poem continues for several more stanzas, the second stanza
emphasizing the boy as fetish:

In Pope's day they would have painted him
with a turban and a plume—a peacock feather
Enriched by the summer night positive sheen of his skin
He would have had a little round cherub face
round as an apple of sard [in the margin Hayden writes, *is sard
    black?*]
Or shaped like an onyx heart
He would be resting his chin in the soft hand of one of those
ladies in opulent satin and rococo. . . .

At the conclusion of this first draft Hayden has written, "Dogs and birds in that fantasy—green space resemble each other and are descendants so of mythic beasts in Breughel, etc. . . . Ectoplasmic." The entry concludes with what is apparently another take on the poem:

> The radium blue giraffe
> and the boy with a [crossed out] glint of a look
> and a sequin of a mouth
> and bright bangles at neck and ankle
> [*lend* crossed out] hire [?] themselves out quite readily
> to speculation and conjecture.

An entry in December adds to the textual sources of "Invisible Circus"; Hayden was impressed by the visual and verbal impact of circus posters:

> "Maximo the Merry. The international pantomimist on the
>   steel thread."
> (from a circus program)
> Immediate and compelling as a circus poster (lithograph)
> A grand parade, an impressive gala display of nouns, adjectives,
>   verbs (in circus advertising)
> ". . . feats by *comiques of the air*" (program)
> Note: alliteration used in description of circus acts and
>   personalities. . . .
> High over the heads of the crowd, upon his filament
>   (gossamer) floss of steel,
> exotic Maximo, the season's novelty, begins to waltz and tilt
>   and reel
> the season's novelty, [*erotico* crossed out] exotic Maximo
> umbrellas of light revolve about clever Maximo.

"Invisible Circus" is not a successful poem, primarily because the figure of the circus child is not clearly delineated. The premise of the poem, that the impoverished child, stimulated by posters of circus gaiety, is compelled to "create our own / comiques and flying devils," suddenly becomes something more sinister, changing from a "Peacock's feather of a boy" to the "Reefer whimsey of a conniving / beast: nocturnal oddment of / a boy," in which the child becomes an object of unspecified cupidity. The two visions of the child are not reconciled.

In the 1950s Hayden began "a series of poems about my life in the slums of Detroit at this time. By then I had enough detachment, I'd gained enough psychic or emotional distance to write these memory poems. I was also becoming a better poet. . . . I hadn't ever thought of this before but it occurs to me now that writing 'Summertime' was the way I achieved it, was part of the process, at least."[19] In the poem referenced "'Summertime and the Living . . .'" Hayden places the "invisible circus" child at the perceptual center of the poem in its opening lines, changing him from subject to object:

> Nobody planted roses, he recalls,
> but sunflowers gangled there sometimes,
> tough-stalked and bold
> and like the vivid children there unplanned.
> There circus-poster horses curveted
> in trees of heaven
> above the quarrels and shattered glass,
> and he was bareback rider of them all.

In his final childhood recollections, "Elegies for Paradise Valley," published in 1977, Hayden completes the circuit of childhood recollection, resolving the images of "ethereal jitterbug" and "nocturnal mood" first sketched in his journal "1946":

> We'd dance there, Uncle
> Crip and I,
> for though I spoke
> my pieces well in Sunday School,
>
> I knew myself (precocious
> in the ways of guilt
> and secret pain)
> the devil's own rag babydoll.

Also first appearing in *The Lion and the Archer*, "Homage to the Empress of the Blues" emphasizes the pictorial qualities of Bessie Smith's performance in its refrains: "She came out on the stage in yards of pearls, emerging like / a favorite scenic view, flashed her golden smile and sang," and, in the concluding lines, "She came out on the stage in ostrich feathers, beaded satin, / and shone that smile on us and sang." The motif of circus posters pasted on ghetto walls recurs with "Because grey laths began somewhere to show from underneath / torn hurdygurdy lithographs of dollfaced heaven."

Offering a healing celebration of black life and culture, "Homage to the Empress of the Blues" is posited in counterpoint to the racist mockery of black life Hayden renders in "A Ballad of Remembrance," permitting the reader to view the complex dimensions of art and identity in black life.

Hayden's condemnation of racial, religious, and political persecution was one of the major themes of his poetry, and it takes on a contemporary, nonpolemical style in *The Lion and the Archer*. He condemned fascism and war in a series of poems in *Heart-Shape in the Dust* (1940), "Words This Spring," "Poem in Time of War," "Prophecy," and "The Wind, the Weathercock and the Warrior's Ghost." In *The Lion and the Archer* Hayden published a poem, "Eine Kleine Nachtmusik," that had first appeared in the *Fisk Herald* in 1947 and was then revised and reprinted in his collection *A Ballad of Remembrance* (1962). Set in Vienna, "Eine Kleine Nachtmusik" depicts the ruins of Europe in the aftermath of Nazi Germany's devastation. The poem is organized in three stanzas. The first introduces postwar Vienna, and the second portrays the central figure, "Anton the student," who is reading in his cold room, "Anton aching reads re-reads the dimming lines, / warms his fingers at the candleshine and turns the page."

Like the other poems in *The Lion and the Archer*, "Eine Kleine Nachtmusik" is cast in a carnival, circus-like motif, and, like them, there is a contrast between the seeming gaiety of these popular entertainments and a somber reality, as seen in the concluding stanza, which imparts a cutting irony to the title taken from Mozart's felicitous serenade:

III.

Now as the ferris wheel revolves to extrovert neomusic
and soldiers pay with cigarettes and candybars
for rides for rides with the famished girls whose colloquies
with death have taught them how to play at being whores:

Now as skin-and-bones Europe hurts all over from the
    swastika's
hexentanz: oh think of Anton, Anton brittle, Anton crystalline;
think what the winter moon, the leper beauty of a Gothic
    tale, must see:
the ice-azure likeness of a young man reading, carved most
    craftily.

"Eine Kleine Nachtmusik" also appears in Hayden's 1946 journal in a longer version that explicitly links Anton to the historical persecution of Jews. This journal entry, deleted from the published version, registers that theme:

> He waits and reads. He is cold and starving and knows he will die
> of hunger and knows there is bread
>   enough and to spare. But this
> *is what* it means to be of Europe and a Jew.
> The lightless chandelier, the reddish walls stained with time
> the candle guttering and the narcotic
> cold, but mostly the lonely unnecessary death
> he sees are variations on the themes
> of Europe and of Jew, redactions of a text
> that has remained the same.

A very early version of "The Rabbi" appears in a journal from 1948, apparently inspired by the first wave of newsreels and other photographic evidence of the Holocaust:

> I cannot get out of my mind that ruin, that heap, that cairn
> Of charred bones, of mouths open as though screaming still,
> Of flesh calcified, tortured and hurt out of all humanhood
> This is all that is left of those who were foolish enough to be Jews.

In the second stanza Hayden links this Holocaust and its victims to childhood Jewish friends from Paradise Valley:

> II

> Oh Molly, Eva, Harry it was you that with a silken [*word illegible*]
> snatched out the poison fangs from Jew
> Despite our elders' fears and warnings, we
> like the spies we used to play at being
> procured, betrayed the secrets of our loving enemies

The remainder of this stanza catalogs their childish pranks and games and ends with a lament for his vanished friends. In the third stanza linkage is made, "I see your faces, oh my dears, how many times— / Nostalgias mingle with the horrors that I feel," and Hayden proceeds with a parallel catalog of concentration camp paraphernalia and atrocities.

With his characteristic fidelity to rendered image, Hayden edits
and revises out all excess of sentiment and detail from these drafts.
In its final version as "The Rabbi," the poem focuses upon the fig-
ure of the rabbi, perhaps the prototype for "others" in Hayden's
poems who pose unsettling questions to received biases and values.
The antinomies of blacks and Jews cataloged in the journal draft are
compressed, "And I learned schwartze too / And schnapps, which
schwartzes bought / on credit from 'Jew Baby.'" The poem con-
cludes with an austere acknowledgment of their mutual separation:

> But the synagogue became
> New Calvary.
> The rabbi bore my friends off
> in his prayer shawl.

The drafts from Hayden's 1946 and 1948 notebooks are reformu-
lated again in the poem "In light half nightmare and half vision,"
first published in *Figure of Time* and included in the *Collected Poems*
as "From the Corpse Woodpiles, from the Ashes":

> From the corpse woodpiles, from the ashes and staring pits
> of Buchenwald, Dachau they come—
>
> *O David, Hirschel, Eva, cops and robbers with*
> *me once, their faces are like yours—*
> from Johannesburg, from Seoul. Their struggles are all
> horizons,
> their deaths encircle me.

In this treatment of modern inhumanity Hayden has widened the
circle of genocide to include South Africa and Korea. Assuming the
persona of the horrified witness, Hayden runs "Through target
streets . . . in light part nightmare and part vision." His final resolu-
tion now is religious, not political; the material motives of bread
and social conflict are gone. The solution lies in his Bahá'í faith, in
the prophet Baha'u'llah, incarcerated in "that cold cloacal cell /
where He, who is man beatified / And Godly mystery, / lies
chained, His pain / our anguish and our anodyne."

The title poem of *Figure of Time*, "Figure," and "In light half
nightmare . . ." are placed on facing pages. In "Figure" the subject
is a lynching victim. One can infer from Hayden's alignment of
these two poems that he regards the issues of America's discrimi-

nation and persecution of blacks and the issues of colonialism and the Holocaust to be linked. The lynching victim is central to contemporary reality, "Is metaphor of a place, a time. Is our / time geometrized":

FIGURE

He would slump to his knees, now that his agonies
are accomplished, would fall but for the chain that binds
him to the tall columnar tree.

His head hangs heavily away to one side; we
cannot see his face. The dead weight of
the quelled head has pulled

The haltering chain tight. A clothesline nooses
both wrists, forcing his arms in an arrowing angle
out behind him. Stripes

Of blood like tribal markings run from naked
shoulder to naked waist. We observe how his jeans are
torn at the groin;

How the lower links of the chain cut deeply into
the small of his back and counter the sag, the downthrust.
And the chain, we observe the chain—

The kind a farmer might have had use for or a man with
a vicious dog. We have seen its like in hardware
stores; it is cheap but strong

And it serves and except for the doubled length of it lashing
him to the torture tree, he would slump to his knees, in
total subsidence fall.

He is a scythe in daylight's clutch. Is gnomon.
Is metaphor of a place, a time. Is our
time geometrized.

Hayden's earlier treatments of lynching in *Heart-Shape in the Dust* are angry and impassioned. "Figure of Time," with its hard-edged accumulation of defining detail, has a sculptured quality and through its tropes imparts a historical depth to the lynching that first begins by suggesting the Crucifixion. The pose itself, of the slumping body half-supported on the "torture tree" by a chain, suggests Jesus' death upon the Cross. While the figure's race is not indicated, the simile "Stripes / Of blood like tribal markings" evokes both an African origin as well as the Antebellum era, at that time *stripes* being a common word for lashes. The chain imagery not only denotes this victim's capture and bondage to the tree, but its repetition emphasizes the primal confinement of slavery and the reification of its values. This black, this "figure of time," is a gnomon, the shadow cast by the style of a sundial to tell the time. The exact description, its understatement, makes concrete the horror of lynching. In his depiction of the tortured black as "metaphor of a place, a time. Is our / time geometrized" Hayden establishes racism as a fundamental moral issue of contemporary America. "Figure" is the expression of Hayden's mature style and vision. He has reined in some of the excesses of his baroque style but has retained the keen imagery, tight rhythm, precise diction, and sense of the defining symbol that characterize his best poetry.[20]

From 1946 through 1948 Robert Hayden transformed his poetry from a Left populist style that favored social commentary to a modernist aesthetic rich in symbolism and surrealist method. The fruition of this effort was *The Lion and the Archer*. Hayden did not relinquish his Left humanist values, although the McCarthyism of the 1950s and the segregated environment of the South constrained their expression. Instead, he increasingly came to focus upon the moral issues that he perceived to be at the center of socioeconomic realities. With "Figure" and "In light half nightmare . . ." Hayden's transition from Left populist poet to modernist is complete, and he proceeded to demonstrate in his later work how effectively this style could address major moral and social concerns.

NOTES

1. Until the advent of the civil rights movement, the majority of black academics found their job opportunities confined to the historically black colleges and universities of the South.

2. Langston Hughes and Arna Bontemps, ed., *The Poetry of the Negro* (Garden City, N.Y.: Doubleday, 1949), 165.

3. Cited in John Hatcher, *From the Auroral Darkness* (Oxford: George Ronald, 1984), 20.

4. Pontheolla T. Williams, *Robert Hayden: A Critical Analysis of His Poetry* (Urbana and Chicago: University of Illinois Press, 1987), 27 28.

5. Robert Hayden, *Collected Prose* (Ann Arbor: University of Michigan Press, 1984), 41–42.

6. Robert Hayden, *Heart-Shape in the Dust* (Detroit: Falcon Press, 1940), 27.

7. Robert Hayden, *Kaleideoscope: Poems by American Negro Poets* (New York: Harcourt, Brace, and World 1967), xx.

8. Steven Vincent Benét, *John Brown's Body,* ed. Mabel A. Bessey (New York: Rinehart and Co., 1941), 339. Hayden, *Collected Prose,* 162.

9. Hayden, *Collected Prose,* 185.

10. Ibid., 186.

11. Federico García Lorca, "The Poetic Image in Don Luis de Góngora," *Poet in New York,* trans. Ben Belitt (New York: Grove Press, 1955), 167–77.

12. Major texts that had been translated include *Lament for the Death of a Bullfighter and Other Poems,* trans. A. L. Lloyd (London: Heinemann, 1937); *The Poet in New York and Other Poems,* trans. Rolfe Humphries (New York: Norton, 1940); *Poems,* trans. Stephen Spender and J. L. Gili (New York: Oxford University Press, 1939), as well as a number of Lorca's plays. At least twelve major articles and reviews about Lorca had been published by 1943, by authors including William Carlos Williams, Arturo Barea, Muriel Rukeyser, and Edwin Honig in journals such as *Poetry, Kenyon Review, New Republic,* and *Horizon.*

13. Herbert Read, "Surrealism and the Romantic Principle," in *Criticism: The Foundations of Modern Literary Judgement,* ed. Mark Schorer, Josephine Miles, and Gordon McKenzie (New York: Harcourt, Brace and Company, 1948), 95–115.

14. Ibid., 111.

15. Published in *Phylon* in 1944, "Middle Passage" preceded *The Lion and the Archer* by several years. It was then published in Edwin Seaver's *Cross Section: 1945.* Evidence from the *Phylon* version indicates that Hayden had reworked "Middle Passage" from earlier versions written in the Left populist style of *The Black Spear.* In his interview with Paul McCluskey, Hayden states that he was working on "Middle Passage" in 1942 but did not complete it in time for inclusion in his 1942 Hopwood manuscript. In the absence of a paper trail of earlier versions of "Middle Passage" one must focus analysis upon the development of Hayden's modernism as seen in *The Lion and the Archer.*

16. Kalamu ya Salaam, letter to author, 14 March 2000. Also see Williams, *Robert Hayden,* 54.

17. Hayden tells of the background to "A Ballad of Remembrance" in his interview with McCluskey (*Collected Prose,* 154–56). Hayden met Van Doren in 1945 at Xavier University in a reading promoting U.S. Treasury bonds, Hayden appearing at the behest of the black author and writer William Dean Pickens, who was an official in the Treasury Department. Van Doren spoke on world peace, and Hayden followed him, reading "Middle Passage." They struck up a conversation afterward (Hayden says he read badly, was flustered, and then was consoled by Van Doren) and tried to have coffee in the French Quarter, but all the facilities were segregated. They did

manage it the next day. Hayden wrote "Ballad" the following summer at Fisk. The poem compresses the events of several days into its kaleidoscopic narrative .

18. Charles Lynch, "Robert Hayden and Gwendolyn Brooks: A Critical Study" (Ph.D. diss., New York University, 1977).

19. Hayden, *Collected Prose,* 138–39.

20. "Figure" is a fully achieved poem, but Hayden chose to omit it from his *Collected Poems.* He retained the chain imagery and reworked it into "Night, Death, Mississippi," in which a lynching is narrated through various voices of white characters.

WILBURN WILLIAMS, JR.

Covenant of Timelessness and Time: Symbolism and History in Robert Hayden's *Angle of Ascent*

I

The appearance of Robert Hayden's *Angle of Ascent* is something of a problematic event for students of the Afro-American tradition in poetry, for, while it gives us occasion to review and pay homage to the best work of one of our finest poets, it insistently calls to mind the appalling tardiness of our recognition of his achievement. A meticulous craftsman whose exacting standards severely limit the amount of his published verse, Robert Hayden has steadily accumulated over the course of three decades a body of poetry so distinctive in character and harmonious in development that its very existence seems more fated than willed, the organic issue of a natural principle rather than the deliberate artifice of a human imagination.[1] But, in spite of official honors—Hayden is now the poetry consultant at the Library of Congress and a Fellow of the Academy of American Poets—and a formidable reputation among critics, Hayden has received surprisingly little notice in print. Unless we suffer another of those sad fits of inattention that have so far limited Hayden's readership, *Angle of Ascent* should win for him the regard he has long deserved. With the exception of *Heart-Shape in the Dust,* the apprenticeship collection of 1940, poetry from every previous work of Hayden's is represented here, and we can see clearly the remarkable fertility of the symbolist's union with the historian, the bipolar extremes of Hayden's singular poetic genius.

Robert Hayden is a poet whose symbolistic imagination is intent on divining the shape of a transcendent order of spirit and grace that might redeem a world bent on its own destruction. His

From *Chant of Saints,* ed. Michael S. Harper and Robert B. Stepto (Urbana and Chicago: University of Illinois Press, 1979), 66–84.

155

memory, assailed by the discontinuities created by its own fallibility, is equally determined to catch and preserve every shadow and echo of the actual human experience in which our terribleness stands revealed. In poem after poem Hayden deftly balances the conflicting claims of the ideal and actual. Spiritual enlightenment in his poetry is never the reward of evading material fact. The realities of imagination and the actualities of history are bound together in an alliance that makes neither thinkable without the other. Robert Hayden's poetry proposes that, if it is in the higher order of spirit that the gross actualities of life find their true meaning, it is also true that that transcendent realm is meaningful to man only as it is visibly incarnate on the plane of his experience.

Viewed as a theory of poetics, Hayden's characteristic method of composition will hardly strike anyone as unique. His preoccupation with the relationship between natural and spiritual facts puts him squarely in the American tradition emanating from Emerson; we are not at all amazed, therefore, when we find correspondences between his work and that of figures like Dickinson and Melville. The brief lyric "Snow," for instance—

> Smooths and burdens,
> endangers, hardens.
>
> Erases, revises.
> Extemporizes
>
> Vistas of lunar solitude.
> Builds, embellishes a mood.

—recalls the Dickinson of "It sifts from Leaden Sieves—."[2] But the brooding presence of death lurking behind the brave outward show of a playful wit that is common in Dickinson is uncharacteristic of Hayden, and a comparison with Melville casts more light on his habitual concerns.

In "El-Hajj Malik El-Shabazz" Malcolm X is likened to Ahab— "Rejecting Ahab, he was of Ahab's tribe. / 'Strike through the mask!'"—and "The Diver" closely parallels chapter 92 of Melville's *White-Jacket*. To be sure, Hayden's speaker and Melville's narrator are impelled by distinctly different motives. The former's descent is a conscious act, a matter of deliberate choice, whereas White-Jacket's one hundred–foot fall into a nighttime sea cannot be as-

cribed to his sensible will, however strong his subconscious long-
ing for death might be. Yet the underlying pattern of each man's or-
deal is the same. The approach to death is paradoxically felt as a
profound intensification of life. Death takes, or at least seems to
promise to take, both men to the very core of life. Thus, White-
Jacket, in his precipitous drop "toward the infallible center of the
terraqueous globe," finds all he has seen, read, heard, thought, and
felt seemingly "intensified in one fixed idea in [his] soul." Yielding
to the soft embrace of the sea, he is shocked into revulsion of death
almost purely by chance—"of a sudden some fashionless form"
brushes his side, tingling his nerves with the thrill of being alive.[3]
In like manner Hayden's diver's longing to be united with "those
hidden ones" in a kind of well-being that lies so deep as to be be-
yond the reach of articulate speech, his passion to "have / done
with self and / every dinning / vain complexity" can be satisfied
only if he tears away the mask that sustains his life. The intricate
contrapuntal development of the poem brings an overwhelming
extremity of feeling to the critical moment that finds the diver
poised between life and death. His going down is both easeful and
swift, a plunge into water and a flight through air. The flower crea-
tures of the deep flash and shimmer yet are at the same time mere
"lost images / fadingly remembered." The dead ship, a lifeless hulk
deceptively encrusted with the animate "moss of bryozoans,"
swarms with forms of life that are themselves voracious instruments
of death. And what liberates the diver from this labyrinthine and
potentially annihilating swirl of contradictory instincts and percep-
tions is never clear. As is the case with White-Jacket, he "somehow"
begins the "measured rise," no nearer to winning the object of his
quest but presumably possessed of a deeper, more disciplined ca-
pacity for experience. (*Measured* is decidedly meant to make us
think of the poet's subordination to the rules of his craft.)

The most fruitful area of comparison between Hayden and
Melville is to be found in their tellingly different attitudes toward
the symbolistic enterprise itself. Committed to reconciling within
the ambiguous flux of poetic language the warring oppositions cre-
ated by the divisiveness of discursive logic, the symbolist finds him-
self necessarily presupposing the very terms of order—subject and
object, mind and matter, spirit and nature—his method seeks to
erase.[4] Because the symbolist's stance is such a difficult posture to
keep, the idea of the artist as acrobat and the conception of his craft
as dance of language are conventional figures in modern literature

and criticism. In Hayden, however, the drama of the symbolist's tightrope walk is objectified infrequently. The symbolist's striving for balance is not seen in what Hayden's speakers do but is heard in how they talk: tone assumes the burden that topic might bear. Hayden's characteristically soft-spoken and fluid voice derives much of its power from the evident contrast between the maelstrom of anguish out of which it originates and the quiet reflecting pool of talk into which it is inevitably channeled. Interestingly enough, when Hayden does write poetry in which the action is clearly analogous to the symbolist's task of wizarding a track through a jungle of contraries, the prevailing tone is not his customary seriousness. In "The Performers" the modesty of two high-rise window cleaners subtly mocks the speaker's misuse of their daring as a pretext for a kind of absurd metaphysical strutting that his own desk-bound timidity will not allow. In "The Lions" an animal trainer whose mentality is a peculiar blend of Schopenhauerian willfulness and transcendentalist vision breaks out into an ebullient speech that is at once divinely rapturous and somehow wildly funny:

> And in the kingdom-cage
> as I make my lions leap,
>   through nimbus-fire leap,
> oh, as I see them leap—
>   unsparing beauty that
> creates and serves my will,
>   the savage real that clues
> my vision of the real—
>   my soul exults and Holy cries
> and Holy Holy cries, he said.

Yet, whenever Robert Hayden loses his artistic balance, his fall is not likely to be in Melville's direction. The enormous gulf between the unified paradise of the symbolistic imagination and the outright hellishness of a world rife with division, the gulf that drew Ahab and Pierre to their deaths and drowned Melville the writer in silence, poses no threat to Hayden. Hayden's peril comes from a different quarter, and it comes disguised as his salvation. It is precisely Hayden's faith in the ultimate redemptiveness of the universal and timeless order of spirit that threatens to kill the life of his art. Insofar as his poetry is concerned, Hayden's God and Devil are one. The blinding light of faith can shrivel up the sensuous specificity of poetry just as surely as it can enkindle the life of the world of inert fact. Hayden's divergence from Melville here is nowhere more apparent than in "Theme and Variation." Readers of Hayden will recognize the voice of the Heraclitus-like stranger who delivers the poem's wisdom as the poet's own:

> I sense, he said, the lurking rush, the sly
> transience flickering at the edge of things.
> I've spied from the corner of my eye
> upon the striptease of reality.
>
> There is, there is, he said, an immanence
> that turns to curiosa all I know;
> that changes light to rainbow darkness
> wherein God waylays us and empowers.

Set these lines against this sentence from the famous last paragraph of "The Whiteness of the Whale" in *Moby-Dick:*

> And when we consider that other theory of the natural philosophers, that all other earthly hues—every stately or lovely emblazoning—the sweet tinges of sunset skies and woods; yea, and the gilded velvets of butterflies, and the butterfly cheeks of young girls; all these are but subtle deceits, not actually inherent in substances, but only laid on from without; so that all deified Nature absolutely paints like the harlot, whose allurements cover nothing but the charnel-house within; and when we proceed further, and consider that the mystical cosmetic which produces every one of her hues, the great principle of light, forever remains white or colorless in itself, and if operating without medium upon matter, would touch all objects, even tulips and roses, with its own blank tinge—pondering all this, the palsied universe lies before us a leper; and like wilful travelers in Lapland, who refuse to wear colored and coloring glasses upon their eyes, so the wretched infidel gazes himself blind at the monumental white shroud that wraps all the prospect around him.

Hayden's stranger reverses Ishmael on every point. His perceptions nourish belief; Ishmael's, skepticism and doubt. He is pious, and Ishmael is blasphemous. Melville's Nature dresses, while Hayden's disrobes. The former's adornment is emblematic

of a diabolical deceitfulness; the latter's nudity points to a sanctu-
ary of grace. Where Melville's eye strips away delusory hues to
gaze in horror upon the "blank tinge" of a "palsied" and leprous
universe, Hayden's eye spies out an indwelling spirit that trans-
forms an undifferentiated light into a sacredly tinged darkness
wherein man discovers his hope and his blessing. But here Hay-
den can no more be accused of a naive optimism than Melville
can be charged with blind cynicism. The ironic intimation of vi-
olent assault reverberating in *waylays* checks the stranger's rush
into the plenitude of divine immanence, maintaining the poem's
complexity and integrity.

Nevertheless, the point remains that the beneficent banditry of
Hayden's divinity has far more in common with the onslaughts of
Donne's Three-Personed God than with anything ever done by the
maddeningly elusive Jehovah of Melville. Hayden's supreme high-
wayman is more apt to strip the poet of his facts than to rob him
of his faith, which might be heaven for religion but certainly hell
for poetry. As much is evident in the increasingly sparing detail and
more cryptic utterance that marks the poet's recent work. At his
best Hayden composes poetry that is paradoxically both rich in
statement and ascetic in temperament. In "Stars" and the Akhen-
aten section of "Two Egyptian Portrait Masks," however, an abstract
and unconvincing expression of acute religious belief shows only a
marginal relation to the concrete particularities of human experi-
ence. The latter verse segment plainly suffers in contrast to the
paean to Nefertiti that precedes it. Meditating on the carving of a
woman

> whose burntout
> loveliness alive in stone
> is like the fire of precious stones
>
> dynastic
> death (gold mask and vulture wings)
> charmed her with so she would never die

the poet tersely harmonizes a succession of discordant sensations.
But in the Akhenaten companion piece, the poet's contemplative-
ness has no equivalent object on which it can focus—admittedly, it
would take an extraordinary imagination to bridge the gap be-
tween the majesty of Akhenaten's dream of human oneness and the

fat hips and bloated abdomens of the Pharaoh's Karnak colossi—
and consequently the poetry lacks force:

> Aten
> multi-single like the sun
> reflecting Him by Him
>
> reflected.
> Anubis howled. The royal prophet reeled
> under the dazzling weight
>
> of vision,
> exalted—maddened?—the spirit moving
> in his heart: Aten Jahveh Allah God.

Certainly, there is nothing in this like the faultless description of
death as "dynastic," a brilliant conceit whereby Hayden associates
the idea of the unbroken hereditary transfer of power from gener-
ation to generation with the eternal dominion of death, thus find-
ing death's very indomitability dependent upon the principle of
generation, or life. What Emerson, the one indispensable figure in
any discussion of American symbolism, once said about the poet's
duty is patently applicable to Robert Hayden, and it can serve both
as an accurate representation of what Hayden does in his best work
and as a necessary corrective to the etherealizing proclivities of
Hayden's symbolist genius:

> The poet, like the electric rod, must reach from a point nearer
> the sky than all surrounding objects, down to the earth, and into
> the dark wet soil, or neither is of use. The poet must not only
> converse with pure thought, but he must demonstrate it almost
> to the senses. His words must be pictures, his verses must be
> spheres and cubes, to be seen and smelled and handled.[5]

II

However much we might like to dwell on the manifold possibili-
ties of Hayden's symbolism, particularly in relation to the practices
of Yeats and Eliot (to whom he sometimes alludes) and to Auden
(whom he has said was a key factor in his growth as a poet),[6] no
discussion of his poetry can avoid the question of the place a sense

of history occupies in his work. Every reader is quick to detect a pervasive sense of the past and a powerful elegiac strain in his work. In the most thorough examination of Hayden's poetry we have, Charles T. Davis has recounted the crucial contribution of Hayden's extensive research in the slave trade to "Middle Passage," and he has called attention to the importance of Hayden's grasp of the Afro-American folk tradition to "O Daedalus, Fly Away Home," "The Ballad of Nat Turner," and "Runagate Runagate."[7] Aware of the paradox, Hayden has referred to himself as a "romantic realist," a symbolist compelled to be realistic, and Michael S. Harper has called him a "symbolist poet struggling with the facts of history."[8]

Now, nothing is perhaps more tempting or more mistaken than to infer from all this that the historian in Hayden is at odds with the symbolist. A close reading of the poetry will not support such a conclusion. Because of the popularity of "Middle Passage" and "Runagate Runagate"—poems unmistakably black in subject matter and sometimes identifiably black in use of language—the historical impulse in Hayden is understandably allied in the minds of many readers with the poet's pride in his own blackness. Since Hayden's recognition of his blackness is widely (and, we think, most aberrantly) perceived as a grudging one, the symbolist in Hayden is often viewed as the enemy of his essentially historical, and black, muse. If that Bob Hayden only knew better, the argument (it is hardly reasoning) goes, he would leave that symbolism stuff alone (the poetry of *The Night-Blooming Cereus,* for example) and get back to his roots. Certainly, Hayden's insistence that he be judged as a poet and not as a Negro poet only exacerbates this misapprehension, and no appeal to the extensive exploitation of symbolism in the spirituals and the blues is likely to quiet the suspicion that Hayden's symbolist clings parasitically to the creativity of his black historian.[9]

But, while it is easy to see that the symbolistic method is operative in poems as disparate as "Middle Passage" and "The Night-Blooming Cereus," it is not so evident that Hayden's historical sensibility is also at work in poems that have no obvious connection with historical incidents. To apprehend the unity of Hayden's entire body of work, it is necessary to understand that his fascination with history is but one part of a more comprehensive entrancement in the mystery of time. Robert Hayden is clearly more intrigued by the process of change, the paradoxes of permanence and evanescence, than the particular substances that undergo change. Here we are interested in the psychological and artistic implications of his dramatic re-creations of historical events and not just in the nature of the events themselves. Throughout the poetry of Hayden we encounter a memory and an imagination pitted against the losses time's passage inevitably entails. We meet a consciousness struggling to retain the finest nuances of its own experience and seeking to enter into the experience of others from whom it is alienated by time and space. The fundamental source of Hayden's productivity, the wellspring of his poetic activity, lies in the ability of the human memory to negotiate the distance between time past and time present and the capacity of a profoundly sympathetic imagination to transcend the space between self and other. The complex interactions generated by the life of memory and imagination define the basic unity of Hayden's work.

Yet, while we think that Hayden's obsession with time is, in a sense, larger than his deep involvement in the Afro-American past, it would be foolish to deny the special place black American history occupies in his development as a poet. The 1940s, the years in which Hayden patiently studied the annals of his black past, are also the years in which he matured as an artist.[10] Simply to live in a culture with a sense of the past as notoriously shallow as this one's is burden enough. A black like Hayden, the fierceness of whose need to know his history is matched only by the ponderousness of the mass of distortion and fabrication under which his past lies buried, finds that even the truthful accounts of the black American experience, which cannot really take him farther back than the eighteenth century anyway, give him the composite picture of a collectivity, rather than detailed portraits of individuals. It can hardly seem an accident to him that historians have until recently slighted the value of the slave narratives, documents that shake him with a revelation more awesome than any truth contained in the most complete compilation of data seen even in the wildest dreams of the maddest cliometrician. When he looks at his mental picture of Representative Afro-American Man, he sees that it is a mosaic formed of bits of the lives of many men, and there are moments when he wonders whether the portrait typifies the truth of art or the deceit of artifice. The face is formed of fragments themselves faceless; the sacred text of his people's experience an accretion of footnotes culled from the profane texts of another's. His past is pregnant with a significance that it is incapable of giving birth to.

It is a speechless past peopled with renowned personalities who are ironically impersonal:

> Name in a footnote. Faceless name.
> Moot hero shrouded in Betsy Ross
> and Garvey flags—propped up
> by bayonets, forever falling.
>
> ("Crispus Attucks")

Viewed in this somber light, the primary significance of Hayden's famous poems of Cinquez, Turner, Tubman, and Douglass resides in the poet's imaginative attempt to reforge his present's broken links with the past. The past, Hayden says, need not be past at all. His speakers confront their history as active participants in its making and not as distant onlookers bemoaning their isolation; the past is carried into the present. Although the poet's mind ventures backward in time, the poems themselves invariably close with a statement or action that points forward to the reader's present. The progress of "Middle Passage" is through death "to life upon these shores," and the reader leaves the poem with his attention riveted to *this* life on *these* shores just as much as it is fixed on the historical reality of the slave trade. The man we leave at the conclusion of "The Ballad of Nat Turner" has his revolution still before him. "Runagate Runagate" ends with an invitation, "Come ride-a my train," whose rhythm subtly anticipates the action to be undertaken and the powerful assertion of yet another intention to act—"Mean mean mean to be free." The accentual sonnet on Frederick Douglass is poetry that moves like the beating of a living heart. The poet emphasizes that the dead hero is still a vital force. The first long periodic sentence seems to resist coming to an end. The poem celebrates not a man who has been but a man still coming into being. Although commemorative in nature, it does not so much elegize a past as prophesy a future. Frederick Douglass, the poet, and all enslaved humanity are united in one generative process.

A great deal of Hayden's success in undoing the dislocations of time and space can be attributed to his poet-speakers' uncanny ability to give themselves over to the actuality they contemplate. They become what they behold; known object and knowing subject unite. Like psychic mediums, his speakers obliterate distinctions between self and other; the dead and distant take possession of their voices. Take, for example, these lines from "The Dream (1863)":

That evening Sinda thought she heard the drums
and hobbled from her cabin to the yard.
The quarters now were lonely-still in willow dusk
after the morning's ragged jubilo,
    when laughing crying singing the folks went off
with Marse Lincum's soldier boys.
But Sinda hiding would not follow them: those
Buckras with their ornery
    funning, cussed commands, oh they were not were not
the hosts the dream had promised her.

The poem is obviously a third-person narrative, but the space
separating narrator and actor is frequently violated. The speaker's
voice modulates effortlessly into the cadences of the slaves. *Marse
Lincum, Buckra,* and *ornery* are words heard in the accents of the
slaves. The pathos of the cry "oh they were not were not" is so
extraordinary because, syntax notwithstanding, it is Sinda's own
voice we hear and not the poet's. In six lines in "The Rabbi"
Hayden gives a virtuoso demonstration of the resources of his
voice:

>   And I learned schwartze too
>
>   And schnapps, which schwartzes bought
>   on credit from "Jew Baby."
>   Tippling ironists laughed and said
>   he'd soon be rich as Rothschild
>
>   From their swinish Saturdays.

In the first two lines the poet's retrospective view of the blacks of
his youth is clearly refracted through the cultural lens of the Jews
he knew. By the end of the third line, however, his perspective has
shifted, and it is now the Jews who are being looked upon from a
black point of view. *Credit* is the pivotal term in this transition, for
it not only allows the speaker to describe objectively the economic
relationship of black to Jew but also lets him draw on the powerful
connotations this word has in the Afro-American speech commu-
nity. The last three lines of indirect quotation, framed by two jocu-
larly incongruous phrases that are clearly of the poet's own making,
indicate that the speaker finally assumes an amused posture inde-
pendent of the viewpoint of either black or Jew but remarkably

sensitive to both. And there is a social morality implicit in this display of Hayden's multivocal talents. What might at first seem to be merely a technical device has enormous ethical implications. When the poet says in the last stanza,

> But the synagogue became
> New Calvary.
> The rabbi bore my friends off
> in his prayer shawl.

he means for us to see that the loss of his childhood friends Hirschel and Molly is part of a wholesale separation of black and Jew, a separation that will brook no opposition from considerations as flimsy as one human being's love for another. "New Calvary," tellingly isolated in a single line, is not only the name of the black church that succeeds the synagogue. It represents, too, a place and an action. It is the hill where Christianity and Jewry part ways, the site where Hayden's ideal of human oneness is sacrificed, a modern reenactment of that old attempt at redemption that ironically, bitterly, only sped man in his fall out of unity into division.

But there is a sinister dimension to this intercourse between self and other, present and past. Robert Hayden knows, and this is a sign of his strength, that openness is also vulnerability, that the past in which one finds possibilities of inspiration and renewal can exert a malignant influence on the present. In "A Ballad of Remembrance" the poet is besieged by specters pressing upon him the value of their individual adaptations to American racism. The Zulu king urges accommodation, the gunmetal priestess preaches hate, and a motley contingent of saints, angels, and mermaids, blind to the realities of evil, chime out a song of naive love. These competing voices drive the poet to the brink of madness. In "Tour 5" an autumn ride into the country becomes a frightening excursion into a surreal world alive with ancient conflicts between black, white, and red men. In "Locus" the Southland lies wasted under the blight of its own history. The present abdicates to the superior force of the past. The redbuds are "like momentary trees / of an illusionist"; there is a "violent metamorphosis, / with every blossom turning / deadly and memorial soldiers." Life here is stunted, reality the bondsman of a dream of disaster. The past forecloses its mortgage on the future:

Here spareness, rankness, harsh
brilliances; beauty of what's hardbitten,
knotted, stinted, flourishing
in despite, on thorny meagerness
thriving, twisting into grace.
Here symbol houses
where the brutal dream lives out its lengthy
dying. Here the past, adored and
unforgiven. Here the past—
soulscape, Old Testament battleground
of warring shades whose weapons kill.

Closely related to Hayden's interest in the cunning ironies of history is his anxiety for the fate of myth and religion in the modern world. This concern provides the motivation of some of his best poetry. Take "Full Moon," for example, which we quote in full:

No longer throne of a goddess to whom we pray,
no longer the bubble house of childhood's
tumbling Mother Goose man,

The emphatic moon ascends—
the brilliant challenger of rocket experts,
the white hope of communications men.

Some I love who are dead
were watchers of the moon and knew its lore;
planted seeds, trimmed their hair,

Pierced their ears for gold hoop earrings
as it waxed or waned.
It shines tonight upon their graves.

And burned in the garden of Gethsemane,
its light made holy by the dazzling tears
with which it mingled.

And spread its radiance on the exile's path
of Him who was The Glorious One,
its light made holy by His holiness.

Already a mooted goal and tomorrow perhaps
an arms base, a livid sector,
the full moon dominates the dark.

The world we encounter here is radically impoverished. The slow process by which the rise of positivistic science has emptied Nature of all religious significance is recapitulated in the fall of childhood's illusions before the advance of adult skepticism. For contemporary man the moon exists only as a means of flaunting the triumphs of his technological vanity. But the poet sees in this diminished moon an analogue to the deprivations death has exacted from him and with this crucial recognition of a mutuality of fates begins the movement toward recovery. Like the breathtaking expansion of meaning we witness in Eliot's "Sweeney among the Nightingales" when we leap from the nightingales "singing near The Convent of the Sacred Heart" to those that "sang within the bloody wood / When Agamemnon cried aloud,"[11] there is a startling intensification of feeling in the transition from a light that "shines tonight upon their graves" to the light that "burned in the garden of Gethsemane." But Hayden knows that this age looks upon Jesus Christ and the prophet Baha'u'llah (The Glorious One of the penultimate stanza and the founder of Hayden's Bahá'í faith) with a cynical regard and that any appeal to them to restore the significance of a degraded Nature would sound highly artificial and entirely unconvincing.

Like Flannery O'Connor, who frequently discerns in overt denials of faith ironic avowals of the existence of God, Hayden subverts the materialism of technology to make a claim for the reality of spirit. The moon that is now meaningless will once again become all-meaningful, he says, not as the throne of a benign deity or as an object of harmless childish fancies but as an arms base that can end all life. The meaning that has been lost to the achievement of science reasserts itself with a vengeance by means of that very same achievement. This ironic turn of events is itself fully in keeping with the traditional view of the moon as the symbol of eternal recurrence. The full weight of this paradox is felt in the critical word *livid,* on which a whole world of ambiguities turns. As meaning "ashen" or "pallid," *livid* is both a forthright description of a full moon and suggestive of the moon's fearful retreat before the press of technology. As meaning "black and blue," *livid,* in conjunction with the reference to the moon as "the white hope of communications men," suggests a moon bruised and discolored by the assaults of the Jack Johnsons of science. As a synonym for *enraged* or *angry, livid* further elaborates upon the implied meanings of this prizefighting metaphor, and, by connecting it to the ominous possibilities of the moon's use as an arms base, subtly transforms the earlier reference to the moon as victim into an image of the moon as aggressor. And when we finally consider *livid* as meaning "red," that satellite's consequence as an object of martial reverence is fully revealed, for the red moon is the moon foreseen by John of Patmos, and its appearance announces the coming of God in His wrath, the destruction of nations and the end of time.

III

When we review the entire course of Hayden's development, the importance of the poet as historian seems to lessen drastically over time. In his last two volumes of verse only "Beginnings" immediately strikes us as aspiring to the largeness of historical vision of a "Full Moon" or the early explorations of the Afro-American past for which Hayden is chiefly known. What we feel is responsible for this change is not something so simple as the symbolist's displacement of the historian but a growing preoccupation in the historian with ever smaller units of time. Having exhausted his examination of the present and past, Hayden's historian is free to chronicle the mystery of change itself. Instead of feeling obliged to overcome the effects of change, he is more and more fascinated by single moments of metamorphosis. This is clearly the case in the poetry of *The Night-Blooming Cereus*. Standing before the "Arachne" of the black sculptor Richard Hunt, the poet is transfixed by the impenetrable mystery of the total change of essence he witnesses. At the same time his language manages to evoke Arachne's terror, it confesses, by the violent juxtaposition of concepts of motion and stasis, the human and the animal, birth and death, the singular incapacity of rational terms to represent adequately such an event:

> In goggling terror fleeing powerless to flee
> Arachne not yet arachnid and no longer woman
> in the moment's centrifuge of dying
> becoming.

The capacity of short-lived and seemingly trivial events to manifest truths of exceptional import is shown in "The Night-Blooming Cereus." The speaker initially anticipates the blooming of that flower with a casual disregard for the miracle it will actually be. He and his companion are, in effect, two decadent intellectuals whose interest in the "primitive" is really just a shallow trafficking in the exotic. For them the blossoming sanctions hedonistic indulgence: they will paint themselves and "dance / in honor of archaic mysteries." Yet so much more than they can possibly imagine depends on the appearance of that blossom. When the bud unfolds, the phenomenon of its transformation enlarges into the enigma of eternal recurrence, the riddle of the cyclical alternation of life and death. And the blasphemous are reduced to near speechlessness:

> Lunar presence,
> foredoomed, already dying,
> it charged the room
> with plangency
>
> older than human
> cries, ancient as prayers
> invoking Osiris, Krishna,
> Tezcátlipóca.
>
> We spoke
> in whispers when
> we spoke
> at all . . .

Just as Hayden's historian's engrossment with the epochal modulates into an absorption with the momentary, there is a parallel shift of his focus away from the history of a people to the biographies of individuals, away from the public figures of the past to persons who are the poet's contemporaries. The boxer Tiger Flowers and the artist Betsy Graves Reyneau take the place of Nat Turner and Harriet Tubman. If the personages that engage him impress us as having little relation to the main currents of our history, they clearly arouse anxieties in him that nothing less than a total reconsideration of the nature of history itself can assuage. Just as Hayden's early historian is compelled to personalize the past he confronts, his later one is compelled to objectivize his own subjectivity. His private anguish never locks him into the sterile dead end of solipsism; it impels him outward into the world. "The Peacock Room," Hayden tells us, grew out of an intense emotional experience. A visit to that room designed by Whistler excited painful recollections of his dead friend Betsy Graves Reyneau, who had been given a party in the same room on her twelfth birthday.[12] Contemplating the rival claims of art and life,

> Ars Longa Which is crueller
> Vita Brevis life or art?

the poet seeks shelter in Whistler's "lyric space," as he once did in the glow "of the lamp shaped like a rose" his "mother would light / . . . some nights to keep / Raw-Head-And-Bloody-Bones away." But he knows that the dreadful facts of the nightmare that is our history—"Hiroshima Watts My Lai"—scorn "the vision chambered in gold." The very title of the poem, however, has already hinted that his meditations will not issue into a simplistic espousal of art's advantages over life. The peacock is an ambiguous figure. The legendary incorruptibility of the bird's flesh has led to its adoption as a type of immortality and an image of the Resurrected Christ; but as the emblem of Pride, the root of all evil, the bird has always had ominous connotations in Christian culture. These intimations of evil remind the poet of the artist driven mad by Whistler's triumph, and the Peacock Room is transformed in his mind from sanctuary to chamber of horrors. The echoes of Stevens's "Domination of Black" and Poe's "Raven" heighten the poet's fears:

> With shadow cries
>
> the peacocks flutter down,
> their spread tails concealing her,
>   then folding, drooping to reveal
> her eyeless, old—Med School
> cadaver, flesh-object
>   pickled in formaldehyde,
> who was artist, compassionate,
> clear-eyed. Who was beloved friend.
> No more. No more.

The paradox of a lasting art that mocks man's fragility at the same time that it realizes his dream of immortality is resolved in the beatific, enigmatic smile of the Bodhisattva ("one whose being—sattva—is enlightenment—bodhi"):

> . . . What is art?
> What is life?
> What the Peacock Room?
> Rose-leaves and ashes drift
> its portals, gently spinning toward
> a bronze Bodhisattva's ancient smile.

In a remarkable way "Beginnings," the first poem of *Angle of Ascent,* reenacts the course of the fruitful collaboration of Hayden's historian and symbolist. The historian summons up the essential facts of the poet's ancestry, and the symbolist immediately translates them into the terms of art:

> Plowdens, Finns,
> Sheffeys, Haydens,
> Westerfields.
>
> Pennsylvania gothic,
> Kentucky homespun,
> Virginia baroque.

As the poem moves forward in time, the ancestors are particularized. Joe Finn appears "to join Abe Lincoln's men" and "disappears into his name." Greatgrandma Easter lingers longer before the poet's gaze, and she is remembered not for the role she took in a historic conflict but for her individual qualities: "She was more than six feet tall. At ninety could / still chop and tote firewood." The progression toward individuation that accompanies the poem's movement to the present—the sharpness of focus of the portrait of an ancestor is a direct function of that ancestor's nearness to the poet's own present—is paralleled by a growth in the poet's awareness of the figurative possibilities of language. As the historian's field of view contracts, the symbolist's artfulness becomes increasingly apparent. As we move from summaries of the entire lives of Joe Finn and Greatgrandma Easter to select moments in the lives of the poet's aunts, the symbolist's reveling in words for the beauty of their sound and rhythm becomes more evident:

> Melissabelle and Sarah Jane
> oh they took all the prizes one Hallowe'en.
> And we'll let the calico curtain fall
> on Pocahontas and the Corncob Queen

dancing the figures the callers call—
Sashay, ladies, promenade, all.

But, when the poet himself finally appears, a curious—but, for
Robert Hayden, characteristic—change occurs. The historian re-
asserts his centrality (the concluding piece is called "The Crystal
Cave Elegy"), and the poem's steady flow toward life and the pres-
ent is momentarily reversed in commemoration of the death of the
miner Floyd Collins. The symbolist's increasing involvement in the
resources of his art does not end in an autistic preoccupation with
the poet's inner life but finally turns outward in prayer for the lib-
eration of Collins. The timeless paradise of the imagination is in-
voked to release humanity from the limitations of time:

> Poor game loner
> trapped in the rock
> of Crystal Cave, as
> once in Kentucky coal-
> mine dark (I taste the
> darkness yet)
> my greenhorn dream of
> life. Alive down there
> in his grave. Open
> for him, blue door.

The province of the poet is neither the realist's moonscape of
inert matter nor the romantic's starfire of pure spirit but the middle
kingdom of actual earth that unites the two. Robert Hayden's sym-
bolist and historian long ago joined hands to seize this fertile terri-
tory as their own. Together they have kept it up very well.

NOTES

1. This meticulousness poses problems for the critic. Robert Hayden
frequently revises his work, and a poem in one collection can appear in
considerably altered form in a later collection. In general Hayden's revi-
sions involve deletions; he characteristically seeks greater economy of ex-
pression. His revisions could form the topic of a separate essay.
2. Thomas H. Johnson, ed., *Final Harvest: Emily Dickinson's Poems*
(Boston: Little, Brown, 1962), 59. The Dickinson influence here might not
be direct. It is quite possible, given the extraordinary likeness Hayden's
"Witch Doctor" bears to Gwendolyn Brooks's well-known "The Sundays
of Satin-Legs Smith," that the Dickinson influence is filtered through

Brooks, particularly the Brooks of *Annie Allen,* in which one finds poems ("A light and diplomatic bird," for example) that are virtually indistinguishable from the work of Dickinson's own hand.

3. Herman Melville, *White-Jacket: The World in a Man-of-War* (New York: Grove Press, 1952), 370.

4. See Charles Feidelson, Jr., *Symbolism and American Literature* (Chicago: University of Chicago Press, 1953), 71.

5. Quoted in F. O. Matthiessen, *American Renaissance* (New York: Oxford University Press, 1941), 54.

6. John O'Brien, ed., *Interviews with Black Writers* (New York: Liveright, 1973), 114.

7. Charles T. Davis, "Robert Hayden's Use of History," in *Modern Black Poets,* ed. Donald Gibson (Englewood Cliffs, N.J.: Prentice-Hall, 1973), 96–111.

8. *New York Times Book Review,* 22 February 1976, 34.

9. Hayden's insistence that he is a poet who happens to be Negro, made most dramatically at the Fisk University Centennial Writers' Conference in 1966, inevitably calls to mind the stance taken by Countee Cullen in the foreword to *Caroling Dusk* (New York: Harper & Brothers, 1927). Hayden was enamored of Cullen as an undergraduate, and the careful reader can detect significant correspondences between "The Ballad of Nat Turner" and "The Shroud of Color." Yet, when Cullen rejected the idea of a black poetry in favor of a poetry written by blacks, his equation of a black movement in poetry with disease clearly indicated how much he underestimated the possibilities for poetry in black American culture and how much he was intimidated by the richness of the Anglo-American poetic tradition: "to say that the pulse beat of their [i.e., the blacks'] verse shows generally such a fever, or the symptoms of such an ague, will prove on closer examination merely the moment's exaggeration of a physician anxious to establish a new literary ailment." Hayden throughout his career has prized his independence, but he has never hesitated to exploit the possibilities for poetry in Afro-American culture. At any rate, Melvin B. Tolson, the magnificent and neglected black poet who rose in opposition to Hayden at Fisk to say that blackness is prior to poetry, has himself been accused of denying his own blackness. No issue in Afro-American letters has to date generated more heat or less light than the question of what *black poet* means.

10. For the assertion that Hayden was especially concerned with Afro-American history during the 1940s, we refer the reader to Davis, "Hayden's Use of History," 97. Proof that Hayden reached his maturity during these years is to be found in the difference between the stiff poetry of *Heart-Shape in the Dust* and the elastic verse of *The Lion and the Archer* (Nashville: Hemphill Press, 1948).

11. T. S. Eliot, *The Waste Land and Other Poems* (1922; rpt., New York: Harcourt, Brace and World, 1962), 26.

12. O'Brien, *Interviews,* 120–22.

LEWIS TURCO

Angle of Ascent: The Poetry of
Robert Hayden

Julius Lester, reviewing *Words in the Mourning Time* for the *New York Times Book Review,* wrote that Robert Hayden was "one of the most underrated and unrecognized poets in America." Until the publication of Hayden's most recent volume, *Angle of Ascent: New and Selected Poems,* this was true. Various reasons might be given to account for this fact, among them foreign publication of two volumes and small press publication of others, with the attendant problems of limited distribution.

Robert Hayden has better insight into the situation, however. In a videotaped interview that he made for the "Writers' Forum" series at the State University of New York at Brockport, Hayden was asked about "Black poetry." His response was that such a term, which has the approval of many militant black poets, was useful to white academics who wish to ignore poetry written by blacks. Hayden contended that most Black poetry was and still is relegated to courses in "Black literature" and is not often taught in the standard English literature syllabus. The inference to be made is that somehow there are special standards to be applied, standards that need not be applied to "White poetry" for one reason or another. Clearly, one of the implications here is that poetry written by blacks is not good enough or not universal enough to be included in the Anglo-Saxon literary canon.

Hayden's poetry had been ghettoized along with the work of the other "Black poets." For proof that this situation remains true one need merely look to the magazines that have so far reviewed *Angle of Ascent* and notice that most, if not all of them, have felt that the book had to be reviewed by another Black.

But Robert Hayden has always wished to be judged as a poet among poets, not one to whom special rules of criticism ought to

From *Michigan Quarterly Review* 16, no. 2 (Spring 1977): 199–219.

be applied in order to make his work acceptable in more than a sociological sense. His stance, reiterated in the Brockport interview, has been well known for a long time both to militant Blacks and to "liberal" whites. Thus, if the latter have relegated Hayden to the literary ghetto along with the other Black poets, the former have seen him if not as an "Uncle Tom," at least as a reluctant resident. Perhaps this situation will best explain why Hayden has been ignored. Yet Hayden has written as much out of his ethnic background as has anyone else. In order to prove this, I intend to examine his work in the light of Stephen Henderson's codification of what constitutes Black poetry, as distinguished from "White poetry." At the same time I will refute Henderson's arguments that there are such things as ethnic "techniques." I propose to show that, in fact, Henderson's techniques are elements of ethnic Black styles and that Hayden, having written in many of these styles, is a paradigmatic poet of the English language who has been true to his roots and history, though not circumscribed by, or limited to, what is merely racial, ethnic, or personal.

In his long scholarly introduction to the anthology *Understanding the New Black Poetry* (1973) Stephen Henderson goes deeply into, as the publisher's jacket blurb puts it, "what is black technique in the poetry." Henderson believes that large questions about the value of Black poetry "cannot be resolved without considering the ethnic roots of Black poetry, which . . . are ultimately understood only by Black people themselves."

I am inclined to agree, as long as it is "ethnic roots" we're talking about. I'd go further: a poem may be so heavily ethnic that most who do not belong to the group could not understand, let alone judge, such a poem. I am well aware that "language is the main cohesive force within a given ethnic group," as Arthur Koestler has pointed out, "but, at the same time, it creates barriers and acts as a repellent force between groups." It is quite possible for Black writers to use English in such ways as to speak directly to a Black audience while, at the same time, the white audience is held at bay. This is done by manipulation of techniques and development of Black styles, not by using particular techniques labeled *Black* as distinguished from others labeled *White*.

The language techniques used in such poems would be analyzable, and the same techniques would appear in many other kinds of poetry.

Henderson says:

Although it is an arbitrary scheme for the purpose of analysis, one may describe or discuss a "Black" poem in terms of the following broad critical categories: (1) Theme, (2) Structure, (3) Saturation.

(1) By *theme* I mean that which is being spoken of, whether the specific subject matter, the emotional response to it, or its intellectual formulation.

(2) By *structure* I mean chiefly some aspect of the poem such as diction, rhythm, figurative language, which goes into the total makeup. (At times, I use the word in an extended sense to include what is usually called genrè.)

(3) By *saturation* I mean several things, chiefly the communication of "Blackness" and fidelity to the observed or intuited truth of the Black Experience in the United States. It follows that these categories should also be valid in any critical evaluation of the poem.

I have no quarrel with the first and third of these categories, nor even with the parenthetical material in the second category. There are obviously many specifically Black themes possible—Hayden uses many. But writers of other ethnic groups could, if they wished, write on these themes as well, and many have done so. Certainly, there are genres, or kinds, of Black writing. With regard to "saturation": it is equally obvious that poetry can be heavily saturated with Black ethnic referents; again, Hayden refers very often to such things, though nearly always in such a way that the general reader of whatever background will understand.

But I call into question many of Henderson's remarks about Black techniques under his heading of "Structure." I'd like to discuss each of his subheadings, the first of which is (1) "Virtuoso naming and enumerating." Though Henderson doesn't say so in so many words, he implies that this is a specifically Black technique, the roots of which "might conceivably lie in the folk practice of riddling and similar kinds of wordplay." As an example, Henderson recommends Ted Joans's "The Nice Colored Man," a portion of which reads,

Nice Nigger Educated Nigger Never Nigger Southern Nigger
Clever Nigger Northern Nigger Nasty Nigger Unforgivable
Nigger Unforgettable Nigger Unspeakable Nigger Rude &
Uncouth Nigger Mean & Vicious Nigger Smart Black Nigger
Smart Black Nigger Smart Black Nigger Smart Black Nigger
Smart Black Nigger.

Henderson is correct in his derivation from folk literature but not in his implication that the folk are Black in particular. Here is number 749 from the Baring-Goulds' *The Annotated Mother Goose:*

> There was a man, and his name was Dob,
> And he had a wife, and her name was Mob,
> And he had a dog, and he called it Cob,
> And she had a cat, called Chitterabob,
> Cob, says Dob,
> Chitterabob, says Mob,
> Cob was Dob's dog,
> Chitterabob Mob's cat.

This nursery rhyme, however, is of later derivation than the sixteenth-century English poet John Skelton's "Ware the Hawk," a portion of which reads:

> Of no tyrant I read
> That so far did exceed,
> Neither Diocletian,
> Nor yet Domitian,
> Nor yet crooked Cacus,
> Nor yet drunken Bacchus;
> Neither Olibrius,
> Nor Dionysius,
> Neither Phalary
> Rehearsed in Valery;
> Nor Sardanapall.

and so on. One might cite other examples, including Whitman, yet my intent is not to do an exhaustive study of such techniques but merely to show that these are techniques of the English language, not of a particular ethnic group. The standard term for this technique is *cataloging,* and in this particular poem of Joans' it is also a form of repetition, particularly incremental repetition. Robert Hayden is no stranger to the technique since he begins *Angle of Ascent* with a set of poems titled "Beginnings," the first section of which reads,

> Plowdens, Finns,
> Sheffeys, Haydens,
> Westerfields.

Pennsylvania gothic,
Kentucky homespun,
Virginia baroque.

Hayden uses cataloging to particularly beautiful effect in "Theme and Variation," a poem of two parts and four stanzas, the first of which reads, "Fossil, fuschia, mantis, man, / fire and water, earth and air— / all things alter even as I behold, / all things alter, the stranger said."

(2) "Jazzy rhythmic effects." Henderson is vague about this technique. He says, "Compare these lines from LeRoi Jones' 'T. T. Jackson Sings' with the traditional dozens lines which are printed just below them.

> I fucked your mother
> On top of a house
> When I got through
> She thought she was
> Mickey Mouse
>
> 𐑀
>
> I fucked your mother from house to house
> Out came a baby named Minnie Mouse."

Both verses are written in the prosody called "dipodics," which is a derivation from Anglo-Saxon prosody. It is notably the "folk" prosody of nursery rhymes, ballads, and riddles—both the nursery rhyme and the Skelton piece I quoted earlier are dipodic. Here is a verse whose rhythms are very close to those of the first example:

> There was a woman
> Got laid in a shoe
> She said, "Chillun,
> Don't never do
> What I do."

The original, of course, was,

> There was an old woman who lived in a shoe.
> She had so many children, she didn't know what to do.

Hayden modulates podic rhythms in part 5 of "Beginnings," "(*The Crystal Cave Elegy*)"—"Floyd Collins oh / I guess he's a

goner, / Pa Hayden sighed, / the Extra trembling / in his hands."
If the rhythms are "jazzy," they are as old as the English language.

Stephen Henderson's other examples are very different, mostly
prose poems, some of them rhymed. It's difficult to see what these
various techniques have in common; they go by different names in
prosodic terminology. One might mention that Poe's "The Bells"
has been discussed in the twentieth century as a "jazz poem" writ-
ten before jazz had been invented.

Henderson mentions "blues" as a quality of jazz in the poems he
cites. Perhaps we can put off till later the question of Black musi-
cal forms as bases for Black techniques.

(3) "Virtuoso free-rhyming." Henderson says in effect that these
examples typify a Black tradition:

> I don't want nothin' old but some gold;
> I don't want nothin' black but a Cadillac!
>
> I can't eat a bite, I can't sleep at night,
> 'Cause the woman I love don't treat me right.
>
> They call me Rap the dicker the ass kicker
> The cherry picker and city slicker the titty licker.

There may be in these fragments identifiably Black themes and
saturations, but no race or ethnic group has a corner on the "free
rhyming" or internal rhyme markets—nor, for that matter, on scat-
ology. Here is Skelton again, in "The Tunning of Elinor Rumming":

> With a whim-wham
> Knit with a trim-tram
> Upon her brain-pan
> Like an Egyptian . . .
>
>
>
> But let us turn plain,
> There we left again.
> For, as ill a patch as that,
> The hens run in the mash-vat;
> For they go to roost
> Straight over the ale-joust,
> And dung, when it comes,
> In the ale-tunnes.

And here is another nursery rhyme, number 751:

> I need not your needles, they're needless to me,
>   For kneading of needles is needless, you see,
> But did my neat trousers but need to be kneed,
>   I then should have need of your needles indeed.

Finally, here's a piece from Robert Burns's "The Kirk's Alarm":

> Dr. Mac, Dr. Mac, you should stretch on a rack,
>   To strike evil-doers wi' terror;
> To join faith and sense upon onie pretence,
>   Is heretic, damnable error.

Burns's poem is, indeed, ethnic but ethnic Scots.

Robert Hayden is not in any way scatological, as Burns and Skelton and the Black fragments cited can be, but I am not at all sure that that is a criticism. Neither is he much interested in rhyming, particularly bumptious rhyming. The closest he comes, perhaps, is in "Incense of the Lucky Virgin," where some consonance is used instead of rhyme, and each stanza uses an incremental repetition as a sort of substitute for rhyme.

(4) "Hyperbolic imagery." Henderson says, "The breathless virtuoso quality of free-rhyming comes from the utilization of a single rhyme sound, the object being to get in as many rhymes as one can." Though he doesn't intend it, Henderson's is about as good a definition of Skelton's dipodic method as one could wish—a method called, after its inventor, *Skeltonics,* or "tumbling verse." "Oratorically," Henderson continues, "this is balanced by a passage in which there is no rhyme at all, and the wit and the energy expend themselves in a series of hyperbolic wisecracks, rooted in the tradition of masculine boasting." He gives an example from the folk tradition:

> I'm the man who walked the water and tied the whale's
>   tail in a knot
> Taught the little fishes how to swim
> Crossed the burning sands and shook the devil's hand
> Rode round the world on the back of a snail carrying
> a sack saying AIR MAIL.

There's nothing new about the "brag"—the Anglo-Saxon poets understood it as a basic convention in the Middle Ages. It should go without saying that *hyperbole* is an ancient Greek term, and this type of stylized American hyperbole is called "the backwoods boast" by folklorists. It was a feature of the westward movement of the nineteenth century. Hayden is acquainted with the tradition and uses it in "Witch Doctor"—"He's / God's dictaphone of all-redeeming truth. / Oh he's the holyweight champeen who's come / to give the knockout lick to your bad luck; / say he's the holyweight champeen who's here / to deal a knockout punch to your hard luck."

(5) "Metaphysical imagery." In speaking of this category Henderson mentions its uses in English literature. He does not, evidently, mean to make a case for this technique's being particularly Black. Hayden often uses the conceit, the extended metaphor. A striking example is his well-known "Zeus over Redeye," in which the classical names applied to rockets are compared with the gods of mythology, who were the weapons' archetypes.

(6) Henderson polishes off "understatement," or litotes, in four lines without making racial claims for it. Used in the proper circumstances, this universal technique can be one of the most effective in the poet's toolbox. Robert Hayden has written one of the most touching contemporary poems utilizing litotes, "Those Winter Sundays," one of his best-known poems also.

(7) "Compressed and cryptic imagery." Henderson here is as cryptic as his subheading. The example he gives is a brag from Ellison's *Invisible Man*. No definition is offered beyond "arcane references to what I have called 'mascon' imagery." I will discuss *masconception* later. Meanwhile, Henderson makes no claims that Black poets can be more obscure than other kinds of poets. Hayden, too, has his obscure moments—he has been called by others a "Symbolist," and some of his more recent poems, such as "Stars," part 2, which appears to have a relation to Hayden's Bahá'í theology, can be baffling:

Betelgeuse Aldebaran

Abstract as future yesterdays
the starlight
crosses eons of meta-space
to us.

Algol Arcturus Almaak

How shall the mind keep warm
    save at spectral
fires—how thrive but by the light
    of paradox?

Altair Vega Polaris Maia

(8) "Worrying the line." Henderson says, "This is the folk ex-
pression for the device of altering the pitch of a note in a given pas-
sage or for other kinds of ornamentation often associated with
melismatic singing in the Black tradition. A verbal parallel exists in
which a word or phrase is broken in order to allow for affective or
didactic comment." Here is an example from Rich Amerson's
"Black Woman":

> Say, I feel superstitious, Mamma
> 'Bout my hoggin' bread, Lord help my hungry time,
> I feel superstitious, Baby, 'bout my hoggin' bread!
> Ah-hmmm, Baby, I feel superstitious,
> I say 'stitious, Black Woman!
> Ah-hmmm, ah you hear me cryin'
> About I done got hungry, oh Lordy!
> Oh, Mamma, I feel superstitious
> About my hog Lord God it's my bread.

Melismatic means, according to the Oxford dictionary, "the art of
florid or ornate vocalization." Henderson makes much, later on, of
musical comparisons between Black poetry and Black music. The
language techniques illustrated by the Amerson passage that Hen-
derson quotes are such things as parallelism, incremental repetition,
orthographical schemas—elision and apocopation primarily. That
Amerson's poem is written in a Black style and tradition is not
open to question, but one can find hundreds of examples of the
same techniques in English poetry from all periods. Hayden, in the
ending of "Runagate Runagate," uses them:

> Armed and known to be Dangerous

> Wanted Reward Dead or Alive

> > Tell me, Ezekiel, oh tell me do you see
> > mailed Jehovah coming to deliver me?

Hoot-owl calling in the ghosted air,
five times calling to the hants in the air.
Shadow of a face in the scary leaves,
shadow of a voice in the talking leaves:

Come ride-a my train

Oh that train, ghost-story train
through swamp and savanna movering movering,
over trestles of dew, through caves of the wish,
Midnight Special on a sabre track movering movering,
first stop Mercy and the last Hallelujah.

Come ride-a my train

Mean mean mean to be free.

At this point in his essay Henderson defines his neologism *mas-con:* "a massive concentration of Black experiential energy." If we look at the poems just cited, by Amerson and Hayden, we must see that they are clearly Black poems. But it is not the techniques that make them Black—*it is how the techniques are applied.* There is "mas-con" in the poems, but the "massive concentration of Black expe-riential energy" is a function of style, not structure.

I don't believe anyone could have faulted Henderson if he had called the second of his three major critical categories "Style" rather than "Structure" or, better, "Styles"—there is more than one Black style of writing, as Henderson recognizes; Hayden is a mas-ter of several. But Henderson's insisting on identifying particular English language techniques as being somehow "Black" confuses the issue, as for instance when he speaks about "the Black oratori-cal technique of repetition."

The oldest prosody in the world—and it is universal—is gram-matic parallelism, which includes the device of repetition. It is to be found in prose poetry as well as in verse poetry—the Bible is full of it, and Henderson gives an example from Martin Luther King's "I Have a Dream" speech. Where does Henderson imagine that the Rev. Dr. King got his oratorical style if not from the King James Bible? That King's adaptation of this prosodic system gives rise to an identifiably Black traditional style is also apparent.

Curiously enough, though Hayden uses parallelism often, I can find no poem in *Angle of Ascent,* except possibly "Witch Doctor," previously cited, that imitates the style of the Negro sermon, though there are references to preachers, as to King himself in "Words in the Mourning Time." This poem, though, is about the Kennedys as well. Hayden has written not only about Christianity but also about Judaism, Bahá'í, and Mohammedanism.

Included in the section on "Structure" in Henderson's essay is a subsection titled "Black Music as Poetic Reference." Henderson says:

> Aside from mascon structure, there are other important ways in which music, Black music, lies at the basis of much Black poetry, either consciously or covertly. I have been able to distinguish at least ten types of usage.

That poetry and music have always been closely associated in all traditions is a truism. Here Henderson is speaking about Black music and poetry:

"In No. 1, *the casual, generalized reference,* there are mere suggestions of Black song types." In Henderson's examples there are mentions of "everlasting song," "Caroling softly souls of slavery," "blues," "jazz," "slave songs," "jubilees," and more generalized musical references. He makes no claim that general reference is a particularly Black technique. Like many other poets of all nations, languages, and times, Hayden uses such allusions in many poems, including "A Ballad of Remembrance," "The Dream," and "Beginnings," part 4.

"In No. 2, there is a careful allusion to song titles." "For a reader familiar with these songs, the titles evoke a more particularized response, and the effect thus borders on the 'subjective correlative' alluded to in type seven." By *subjective correlative* Henderson evidently means an emotional response cued by, in this case, a Black song title. Particular songs and singers carry loads of cultural and ethnic associations and overtones for American Blacks. Plainly, though, the technique of allusion is not racial. I will discuss the subjective correlative when we come to item no. 7.

In no. 3 "*Quotations from a song* are incorporated into the poem." My comments regarding no. 2 apply.

No. 4 is "Adaptations of song forms," which "include blues, ballads, hymns, children's songs, work songs, spirituals, and popular songs." Henderson says that in particular the ballad, the hymn, and the blues are "numerous and easily recognizable." He continues: "The first two have numerous parallels in other literary traditions.

But the blues as a literary form was developed and refined by Langston Hughes and later by Sterling Brown, though Hughes clearly overstated his case for the fixity of the blues form in his preface to *Fine Clothes for the Jew*."

There is a difference between *technique* and *form*. Techniques are universal within a language—often just plain universal, but specific forms may develop in any culture or social heritage. I am willing to grant Henderson his claim that the blues and jazz are specifically Black American forms, despite Poe's "The Bells" and Browning's "A Toccata of Galuppi's."

Henderson mentions the "'classic' twelve-bar, three line form" of the blues, as in Eddie "Son" House's "Dry Spell Blues":

> The dry spell blues have fallen, drove me from door to door.
> Dry spell blues have fallen, drove me from door to door.
> The dry spell blues have put everybody on the killing floor.
>
> Now the people down south sure won't have no home.
> Now the people down south sure won't have no home
> 'Cause the dry spell have parched all this cotton and corn.

And so forth. Here is a portion of the Browning poem:

> Here you come with your old music, and here's all the good it
>   brings.
> What, they lived once thus at Venice where the merchants
>   were the kings,
> Where Saint Mark's is, where the Doges used to wed the sea
>   with rings.

The rhythms and rhymes are the same. The only thing missing from the Browning poem is the formal repetition. The main point is that, though the *forms* differ slightly, the *techniques* are the same. The *styles* are completely different.

That Hayden has been influenced by the "song forms" Henderson mentions is quite obvious. It is equally obvious that many other poets have been likewise so influenced. But Hayden is usually not content merely to be influenced by a form; he transforms it into something uniquely his. Though "The Ballad of Nat Turner," for instance, looks typographically like a traditional ballad and might even fool the casual reader into thinking that it is one, in fact it does not rhyme as most ballads do, it consonates, and, though repetition is sometimes used as a substitute for rhyme, there is no ballad refrain. Some stanzas do not even consonate or have repetition, yet the whole poem has the effect of a unified narrative song. This is a masterful wedding of tradition with personal style.

"Device No. 5 is the practice, with considerable variety, of *forcing the reader to incorporate into the structure of the poem his memory of a specific song or passage of a song, or even of a specific delivery technique.* Without this specific memory the poem cannot be properly realized." Evidently, this particular Black technique depends heavily either on a shared live experience or on the reader's having a phonograph record of a particular Black musician.

Henderson expends a great deal of energy in elaborating on this "device" of "arcane" allusion (the quoted words are his), ranging from Percy Johnson's "Number Five Cooper Square"—

> I remember Clifford tossing
> Bubbles, Scit! Whoom!, from an
> Ante-bellum moon. Scit! And
> Killer Joe's golden chain, Scit!
> While Ornette gives a lecture on
> A Sanscrit theme with Bachian
> footnotes, scit.

—to "Don Lee's famous poem 'Don't Cry, Scream,'" which contains "the stylized *visual* representation . . . 'sing / loud & / high / with / feeling' and 'sing / loud & / long / with feeling'" to "the *stylized* [my italics] rendition of the Coltrane sound":

> i can see my me, it was truth you gave,
> like a daily shit
> it had to come.
>
> can you scream————brother? very
> can you scream————brother? soft
>
> I hear you.
> I hear you.
>
> and the Gods will too.

The twentieth-century British poet Dame Edith Sitwell has done similar things in "Polka" from *Facade:*

"As they watch me dance the polka,"
Said Mr. Wagg like a bear,
"In my top hat and my whiskers that—
Tra la la la, trap the Fair.

Tra la la la la-
Tra la la la la-
Tra la la la la la la la la
    La
    La
    La!"

Henderson speaks about references to Black music forms, performers, and performances, but one can use this technique to refer to any sort of music that may be familiar to an audience, as W. S. Gilbert did in *H.M.S. Pinafore:*

When the foeman bares his steel,
    Tarantara! tarantara!
We uncomfortable feel,
    Tarantara!
And we find the wisest thing,
    Tarantara! tarantara!
Is to slap our chests and sing
    Tarantara!
For when threatened with emeutes,
    Tarantara! tarantara!
And your heart is in your boots,
    Tarantara!
There is nothing brings it round,
    Tarantara! tarantara!
Like the trumpet's martial sound,
    Tarantara! tarantara!
Tarantara-ra-ra-ra-ra!

In the eighteenth century Christopher Smart wrote a poem that is practically a treatise on this sort of thing, and, rather than quote it here, I recommend it to the reader as an interesting glimpse into the nature of the language. Its title is "Of the Spiritual Musick"— lest that turn anyone away, let me add that it is a prose poem. Robert Hayden uses many of these so-called techniques in such poems as "Soledad" and "Homage to the Empress of the Blues," from which I quote the first stanza.

> Because there was a man somewhere in a candystripe silk shirt,
> gracile and dangerous as a jaguar and because a woman moaned
> for him in sixty-watt gloom and mourned him Faithless Love
> Twotiming Love Oh Love Oh Careless Aggravating Love . . .

and so forth. Hayden's intent here, however, is not to appeal to one ethnic minority above another but to build a context for such allusions that enables any reader to understand the situation and emotion of the narrator.

"In the sixth kind of musical referent," Henderson continues, *"precise musical notation is incorporated into the text of the poem."* It seems to me that this device goes back as far as the invention of musical notation. Certainly, texts have always been written for music and vice versa. William Walton wrote music for Sitwell's *Façade,* and there is a recording of her reading the poems to his music—not singing them, *reading* them. Thomas Campion published his first *Book of Ayres* in 1601 and a treatise on *Counter-Point* later on. The connection of music with poetry is ancient and continuing—Sidney Lanier, the poet-musician, had a theory of the "symphonic poem" in the nineteenth century. At any rate, Robert Hayden does not use this device, evidently preferring his language music to stand on its own on the printed page.

In device no. 7 the reader's *"emotional response to a well-known song is incorporated into the poem* in a manner resembling the use of a 'rest' in music or an assumed 'obbligato.'"* I shall let Henderson's use of traditional musical terms speak for itself. This is merely an elaboration of device nos. 2–5, with the addition that a cue word or phrase is used as a refrain, as in the example he gives from Robert Terrell's "Asian Stew," with its play on the word *jelly.*

> Wit rice-n-mud-n-bamboo shoots
> Wit sizzled hairs-n-human eclairs
> Wit shrapnel-n-goodwill-n-jelly
> jelly jelly

In "O Daedalus, Fly Away Home" Robert Hayden uses such words as *juba* and *conjo* in similar ways, building a beautiful and, simultaneously, sad song of loss, beginning:

> Drifting night in the Georgia pines,
> coonskin drum and jubilee banjo.
> Pretty Malinda, dance with me.

Night is juba, night is conjo.
Pretty Malinda, dance with me.

The poem turns to the thought of "home"—Africa—and of death as a release from longing for rest, ending with:

Night is a mourning juju man
weaving a wish and a weariness together
to make two wings.

O fly away home fly away.

No poet I know of is so capable of couching the American Black's experience and situation, emotion, and ambience in language that is accessible to everyone.

Henderson says in this regard, "Since the reference is to a state of mind or feeling instead of to an object or structure, the technique could be called the use of the 'subjective correlative,' in contrast to the 'objective correlative' of the New Criticism."

Subjective correlative is an impressive term for *cue* or *cue word.* Such words are intended as automatic triggers for a culturally conditioned emotional response. The technique is no different in kind from the use of the words *apple pie, motherhood,* or *Old Glory* in a political speech. It is not particularly a poetic device but a rhetorical one. It is, in fact, rather antipoetic in that it requires little skill on the part of the writer; all he needs is to be tapped into the ethos of his audience in order to find the particular word that will set off the response he wants. The question, then, is whether the poet will settle for the effect of the word alone or, like Hayden, build a context for it that provides the alien reader with points of reference that will allow him to understand some of the overtones with which the cues are laden. Hayden does the latter in poem after poem; he cares about the reader, whoever he may be, for Hayden knows that, though there are many forms of humanity, they are all, finally, human and capable of communication. It is the writer's job to help people to understand one another.

In the eighth of Henderson's devices "the musician himself functions as subject, poem, history, or myth." This technique is the same in all cultures: reference to a culture hero of some sort. That in this case the referent is a musician is a very slight reason for the critic's listing it here.

Device no. 9 is "language from the jazz life or associated with it, commonly called 'hip' speech." There is nothing new about dialect poetry nor even slang poetry. One of Hayden's finest poems is full of nineteenth-century Negro southern dialect: "The Dream" alternates narration regarding a character named Sinda with Black letters from the Civil War front. It is the most effective dialect poem I have ever read, though Hayden claims that many people have misinterpreted it. This puzzles me, and the only reason I can think of for it is that the unexpected person dies.

I cannot think why Henderson lists this device, for the only excuse conceivable seems to be that "hip" talk uses a number of jazz musical terms, and Henderson seems intent upon distinguishing jazz, for cultural reasons, from other forms of music. But where does that leave the other Black musical forms he listed earlier—the spirituals and so forth?

Henderson writes, "In the tenth category, *the poem as 'score'* or *'chart,'* we move to the most challenging aspect of Black poetic structure [he is still saying "structure," not "style" or "tradition"]— the question of limit, or performance of the text." Later Henderson writes:

> A poem may thus differ from performance to performance just as jazz performances of "My Favorite Things" would. Moreover, it implies that there is a Black poetic mechanism, much like the musical ones, which can transform even a Shakespearian sonnet into a jazz poem, the basic conceptual model of contemporary Black poetry. The technique, the fundamental device, would be improvisation, lying as it does at the very heart of jazz music.

Neither in music nor in poetry is improvisation in any way linked merely to jazz or to a specific ethnic group. The Anglo-Saxon knights were expected to be able to compose extemporaneous verse brags in the mead hall after a battle, and the official bards had to be ready on command to compose in public a poem on any subject, with musical accompaniment. None of these compositions was written down until much later, if ever. The "scores" existed only in the oral tradition.

The Arabic *qasida* is a form dating from prehistoric times, and its essence is improvisation. The technique as it is described in Preminger's *Encyclopedia of Poetry and Poetics* is a model for the

composition of poetry in many ancient societies, including that of
the English:

> Only by considering how poetry is composed in Arabic can
> the evolution of the qasidah be reconstructed. In its simplest
> form, verse is composed extempore, sung to some traditional
> tune, in one *bait* at a time; it is then taken up by the company,
> sung to rhythmical movement and hand clapping. Until the poet
> warms to his work he casts about among the many traditional
> themes in his conscious and subconscious memory—which
> doubtless explains the qasidah sequence and the recurrent
> clichés of both classical and colloquial versification, for in Ara-
> bia mere originality for its own sake is not sought. When visited
> by Inspiration—which the Arabs conceive as supernatural, a
> species of demon—the poet now turns to the theme he wishes
> to treat.

One of the purposes of Henderson's book, evidently, is to pro-
vide young Black poets with an arsenal of weapons to use in writ-
ing poetry that is acceptably ethnic. But I am sure that Robert
Hayden would feel that it is important also that young poets un-
derstand the differences between "styles" and "techniques." A style
is something that develops with skill, experience, and personality;
technique, on the other hand, can be studied and learned. To con-
fuse the two things, as Henderson does and as Hayden obviously
does not, is to do a disservice to developing poets by making some-
thing racial of the elements—I should say some of the elements—
of the English language.

If young Black poets believe there are "Black" techniques and
"white" techniques, it is likely that they will turn away from the
conscious development of skills in the language they must use and
turn, instead, to imitations of approved styles already developed and
patented by their predecessors and elders. If such a situation devel-
ops, the danger exists that there will be a generation of Black writ-
ers who are imitators rather than poets. Hayden, being a teacher, is
well aware of this, and he argues against the ghettoizing of poetry
in the classroom and, by superb example, in his poetry.

Blake said in the first preface to his *Jerusalem:*

Poetry fettered, fetters the human race. Nations are destroyed or
flourish in proportion as their poetry, painting, and music are

destroyed or flourish. The primeval state of man was wisdom, art, and science.

There are wisdom, art, and the science of language in the poetry of Robert Hayden. His work is unfettered in many ways, not the least of which is in the range of techniques available to him. It gives his imagination wings, allows him to travel throughout human nature. Yet he is in no way untrue to his personal heritage nor to the heritage of American Blacks. His style is Protean, capable of change and growth as he develops from book to book, poem to poem. If his work has been overlooked in the past, it has been for the smallest of reasons; it is because he has been willing to be neither a propagandist nor a dweller in a literary ghetto. He has preferred to be a poet.

CONSTANCE J. POST

Image and Idea in the Poetry of Robert Hayden

In Robert Hayden's "Kodachromes of the Island" the speaker of the poem roams about, thinking of Yeats's passionate search for a theme while seeking one of his own. For both men the search came long after their careers as poets had been established. Yeats, it will be recalled, wrote "The Circus Animals' Desertion," the poem in which he discusses his search for a new theme, fifty years after the publication of his first book of poetry. In Hayden's case the search came in the middle of his career, after he had already written some of his most celebrated poems, such as "Middle Passage," "Runagate Runagate," and "Frederick Douglass." These and other poems were included in his second book of poetry, *A Ballad of Remembrance,* published in 1962, ten years before the collection in which "Kodachromes of the Island" appears, *Words in the Mourning Time* (1972).

Both men pursued the quest with dogged persistence. According to Yeats, the search preoccupied him daily for more than a month and culminated in his enumeration, resignedly, of old themes, among them the reconciling of what he called the three islands of incompatible things, "Vain gaiety, vain battle, vain repose." Hayden, eschewing any such enumeration, leaves it up to the reader to judge the degree of his success. Elsewhere, however, a clue is provided in an interview conducted with him by John O'Brien. Having acknowledged how stale and repetitious he thought his poetry had become, Hayden affirms that *The Night-Blooming Cereus* represented a real breakthrough for him.[1] After that, he says, "I began to move in a new direction and to consolidate my gains, such as they were."

A careful study of Hayden's poetry will reveal, I believe, that any

From *CLA Journal* 20 (December 1976): 164–75. Reprinted with permission of the College Language Association.

new direction he might have taken was primarily in the area of consolidation, if only to look at his old themes from a new angle. By his so doing, a thread of continuity is woven throughout his entire work, giving it a unity and a coherence it otherwise would lack. This is true in general of his themes and the means he uses to develop them, especially of his imagery. Considered together, his lyrics take on an almost epic quality. They therefore support Donald Stauffer's thesis that the imagery of some poets, whether consciously or unconsciously, is organized in such coherent patterns that an epic effect is achieved.[2]

Struggle, for example, is a common theme running through Hayden's poetry, fortified not only by his choice of imagery but through his use of paradox. His chief symbol for it is the star. In the poem entitled "Stars" he refers to the starlight that "crosses eons of meta-space to us" and asks, "How shall the mind keep warm / save at spectral / fires—how thrive but by the light / of paradox?" The light of paradox *is* about speed, distance, and time just as paradox, literally meaning "beyond opinion," contradicts our expectations. (*Meta* and *para* share the same meaning of "beyond.")

The star, moreover, is a paradox because of its physical properties. It exists only because of the careful balance of contradictory forces whereby "the energy generated by nuclear reactions in the interior is balanced by the outflow of energy to the surface"; similarly, "the inward gravitational forces are balanced by the outward-directed gas and radiation pressure" (*American Heritage Dictionary*). When such a balance of opposites is no longer present in the star, it collapses within itself. Starlight can thus be seen as a means of keeping the mind warm and thriving.

What additional meanings does Hayden attach to the stars? Of central importance in understanding the significance of the stars to him is the connection he makes between them and the Bahá'í faith.[3] In section 5 of "Stars" he mentions many different kinds of stars and then singles out the Nine-Pointed Star, "sunstar in the constellation / of the nuclear Will." A symbol commonly used by the Navajo Indians, the nine-pointed star represents perfection according to Bahá'ísm, since after nine all numbers are repetitious. Furthermore, the number nine is seen as the numerical manifestation of the Greatest Name, Baha, says A. Q. Faizi, who gives the numerical value of the name Baha, based upon the Arabic alphabet, as follows: $B = 2, A = 1, H = 5, A = 1$ for a total of 9.[4]

In section 3 of "Stars" the number 9 also assumes importance as Hayden, in groups of two, three, and four, mentions the names of nine stars of various colors and constellations. All share one thing in common, however, and that is brightness. Five of the nine stars— Aldebaran, Arcturus, Altair, Vega, and Polaris—are among the brightest stars in the sky, visible at latitude 40° N. Another two, Betelgeuse and Algol, are two of the brightest variable stars; even though their brightness fluctuates, it nevertheless exceeds that of most of the other six thousand stars in the sky that are visible to the naked eye. Also visible without the use of a telescope are the last two, Almaak (also known as Almach) and Maia, the star for whom Hayden's daughter is named.

The significance of nine for Bahá'ísm, other than that already mentioned, varies somewhat. Because every Bahá'í temple has nine openings and since the one in the United States, located in Wilmette, Illinois, has nine sides, a common interpretation among Western Bahá'ís is that each side represents one of the major religions of the world: Hinduism, Confucianism, Taoism, Buddhism, Judaism, Islam, Christianity, Zoroastrianism, and Bahá'ísm.[5] The last religion, that of Bahá'ísm, is considered therefore by some as the latest in a series of manifestations of God, though not necessarily his final revelation to man. Baha'u'llah himself gave a different interpretation to the significance of the nine openings. According to his teachings, the temple of wood or stone is but a correspondence of the human body, itself the temple of God, which has nine openings. In either interpretation the salient point is that God is not limited in the ways he manifests Himself. Our minds can thus be illuminated by any one of the nine stars or by the Nine-Pointed Star itself, "whose radiance filtering down to us lights mind and spirit, signals future light."

That explains why in section 1 of the poem, Orion, the giant hunter who pursued the Pleiades, is praised. As the lover of Eos, the Greek goddess of dawn, he represents, in a larger sense, those who love the dawning of this new manifestation of God. In Hayden's poem "Baha'u'llah in the Garden of Ridwan" he is equated with the auroral darkness. Aurora, the Roman equivalent of Eos, figures significantly in the Bahá'í faith since the term *Dawnbreaker* has often been used to refer to thousands of early Persian Bahá'ís who were martyred. (A literal translation of the term from Arabic is "the Rising Place of the Lights of the Sun.") In the garden all of nature joins in praising the Dawnbreaker Baha'u'llah. "Energies / like an-

gels dance // glorias of recognition," their radiance as much an il-
lumination as the pulsars and quasars of section 4 in "Stars."

Coming down to earth, we find that even the rocks praise Ba-
ha'u'llah as "Within the rock the undiscovered suns release their
light." A mineral silicate, common in igneous and metamorphic
rock, is called mica. The word *mica* is influenced by the Latin *mi-
care,* meaning "to shine." Bearing a brightness similar to that of the
stars, it participates in the general awakening of nature that accom-
panies the arrival of the Dawnbreaker.

Mica is used elsewhere by Hayden to refer to the sea and to the
sky. In "Gulls," for instance, he speaks of the "mica'd fall of the sea,"
using mica to describe the dark sea as the waves, breaking upon it,
appear as little suns. Thus mica, based upon a metaphor derived
from the stars, is first transferred to rock and then to the sea and fi-
nally, to complete the circle, back to the sky again.

"The birds explode / into mica sky," writes Hayden in "A Plague
of Starlings," a poem that describes the attempts of workmen at Fisk
University to get rid of the troublesome birds by shooting into the
leaves at evening time. Starlings themselves are reminders of the stars
in their dark, often iridescent plumage. The irony that they present
is not lost upon the speaker in the poem as he tries to avoid their
carcasses while walking to class to lecture on what Socrates had told
his friends about the migratory habits of the soul.

Not only do the rocks and the sea reflect the light of the stars.
So do people. In "Runagate Runagate" Hayden praises Harriet
Tubman, leader of the Underground Railroad, as a "woman of
earth, whipscarred, a summoning, a shining." She, like Sojourner
Truth, is a star, summoning others to her light as well as being the
light. Similarly, Akhenaten in "Two Egyptian Portrait Masks" is
spoken of as "O Lord of every land / shining forth for all." Finally,
Baha'u'llah is the supreme reflection of that light. Of him Hayden
says, "who by the light of suns beyond the suns beyond the sun and
stars . . . alone can comprehend . . . and stars and stones and seas
acclaimed."

Hayden's theme of struggle draws support not just from his im-
agery of the stars and other celestial bodies, as well as their corre-
spondences in other aspects of Nature. Equally significant is his use
of oxymorons, whereby he achieves the maximum effect of com-
bining opposites with a minimum number of words. For example,
Sojourner Truth is called a "childless mother" in section 3 of "Stars."
An apparent contradiction, it can be resolved by one's remembering

that Hayden refers to this freed slave, originally called Isabella, as one who was following the star, her mind a star. Believing that she had received a special message from heaven, she left her job in New York, adopted the name Sojourner Truth and traveled throughout the North preaching emancipation and women's rights. By shedding light upon others, she consequently became the mother of countless children, her own and those who would not have been conceived without her efforts.

Likewise, the apparent contradiction contained in Hayden's reference to Akhenaten as "multi-single like the Sun" can be resolved by the examination of the image closely in the poem "Two Egyptian Portrait Masks." Akhenaten, king of Egypt from c. 1375–c. 1358 B.C.E., believed, as the name he adopted suggests (*Aten* meaning *sun*), that the sun was god and god alone. The universe was filled with his beneficent light, and by it everything that lived had its being. So convinced was Akhenaten of the truth of his solar monotheism that, in addition to taking a new name, he also established a new capital. The spirit in his heart, says Hayden, was that of "Aten Jahveh Allah God." Akhenaten can therefore be multi-single because he contains within himself the spirit of God in several of its manifestations besides his own: that of Yahweh, worshiped by Jews; Allah, by Muslims; and God, by Christians, among others. Akhenaten is thus seen as one of the royal prophets in the progressive revelation of God.

Two of Hayden's oxymorons are somewhat similar in content, although the position of the terms has been reversed. A striking contrast can thus be observed between *eudaemonic pain* in the poem "Witch Doctor" and *pained amusement* in the poem "Sphinx." In the first of these two poems the witch doctor, a religious leader, is considering what new device he can use in order to "enmesh his flock in theopathic tension." The degree of his success is attested by the "cries of eudaemonic pain" from the audience, a pain that is happy since it comes from having a good spirit.

Just as pain may be accompanied by happiness, so happiness may be accompanied by pain, according to Hayden. The latter is illustrated in the second poem in which the Sphinx says that eventually "you will come to regard my questioning / with a certain pained // amusement." Causing pain, the Sphinx's riddle may concomitantly be a source of gaiety, enabling a person to tolerate a paradox. By the poet's own admission this poem suggests that "something fundamentally negative, or apparently so, may be used in a positive, a creative way."[6] Turning adversity into advantage is vintage Brer Rabbit, of course, and serves to remind us of the degree to which folk material from Hayden's Afro-American tradition permeates his poetry.

An apparently insolvable question also puzzles the participants in "Electrical Storm." In that poem the speaker muses over whether it was chance or choice that saved himself and others in the storm that killed several persons. While he is content to leave the question dangling like the electrical wires strewn about the ground, he feels confident that he knows "what those / cowering true believers would have said." True believers—the phrase is used by Eric Hoffer as the title of his book on religious fanaticism—supposedly do not find it necessary to cringe or shrink in fear. In this case the speaker in the poem appears certain that the believers would have insisted that heavenly design determined who would be saved. The irony in this poem is that those who don't know the answer to the riddle can nevertheless live with it better than those who are so sure they have the answers.

The oxymorons in "Theme and Variation" will serve as the final examples of the compact paradox as used by Hayden. In this poem the speaker, identified as a stranger, ponders life's ephemerality. Referring in the first line to the four major categories of life—animal, plant, insect, and man—and in the second to the four elements (earth, air, water, and fire), the stranger avers that these "Are the reveling shadows / of a changing permanence." This idea, at least as old as Heraclitus, has been advanced more recently by the twentieth-century philosopher Henri Bergson. According to his views, change takes on the pervasive character of reality. Such a constantly altering state of things makes man a voyeur, spying "upon the striptease of reality," says the stranger. Continuing to employ sexual imagery, he comments, upon seeing the transience occurring at the edge of things, that such an impending change turns to "curiosa all I know."

Such an immanence, moreover, "changes light to rainbow darkness / wherein God waylays us and empowers." The oxymoron *rainbow darkness* is strikingly similar to the *golden darkness* found in the poem "The Ballad of Nat Turner" and the *auroral darkness* of the poem "Baha'u'llah in the Garden of Ridwan." The use of the word *rainbow*, however, adds a note of promise to this image, as Noah was given the rainbow as a sign of God's avowal not to destroy the earth again by water. In such a darkness God waylays and empowers.

Reminiscent of the sexual imagery used by Donne and Crashaw, Hayden here depicts God as one who ambushes—*ambush* being synonymous with the word *waylay* but also suggestive of a sexual overpowering.

Hayden also makes additional use of paradox in his frequent treatment of the theme of struggle, often associated with metamorphosis. Thus, the energies of a paradox, resting in tension as they do in the stars, serve to inform much of Hayden's poetry. In "Richard Hunt's 'Arachne,'" for example, Hayden focuses on the precise moment when Arachne is changed from a woman into a spider. Arachne, according to Greek myth, had challenged Athena to a weaving contest and was subsequently metamorphosed by her into a spider for her temerity.

Hayden stresses the tension of the moment structurally in at least two ways. First, by using present participles throughout the poem, as well as gerunds, he rivets the reader's attention on the metamorphosis itself:

> Human face *becoming* locked insect face
>   mouth of agony *shaping* a cry it cannot utter
>   eyes *bulging* brimming with the horrors
>   of her *becoming*
>
>   Dazed crazed
>   by godly vivisection *husking* her
>   *gutting* her
> *cutting* hubris its fat and bones away
>
> In *goggling* terror *fleeing* powerless to flee
>   Arachne not yet arachnid and no longer woman
>   in the moment's centrifuge of *dying*
>   *becoming.*
>
> (Italics mine)

A second device used by Hayden to create structural tension in the poem is variation in the indentation pattern of the lines. The poem, composed of three stanzas of four lines each, is organized in the following manner: stanza 1 is indented so that each line following the first is indented a few more spaces to the right. The second stanza is indented in just the opposite manner: the first line is indented far to the right, and each successive line indented a bit farther to the left side of the page. The third stanza repeats the pattern of the first. A zigzag effect is thereby achieved that graphically outlines the wrenching force of Arachne's metamorphosis.

In "The Night-Blooming Cereus" Hayden again focuses on the moment of metamorphosis. Waiting night after night to see the tropical cactus burst into flower, the onlookers have been partially rewarded already by the growing awareness of the "rigorous design" governing the process to which they bear witness. Even before the flower appears, it prompts the desire "to celebrate the blossom, / paint ourselves, dance / in honor of / archaic mysteries," just as in the poem "Full Moon" Hayden fondly remembers agrarian peoples who worshiped the moon and regulated their lives by it. When the onlookers "beheld at last the achieved / flower," they were filled with reverence, recognizing the awful struggle by which so grand a moment had been attained. Thus, the cereus, whose name comes from the Latin word for *candle* (because of the similarity in shape), sheds a light that, though ephemeral, stirs man's deepest religious impulses. In so doing, it achieves a glory worthy of the struggle.

A glorious struggle is also recorded by Hayden in "The Ballad of Nat Turner,"[7] in which he achieves a dramatic tension of the first magnitude. At the beginning of the poem Nat Turner wanders into the Dismal Swamp, sees trees "where Ibo warriors / hung shadowless," and wonders if it is the sign promised him by God. The sign he awaits is a go-ahead that the Day of Judgment is at hand, which he is to lead. From his confession we know that he had been identified as a prophet early in his life and that he believed God had ordained him for some great purpose. Such a conviction impelled him, said Turner, to return to his master after a successful escape.

The tension of the poem is heightened considerably through the use of dialogue in the first nine stanzas. When Turner cries in the second stanza, "Speak to me now or let me die," an immediate reply is not forthcoming. In the fifth the blackness whispers, in response to the same question, "Die." Later on, in the ninth stanza, he cries to the rock and the bramble, "Hide me," and they in turn antiphonally utter the same cry, so dazzling is the vision that Turner beheld.

Of equal if not greater importance in establishing tension throughout the poem is Hayden's use of repetition, particularly of the word *and*. Having already used it eight times by the ninth stanza, he then repeats it an additional twenty times in the last eight stanzas. Seven uses of *and* occur at the beginning of sentences; the other thirteen are used as connectives in phrases and dependent clauses. Hayden thereby heaps image upon image, accelerating the action in such a way that the reader reels from its cumulative force much as Turner reels from his vision of the dazzling combat of the angels.

For Hayden the struggles of others may also help us in our own. In recalling the deaths of Martin Luther King, Jr. and Robert Kennedy, he suggests that words in the mourning time may be transformed into a morning time. Through the Dawnbreaker's transilluminating word, these deaths become the "major means whereby, / oh dreadfully, our humanness must be achieved." Likewise, in Hayden's celebrated poem "Middle Passage," Cinquez's "voyage through death / to life upon these shores" is the life that now transfigures many lives, serving, as do the lives of King and Kennedy, as the means whereby others may effect their own metamorphoses.

Another example of such a transformation can be observed in the poem "El-Hajj Malik El-Shabazz." There Hayden traces the gradual metamorphosis of Malcolm X from his memory of the racist murder of his father when Malcolm X was quite young to his subsequent rise as a leader in the Black Muslim movement. His metamorphosis was not complete, says Hayden, until Malcolm recognized "Allah the raceless in whose blazing Oneness all / were one."

Hayden's concern for the struggles of mankind is not limited to publicly acclaimed figures. In "The Diver," for instance, the speaker in the poem says that he strove against the conflicting desires to live and to die. He did so in "languid frenzy," the phrase itself indicative of his contradictory feelings. Somehow, though, he began the "measured rise," finding in order the means whereby to contain his chaotic, opposing feelings. A similar struggle marks the attempts of the old man to fly again in the poem "For a Young Artist." After many painful attempts, he succeeds: "the angle of ascent / achieved." Rising, whether from the bottom of the sea to its surface or from the earth to the sky, depends upon the struggle to establish the proper balance. For the diver it means gauging the speed of his ascent; for the old man, finding the right angle.

Here Hayden is dealing not just with the struggle of a lone individual but with the struggle of the artist. Such a balancing act is much like walking a tightrope. "Death on either side . . . the way of life between," the man in the hospital room in "The Broken Dark" recalls the rabbi saying. The man is also reminded of Baha'u'llah's words, "I have come to tell thee of struggles in the pit."

Not just a figure of speech, the pit refers to an underground dungeon in Tehran, where Baha'u'llah spent four months in heavy chains. Called "The Black Pit," the room had only one opening and was crammed with more than a hundred murderers and thieves. Elsewhere, however, Hayden does refer to the pit in a figurative sense. In the poem on Malcolm X he says that Malcolm's vision of a racist Allah "could not cleanse him / of the odors of the pit." Representing the stench and foulness of hatred, the pit symbolizes for Hayden what we must struggle to extricate ourselves from, despite the pain it may cause us.

The consideration of the way Hayden uses struggle in his poetry must finally rest upon his tragicomic view of life. In "'Lear Is Gay'" Hayden, recalling Yeats's "Lapis Lazuli," praises that gaiety found in an old man who "can laugh / sometimes // at time as at a / scarecrow whose / hobo shoulders are / a-twitch with crows." Dedicated to his friend Betsy Graves Reyneau, the poem expresses admiration for someone whose attitude toward irrevocable defeat is tempered with gaiety. The defeat may be the physical deterioration of the body as one is metamorphosed into a "tattered coat upon a stick," to draw a relevant image from Yeats. Or, generally speaking, it may be anything that is reduced to ineffectuality, which Hayden captures precisely in his image of the scarecrow that can no longer scare a crow.

For Hayden to be able to laugh at the ravages of time is an achievement of the human spirit secure in the knowledge that everything alters even as we behold it. Thus, as the jilted lover and the soul-weary people behold the singer in "Homage to the Empress of the Blues," their sorrow is transformed by the power of her song. She not only "flashed her golden smile," lustrous and radiant, but "shone that smile on us and sang." The light of the stars, their tension in delicate balance, is thereby reflected as she sings the blues. Her song thus embodies Hayden's imagery of the stars, his theme of struggle, and his use of paradox, bearing eloquent testimony to Hayden's artistry as well as to her own.

NOTES

1. John O'Brien, ed., *Interviews with Black Writers* (New York: Liveright, 1973), 13.

2. Donald Stauffer, *The Golden Nightingale* (New York: Macmillan, 1949).

3. The Bahá'í faith was founded in the nineteenth century by Ba-ha'u'llah, a member of the Iranian nobility. His message, first heralded by the Bab in 1844, met with strong opposition from the start. As a result, Ba-ha'u'llah spent much of his life in prison (see Gloria Faizi, *The Bahá'í Faith: An Introduction* [New Delhi: Bahá'í Publishing Trust, 1971]). Among the central tenets of this religion are the belief in one God, the unity of mankind, sexual and racial equality, universal compulsory education, and a universal auxiliary language. The religion has no formal creed and no or-dained clergy. Its sacred writings are the one hundred volumes written by Baha'u'llah.

4. A. Q. Faizi, *Explanation of the Symbol of the Greatest Name* (New Delhi: Bahá'í Publishing Trust, n.d.), 18.

5. This interpretation may be justified since each interior side of the temple in Wilmette has inscribed upon it a symbol of one of the nine major world religions.

6. O'Brien, *Interviews,* 120.

7. Hayden relied upon two sources for his material in this poem. The first is Nat Turner's reputed confessions, reprinted in Herbert Aptheker's *Nat Turner's Slave Rebellion* (New York: Humanities Press, 1966), 127ff. The second is the Book of Ezekiel, attributed to a Hebrew prophet by that name who lived in the sixth century B.C.E. Living in the exiled Jewish community in Babylon, he had predicted the fall of Jerusalem, just as Nat Turner predicted the fall of Jerusalem, Virginia, against which he led the re-volt in 1831.

MELBA JOYCE BOYD

Poetry from Detroit's Black Bottom: The Tension between Belief and Ideology in the Work of Robert Hayden

I met Robert Hayden one October day in 1978 as I got onto the elevator in Haven Hall at the University of Michigan. He had just returned to campus after a two-year appointment as poetry consultant at the Library of Congress, and I, a doctoral candidate in the English department, had hoped to study creative writing with him. But his residence in Washington, D.C. coincided with my graduate tenure in Ann Arbor. A few days before this chance meeting on the elevator, I had attended his poetry reading at the Detroit Public Library for the dedication of the Jacob Lawrence exhibition of *The Legend of John Brown,* containing twenty-two screen prints. Hayden was commissioned to write a poem for the occasion and the publication about the John Brown series. It was one of the most memorable poetry readings I have ever experienced. The audience was mesmerized by his imagery, hypnotized by words that pierced our fragile fears and that empowered our bewildered humanity. It was as if Hayden had evoked the spirit of John Brown into the auditorium. As he read "John Brown," we gave witness and wept for this sacrificial figure:

> And now
> these mordant images—
>
> these vibrant stainedglass
> colors, elemental shapes
> in ardent interplay
> with what we know of him
> know yet fail to understand—
> even we
> for whom he died:
>
> (Shall we not say he died
> for us?)

Hanged body turning clockwise
in the air
            the hour
speeding to that hour
his dead-of-night
sorrows visions prophesied:

And now
            these haunting stark
torchlight images

But the same man whose words had engulfed an auditorium
and left hundreds breathless fluttered like a delicate hummingbird
in the small quarters of the elevator, startled by my surprise and ex-
citement upon seeing him. This seeming contrast of power and
shyness was a reflection of a unique sense of being. Like the ten-
sion between poetry and audience, Hayden was oblivious to pos-
ture and pretension and understood the terrible beauty that lives in
the song and the saying. According to Ellen Sharp, the curator of
graphic arts at the Detroit Institute of Arts:

> It was difficult for him [Hayden] to come to terms with the enig-
> mas and paradoxes in the character of John Brown, and he could
> not stomach the violence and bloodshed of Brown's activities in
> Kansas. However, after receiving the commission for the poem
> from the Art Institute, he studied the gouaches closely; somehow
> this aided in resolving his difficulties with the subject.[1]

Hayden explained the creative process in writing the poem
"John Brown" to television journalist Ron Scott:

> I studied the pictures and I did some more reading. And then
> I spent a great deal of time thinking about John Brown, what he
> represented, just what kind of man he must have been. I tried to
> understand what must have drove him. I reached the point where
> I stopped reading and I did a lot of thinking. I had a chance to
> see the pictures again, and eventually I got the poem together. It
> called for a considerable amount of work.[2]

Sharp's discussion provides a more detailed analysis of Hayden's
aesthetic interaction with Lawrence's paintings:

He also responded to the artist's symbolic use of color and form, which is paralleled in his own work in the utilization of the sounds of words and rhythm of phrases. Hayden liked best the images of the series that are the least realistic and that suggest rather than illustrate their subject. Most appealing to him were images such as number 8, with its jagged interlocking shapes in shades of green, black, and deep brick red, which depict a mountain range, or number 19, in which the company of men who marched on Harpers Ferry are reduced to a row of bayonet spikes silhouetted against a clouded night sky.[3]

It is this oblique, asymmetrical view of the world that provides the consequence of experience, whence poetic meaning is drawn. It is the tension in the poetry of Robert Hayden, the conflict between the beliefs of the poet struggling with the ideologies of oppression. This conflict is the essence of aggravation, motivating the muse to release its disgruntled soul. Hayden explains it thus:

> As a poet, I'm always trying to get to what is human, and what is fundamental. I think poetry does this. People think of poetry as being light and frivolous and spontaneous. And poetry is none of this. Any man or woman who devotes a life to poetry is trying to get down to something very, very fundamental. Trying to say what cannot be said.[4]

Beginnings in Black Bottom

Robert Hayden was born into a torn country, a nation divided by social ideologies that espoused the myth of race, that constricted social mobility, that repressed human sexuality, and that stacked human worth and work into tiny, narrow boxes. Contrary to this constrained setting, his writing was an act of resistance, a struggle to defy the ideas that undergirded oppression. Hayden grew up in an area in Detroit that no longer exists. It was called *Black Bottom,* a term that identified a section of fertile farmland of eighteenth- and nineteenth-century Detroit. As the automobile industry expanded, black laborers crowded into this space and it became a fertile field for African-American artists, educators, and politicians to till their talents. It became the main black section of the city, and Paradise Valley became the cultural center, where the blues and jazz clubs were located. Hayden, like most poets, drew some of his strongest imagery from his origins:

One lives in a situation. One lives in an environment. One isn't always aware of the impressions one is gathering. I don't have romantic yearnings for the past. I miss the people. I sometimes have nostalgia for people I knew and loved [my italics].[5]

The poem "Those Winter Sundays" conveys the love and hardship of his childhood in a portrayal of his father's strength and tenderness weathered and toughened by a cold and harsh reality. Hayden's imagery is an amazing juxtaposition of contrasting elements of sound, light, color, and texture. Within the primary imagery of a man building a fire, Hayden constructs an engaging dialectic by interfacing hard with soft, cold with warm. The poem swells and expands into a poignant and vulnerable portrait of a misunderstood and misshapen man.

There are certain things in my childhood, certain things in my background that I cherish that I find very interesting. But I'm aware of all things, of certain grim realities I had to live through. The fact of being poor, which being of itself is not bad, but being miserable because of unhappy family situations and because of the whole color problem in the United States. But as poor people living in a certain section of Detroit and having suffered particular conditions, we had certain idioms and certain ways of life which were different than say people of the same race living on the Westside of Detroit. We were closer to the folk milieu.

This is one of the poems from a series I've written called "Paradise Valley." The people mentioned are real enough. I knew some and some are composites. They are people I knew and saw every day of my childhood.

> And Belle the classy dresser, where is she,
> who changed her frocks three times a day?
> > Where's Nora, with her laugh, her comic flair,
> > stagestruck Nora waiting for her chance?
> Where's fast Iola, who so loved to dance
> she left her sickbed one last time to whirl
> in silver at The Palace till she fell?

Where's mad Miss Alice, who ate from garbage cans?
Where's snuffdipping Lucy, who played us "chunes"
on her guitar? Where's Hattie? Where's Melissabelle?
Let vanished rooms, let dead streets tell.

I had Beacon Street in mind when I wrote the poem, "Dead Streets" because there are no people there now. An old street lamp shown into the bay window of my house at night. I think something that was familiar and dear to me ended and something else began. Both ending and beginning. I recall in early years when Hudson's [Department Store] built its warehouse on Beacon Street, and then houses were torn down to make way for a power plant. A neighborhood which had been fairly cohesive had been destroyed and the families on Beaubien [Street] and other areas went different ways. Most of us never saw each other again. That was certainly a drastic change.

St. Antoine I remember as a very colorful street, no pun intended. It was a lively street with barbershops and pool halls and restaurants and drug stores, and I suppose gambling joints too. In the summer, people used to stand out in front of the various places there and greet their friends. It was said if you wanted to find a friend you hadn't seen for many years, all you had to do was to stand on the corner of St. Antoine and Adams and pretty soon you were bound to see your old friend.

I remember Halloween on St. Antoine. People used to dress up and come out to parade up and down. I remember when Joe Louis fought Schmeling. That and other victories were celebrated on St. Antoine Street. And people marched up and down the street having a good time. It was a colorful street, and it was considered by some people to be a wicked street because gamblers and the so-called "sporting class" took St. Antoine as its main thoroughfare. About 1940 Billie Holiday came to sing at the Club Plantation. I remember Dudley Randall and I went to hear her sing. I remember how she looked. She was quite striking. She always affected a flower in her hair, and she sang in a very moving way.[6]

Because there was a man somewhere in a candystripe silk shirt,
gracile and dangerous as a jaguar and because a woman moaned
for him in sixty-watt gloom and mourned him Faithless Love
Twotiming Love Oh Love Oh Careless Aggravating Love,

> She came out on the stage in yards of pearls, emerging like
> a favorite scenic view, flashed her golden smile and sang.

Hayden's poetic language in "Homage to the Empress of the Blues" combines the mellow tones and messages of Billie Holiday and Bessie Smith with the progressive, insightful politics of the workers movement of the 1930s and 1940s. The circular phrasing of the blues lyrics sung on Hastings Street was translated into the geometrical imagery of modernism. The language hinges on the very tension that distanced the origins of these distinct cultural expressions and class experiences, and, despite or because of these differences, this cultural marriage produces a rich sound and oblique, complex imagery:

> Because grey laths began somewhere to show from underneath
> torn hurdygurdy lithographs of dollfaced heaven;
> and because there were those who feared alarming fists of snow
> on the door and those who feared the riot-squad of statistics,

> She came out on the stage in ostrich feathers, beaded satin,
> and shone that smile on us and sang.

The divergent languages, angles of perception, and rhythmical timing resolve a translucent experience. Hayden's poetry brings to Billie and Bessie a broader contextual understanding of the suffering, of the blackness, in the blues. He frames raw sexual truth with historical insight, thereby extending the blues legacy and deepening our knowledge of the source and the force of the pain. "Mourning Poem for the Queen of Sunday" not only reflects Hayden's upbringing in the church, but it represents his capacity to synthesize the sounds and signs of the black oral tradition into poetic form. He merges the Baptist sermon, the Negro spiritual, and the blues into a free verse poem by adapting characteristic elements of call and response, end rhyme, repetition, and refrain.

> Lord's lost Him His mockingbird,
> His fancy warbler;
> Satan sweet-talked her,
> four bullets hushed her.
> Who would have thought
> she'd end that way?

Four bullets hushed her. And the world a-clang with evil.
Who's going to make old hardened sinner men tremble now
and the righteous rock?
Oh who and oh who will sing Jesus down   ·
to help with struggling and doing without and being colored
all through blue Monday?
Till way next Sunday?

Rhythmic phrasing determines the variation in sound patterns, while rhyme and repetition construct the time frame. The inclusion of rhetorical questions emulates a preacher's eulogy calling to the congregation, while the refrain reiterates the conflict between good and evil, God and the devil, supplying the response to the preacher's call. The poem also demonstrates the similarities between the spirituals and the blues as the violent death of a churchwoman is refracted through irony and pathos.

Although college educated (Wayne State University and the University of Michigan), Hayden's keen sensitivity is deeply rooted in the blue/black beginnings of Detroit's emerging proletarian culture. He writes in and out of the vernacular with precise phrasing and exquisite finesse. In order to accomplish this, his language is bidialectic and dialectical. Like Bessie, for those of us who can hear, Hayden extracts the mood and music of the culture with timeless historical vision and lifts us above our suffering. But for those of us who can see through feeling, Hayden shows us the light beyond the circle of dark entrapment.

Being a Detroiter, Hayden has a very special place in my poetry and in my literary consciousness. He is legendary in community lore, and my knowledge of his legacy has been largely transmitted though my life experiences with Dudley Randall, another legendary figure in the culture. Randall and Hayden were close friends for almost forty years. Both of them grew up in Black Bottom and were close to the movers and shakers at the helm of black Detroit's cultural and labor movement politics.

The poetry of both poets exhibits knowledge of black oral folk culture and a mastery of the English language and poetics. In a conversation I had with Dudley Randall in his home in August 1981, he talked about his friendship with Hayden and about Hayden's conflicted relationship with his first book, *Heart-Shape in the Dust*. Randall said he was introduced to Hayden in the 1930s:

Probably the later part of the 1930s. I used to go to the YMCA where they would have programs at different times and a friend there said, "Since you are interested in poetry, you ought to meet this guy named Robert Hayden. He's a poet too." So we were introduced and we would talk about poetry and would show each other our poems. I was more interested in sound at first, and Hayden was more interested in metaphor and in phrasing. He would always say, why don't we collaborate and do a book together, but we never did. But I was interested in his career and admired him.

When Hayden expressed interest in a poetry contest, Randall assisted him by typing up the manuscript. Although Hayden did not win the prize, this manuscript became his first published book when the labor leadership in the black community financed the publication of *Heart-Shape in the Dust*. Randall described the importance of this work locally and nationally:

> Some of his friends, some of whom were in the union, donated money and it was printed by the Leathermen. They made up a fictitious name for the publisher, something like Falcon Press. Those were his earliest poems, and he may have disavowed that book because later [as the publisher and editor of Broadside Press] I asked to reprint some of the poems from the book and he said: "No! No! No! No! I wrote those poems when I was an apprentice." And he refused to allow those poems to be reprinted. I really don't agree with him because some of those poems are very beautiful. This book was reviewed in *The Detroit News* and they praised some of the poems. Some of those early poems you can find in *The Negro Caravan,* and he was called by the editors, Sterling Brown and Ulysses Lee, "one of the most promising younger poets."[7]

Hayden and the Black Arts Movement

The exchanges and influences between Hayden and Randall, as transmitted through their work and my apprenticeship with Randall, resolved for me the conflict between poet and society, the politics of aesthetics. There is no inherent contradiction between the humanity of African Americans and this nation. Our special plight is yet another paradox that will ultimately be resolved through struggle as part of humanity's inevitable progression. Unfortunately, too many writers of the 1960s were not open to the depth and breadth of humanity's possibilities as revealed in the poetry of Hayden.

Hayden's egalitarianism and Bahá'í faith were antithetical to the competitive and hostile temperament of many of the younger, militant writers of the Black Arts Movement. Because he would not subscribe to political dogma espoused by the "dictatorship of the black aesthetic," his artistic philosophy grated upon the limited vision and selfish ideals of a more didactic and antagonistic literary sector. Because of his prominence as a poet and because of the intensity of the times, his concerted efforts to disengage himself from this polemical debate were futile. As the debate gained momentum, the tension increased. Attacked by innocent ignorance in some cases and maligned by opportunistic outrage in others, the radical politics in his poetic themes and personal history were ignored, and stones were cast against his image. His stance on artistic freedom was regarded as an escape from political responsibility in the freedom struggle. He became the primary target for ideological ridicule and the recipient of considerable outrage.

At the 1966 Black Writers' Conference at Fisk University the cultural nationalists (left unnamed in this essay to protect the guilty) verbally assaulted Hayden. Dudley Randall attended the conference and in fact was a guest in the Hayden home. While most of the attendees said they were black first, Hayden was criticized for saying, "First, I'm a writer." Randall discussed the confrontation and the uproar it caused at the conference:

> Hayden was on a panel and he made his usual statement that he believed poetry should be judged by its merits as poetry, not for its political utterances. And he was strongly attacked from the floor by many of the students at Fisk. He was a professor of English at that university. I don't remember the exact words, but it was clear they were against him. But he stood up for what he believed. That night, he read his poems of the black experience. He read "Runagate" and "Middle Passage" and other poems. Everybody was moved, even those who had been attacking him. So the whole audience spontaneously gave him a standing ovation. Offstage, he leaned against the wall exhausted, there were tears in his eyes. I told him it was a good reading and he replied, "Yes, it was very moving."[8]

Endings

Robert Hayden returned to the Detroit area in 1969, when he took a professorial position at the University of Michigan. Randall and Hayden tried to coedit a black poetry anthology, but Hayden abandoned the project because he could not commit to a collection that included certain Black Arts poets. He could not overcome the tension between his beliefs and their ideology of poetics. But this tension never came between their friendship. Randall reminisced:

> The last time I saw him was two days before he died. There was a program in honor of him at the University of Michigan in February 1980, on a Sunday. I went to the program, but he was not able to come because he was sick in bed. He had the flu, and later that evening after the program, some of us went to his house. It came out later that he had cancer. I was able to see him then and give him a couple of volumes of his poetry—he had complained he had written the book, *Night-Blooming Cereus,* and he didn't have any copies of it. On Tuesday, one of the women who was there called me and told me that Robert died on Monday.[9]

In an "angle of ascent" Hayden's poetry is committed to the whole of humanity. His thematic concerns reach into the "dead streets" of Paradise Valley, into the heart of Black Bottom, and resurrect those spirits. He illuminates these ghosts and writes them into the stars. Like King and Kennedy, they too are the specters of grief that America confronts as a consequence of its ambiguous heritage. In "Words for the Mourning Time" Hayden portrays our self-destructive nature and reveals why we are the victims of ourselves, unable to save our country from the unseen forces attacking us from within and without:

> For King, for Robert Kennedy,
> destroyed by those they could not save,
> for King for Kennedy I mourn.
> And for America, self-destructive, self-betrayed.
>
> I grieve. Yet know the vanity
> of grief—through power of
> The Blessed Exile's
> transilluminating word.

The vision that dwells in the iris of Robert Hayden's poetry holds a power of human memory that cannot be easily translated through critical discourse or entrapped for political co-optation. The thick, Coke bottle lenses of his glasses seemed to have protected him from the vanity of popularity or the arrogance of artistic contrivance. The then and the thereafter pivot in the agony of his knowing. Through his poetry we reenter the bowels of the slave ship and cleave to memory in this quest to be free.

The last time I saw Robert Hayden I was dreaming. I was seated amid other scholars with heads bent over a large rectangular table in the Library of Congress. I was anguishing over my research on Frances Harper. I glanced over the bowed heads into the all-knowing gaze of Robert Hayden's ghost, and I was blessed by his affirmation. It was the unspoken, unwritten word that only the ultimate experience of death brings.

It is not our words that live beyond our lives but the spirits those words evoke and liberate. The power of Robert Hayden's poetry rises from the page, through human memory, through him, and through us all.

NOTES

1. Ellen Sharp, "Introduction," *The Legend of John Brown. Jacob Lawrence: John Brown, 22 Gouaches* (Detroit: Detroit Institute of Arts, 1978), 13.
2. *Robert Hayden: America's Poet Laureate,* documentary film by Ron Scott, *Detroit Black Journal,* WTVS, Channel 56, 1978.
3. Sharp, "Introduction," 13.
4. Scott, *Robert Hayden.*
5. Ibid.
6. Ibid.
7. Dudley Randall, interview with the author, Detroit, July 1981.
8. Randall, interview with the author, Detroit, August 1985.
9. Dudley Randall's Broadside Press distributed *The Night-Blooming Cereus* in the United States for the Paul Breman Heritage Poetry Series based in London. Interview with the author, Detroit, August 1985.

REGINALD GIBBONS

A Man That in His Writing Was
Most Wise

If by *civilized* we mean neither an empty courtesy nor a bland neutrality nor an isolation from life in favor of books but a focused compassion and sympathy, an understanding of how social forces drive personal relationships and how others require our compassion and sympathy partly on that very account, then Robert Hayden was one of the most civilized poets we have had among us. Every citizen, every *civis,* is a member of Hayden's household, and to everyone he extends not only a refined sensibility but a genuine interest both curious and responsive, an interest that has been educated by life and by reading.

Several times in his poems what appears to be a mild habitual civility is transformed into a trenchant and deeply felt sense of wonder at all human transactions—and it is not always himself whom Hayden puts into the position of seeing deeper or feeling more keenly. He has too much self-knowledge for that. On the contrary, he uses others to illuminate the reaches into which he wants to extend his own emotional understanding, as when, at the end of "The Performers," the onlooker thanks the window washers reentering the safe world through his window.

> A rough day, I remark,
>
> for such a risky business. Many thanks.
> Thank *you,* sir, one of the men replies.

He thus makes his daydreaming transformation of them into "minor Wallendas" a reciprocated human exchange of feeling, and they gain dignity from acknowledging that they have a sense of

From *Obsidian: Black Literature in Review* 8, no. 1 (Spring 1981): 182–87.

themselves as performers occupied in a daily labor that they have transformed into mastery. They acknowledge the onlooker as a spectator, and they validate, beyond the extent to which his reverie could do so, his admiration of them. The quiet gesture that yet contains a powerful revelation is typical of Hayden's poetic manner.

Perhaps, out of the complex struggles and doubts that attended Hayden's thinking about his own origins and childhood—personal and social spheres of irony, disappointment, difficulty, accomplishment, and love, nested one inside the other—Hayden was particularly sensitive to feelings both of dislocation and of the humiliation that comes with dependence. He sought to balance these with a sense of identity. To quote the ending of another poem is to reveal a turn in this direction. In "'Mystery Boy' Looks for Kin in Nashville," after creating the disoriented and fearful mood that surrounds the wandering lost child, and in which voices are calling to him in a way that frightens rather than comforts, Hayden has the "dollbaby wife" point him toward a solution to the great riddle: "We'll go and find them, we'll go / and ask them for your name again."

We will return to the importance to Hayden of names, but for now let us note that it is a similar gesture, in this case honoring an unselfconscious identity, that shifts the narration of "Aunt Jemima of the Ocean Waves" from the expected to the unexpected, from the observer of the seaside carnival, whose attitude is uncertain and shot through with knowledge of historical ironies and indignities, to "Aunt Jemima" herself, whose presence is built out of concrete personal history—her travels and loves, her triumphs and humiliations, her delicate and dignified acceptance, her wisdom. And these are not spelled out by Hayden as the requisites of an adequate personal response to a social reality but are presented through *her* speech, in those characteristically Haydenesque stanzas that give the impression of formality while capturing the vital breath of speech rhythms. Aunt Jemima is the full image for the malaise the onlooker feels, and she is also the cure.

Never an effusive poet, always spare and precise, working to control the emotional response that a poem realizes, Hayden at moments of greatest intensity will cut back to the sparest lines of all, letting an image—in the purely visual sense—stand for everything he does not wish to state explicitly. "Kodachromes of the Island," a poem that is one version of a poetic impulse Hayden seems to have honored more than once ("An Inference of Mexico," "Islands," for example) is characteristic. The poem is divided into three sections, each of four stanzas, each stanza of three lines. Part 2 ends:

> On the landing, women
> were cleaning a catch and
> tossing the guts to
>
> squealing piglets. A tawny
> butterfly drunkenly circled
> then lighted on offal.

This is one way to bring an irony to bear, in a poem. But that isn't enough for Hayden, as it shouldn't be. The third section is far more weighty; in it the photographic sharpness of the description leads not to another final image (which, after all, gains its strength by virtue of its very partiality, its incompleteness, because it stands for *what is not said:* a kind of metonymy that should be considered further, perhaps) but to a consideration of self, in the photographed landscape. Hayden evokes a poetic kinsman, whose own anguish over the adequacy of poetry to speak of the life of men and women in extreme circumstances is often echoed in his work:

> Alien, at home—as always
> everywhere—I roamed
> the cobbled island,
>
> and thought of Yeats,
> his passionate search for
> a theme. Sought mine.

It is worth noting that the last two words affirm not only a kinship with Yeats but a distinction between Yeats's theme and Hayden's. George Seferis says, "*In essence,* the poet has one theme: his live body." If that is true, it is nonetheless true that for Hayden and Yeats the exact contours of identity and morality are very different.

But what precisely is Hayden's sense of image? I think he experiments in moving between two poles and decides resolutely— without calling into question the other extreme—in favor of a sense of image that again returns us to Yeats. Let me quote from Yeats's poem "Ego Dominus Tuus," one of his various castings of an ars poetica. It is in the form of a dialogue between figures called simply by the Latin *hic* and *ille:* the one and the other.

> Ille.   By the help of an image
>   I call to my own opposite, summon all
>   That I have handled least, least looked upon.
> Hic.   And I would find myself and not an image.
> Ille.   That is our modern hope, and by its light
>   We have lit upon the gentle, sensitive mind
>   And lost the old nonchalance of the hand;
>   Whether we have chosen chisel, pen or brush,
>   We are but critics, or but half create,
>   Timid, entangled, empty and abashed,
>   Lacking the countenance of our friends.

The special importance to Yeats of inspiring friendship needs no comment here; what I want to point out is that this rejection of "the gentle, sensitive mind"—a gesture rather harsher in Yeats than in Hayden, certainly—is in favor of a special sense of the "image." That is, the image takes the poet out of himself, into others, and makes possible love and friendship and helps him come to understand his own identity among men and women. And by *image* Yeats does not mean the vague floating oddity that fills many contemporary poems nowadays, the ropes of silence and the stones of loneliness and the water's sad shadow, etc. Yeats means among other things a living face, like the one Dante saw and dedicated his poem to, like Hayden's "Aunt Jemima," like the faces of the gone dead in Hayden's "Elegies for Paradise Valley." Yeats's poem answers another objection as well:

> The rhetorician would deceive his neighbors,
> The sentimentalist himself; while art
> Is but a vision of reality.
> . . . .
> Those men that in their writings are most wise
> Own nothing but their blind, stupefied hearts.

The various parts of "Elegies for Paradise Valley" gloss these assorted lines from Yeats's poem. They establish the living face—with a *name*—as Hayden's necessary poetic image. The beautiful section 5 is not only Hayden's version of Villon's "Ballade des Dames du Temps Jadis," as Donald Davie has pointed out, but also a gathering of images in the Yeatsian sense. Hayden not only eulogizes others but works, in this poem, toward an understanding of himself, by using the Yeatsian sense of the image. This progress is worth noting in some detail.

Section 5 asks the unanswerable question, Where *are* the dead? The last line says, as both an answer and, as we will note, yet another question, "Let vanished rooms, let dead streets tell." Hayden makes us realize that this answer is itself a question: "Tell of what?" He does this by making the first line of the next section provide the next answer, "Of death. Of loving too." That is followed by section 7, which finds its Yeatsian image in the Gypsies—a wonderfully complex and sympathetic shift of perspective, full of ironies and compassion. Section 8, after this interlude, answers that implied question of section 5 again: "Let vanished rooms, let dead streets tell."

> Of death, of loving,
> of sin and hellfire too.
> Unsaved, old Christians
> gossiped; pitched
>
> from the gamblingtable—
> Lord have mercy on
> his wicked soul—
> face foremost into hell.
>
> We'd dance there, Uncle
> Crip and I,
> for though I spoke
> my pieces well in Sunday School,
>
> I knew myself (precocious
> in the ways of guilt
> and secret pain)
> the devil's own rag babydoll.

Why does the question of section 5 receive another answer here? I think it is because of Hayden's feeling that his own identity—which is the ground note of the poem, over which the elegies are sung individually—must still be sought among those who are dead. Earlier I mentioned Hayden's sensitivity to a sense of dislocation. Here he is at pains to present himself, as a child, in a light of intense self-consciousness, as he tries to forge a connection to Crip and to the others. This self-consciousness does not diminish the joy of remembrance: like Roethke waltzing with his papa, Hayden does dance with Uncle Crip and the dance is both joyous and frightening, for, if they seem to be dancing round the gambling table, they are also, given the poem's careful double implication, dancing already in hell—where some of those dead of section 5 must now reside. Hayden, seeking a final image, moves, however, from the resurrected Uncle Crip (whose funeral we have already seen in section 3), to himself as a child. This movement is not merely a return to the child who appeared earlier in the poem but from that child's relatively unselfconscious voice (especially of sections 3 and 4) toward much greater consciousness. This is enacted by the syntax and line-breaks of the last stanza. The effect of the parenthesis and the end of the first line of that stanza is to open a possibility with this last sentence, something first considered and then rejected. "I knew myself (precocious" seems to answer to Yeats's *Hic,* who says, "I would find myself and not an image." In this line the poem proposes merely a knowledge of self—if not then, then now, looking back. But knowing the self isn't enough, and the continuation of the sentence, after the pause enforced by the end of the line, provides us with a possibility that is more important. Knowing one's self won't take one *outside* the self, to where others are. It isn't, in fact, a dislocation—for Hayden's discovery seems to have been, in several poems ("Alien, at home—as always / everywhere") that dislocation as an existential predicament can also be a poetic method. "By the help of an image / I call to my own opposite," Yeats wrote. Hayden effects a dialectical reversal, to make use of dislocation much the way Williams made use of failure in "The Descent":

> No defeat is made up entirely of defeat—since
> the world it opens is always a place
> > formerly
> > > unsuspected.

The last sentence of the "Elegies," and the stanza, completes itself by saying, "I knew myself [to be] the devil's own rag babydoll." Shifting the syntactical perspective, changing *knew* from a reflexive verb of self-knowledge to one that leads us on to the predicate nominative, "the devil's own rag babydoll," Hayden makes us go through a cognitive shift to seeing that the self is *something else,* that it is an image.

In a number of poems Hayden perceives himself as an other—from the poem in which the lost "mystery boy" is waiting to discover his name to the poem that follows "Elegies," "Names," in which Hayden's discovery of his true parentage provokes a profound sense of nonidentity, as if the real Hayden were someone else, *out there,* who really did exist, unlike the one writing the poem. Am I, he asks, merely the ghost or alter ego of that *other?* In this last stanza of "Elegies" what happens is that a syntactic and poetic device stresses this sudden sense of being transformed into an *other,* subject to force and the will of others. It is not unambiguous: it gives the poet the image he needs, at the same time that it takes from him a sense of security in his identity. But it is the double motion that perhaps provides the strength of the poem: in remembering those who are gone, the poet goes into them, until remembering himself, he too is gone, and at last suitably transformed into an image in the poem, given the kind of power and representativeness that a mere narrator may not achieve. Hayden becomes one of his own images and is both released from grief and sorrow and confirmed in compassion and sympathy.

I hope this does not seem too great a philosophical or poetic weight to put on this delicate stanza with its subtle undermining of our first expectation. A poet's vision is as much built up out of local poetic triumphs as it is imposed out of a pre-poetic understanding. And in Hayden's work I believe I see a compellingly honest, even modest, openness as the poet carries out the never-ending search for figures of men and women who will be the emblems of his loss and his joy. Hayden's accomplishments as a poet are considerable and lie in every good line, in his scrupulousness as an artist, and in the great value of the poetic tasks he sets himself in each poem. The theme he sought is the simple necessary one of the man who must make his way through the world's sorrows and take heart from those he meets there, all the while struggling with his own sense of himself. Much remains to be said about Hayden's poetic technique, about his vision, about the special quality of his work, that I have called "civilized"—a quality always in short supply. And, if readers continue to come to his work with the sort of humane sympathy that Hayden himself offers to *them,* then his poems will continue to be read and will continue to instruct us all.

W. D. SNODGRASS

Robert Hayden: The Man in the Middle

Robert Hayden's mother, a glamorous woman of mixed race, appeared to be white; his father, Asa Sheffey, was a black laborer. That marriage failed, and, at eighteen months, Robert was given to be raised by Sue Ellen and William Hayden. At that time he was rechristened; some question arose whether he had been legally adopted. A long and damaging struggle for his custody and loyalty ensued. Late in life he considered changing his name back to Asa Bundy Sheffey.

The Hayden household was, moreover, troubled with poverty and its own internal struggles. Robert's foster-father, another black laborer, was sternly patriarchal; his wife had previously been married, perhaps to a white. According to Hayden's biographer, the wife "could never forget [her first husband] and, unfortunately, never let William Hayden forget him either." In any case, Robert had ample cause to be aware of race and racial mixtures; he himself said that he was nearly as light-skinned as Italian or Jewish playmates in their mixed neighborhood.

Not only in matters of race did he find himself between stools. Like many intellectuals at that time, he felt a sympathy for Marxist theory and politics but quickly became disillusioned with the Communist Party. Raised a strict Baptist, he later converted to Bahá'í, a faith that recognizes the viability of all the major religions. Though he was a devoted husband and father, some cryptic poems allude to a bisexual condition. His literary allegiances were similarly divided. He never lost his early love for the black poets Paul Laurence Dunbar, Countee Cullen, Langston Hughes; in time, however, he came also to admire, and learn from, Keats, Auden, Yeats, Eliot.

Most of this information comes from Pontheolla Williams's

From *Field* 47 (Autumn 1992): 20–30.

admirable study *Robert Hayden: A Critical Analysis of His Poetry.* Williams notes that, though he often felt torn between antagonistic races, competing families, religions, political groups, and artistic traditions, such a position has, for an artist, peculiar advantages. We might recall Isaiah Berlin's recognition that we all make our decisions, define our lives, under the influence of competing systems of value. Just as Hayden's familial division caused him lifelong pain, he must often have longed for an exclusive racial, political, or philosophical commitment—to be a hedgehog, not a fox. Yet that would have meant suppressing some part of his background, so of himself. In a lesser person this might have led to a desperate clutching at some narrow code of allegiance and self-definition. For a man of Hayden's compassion and honesty, it led to a recognition of his pivotal position as an American, himself the "melting pot" of multiple demands, influences, and traditions. To his work it brought the kind of "negative capability" so much admired by Keats—a willingness to see the many sides, the complex relativity of our situation, a freedom from any "irritable reaching" after some comforting dogma.

I shall aim here to take this aspect of Williams's argument and to demonstrate, in greater detail than she could spare, how this broader humanism informs three of Hayden's best-known and most admired poems.

"Those Winter Sundays," deservedly famous, describes William Hayden, the foster-father with whom Robert did not always get along. Yet, despite the family's grinding poverty and his own lack of education, he made it possible for Robert to continue his schooling at Detroit City College (now Wayne State University) and the University of Michigan. It remained a matter of constant self-reproach to Robert that he had never adequately shown the gratitude he felt.

The poem displays an almost uncanny skill in handling its subject. In its very first line a wealth of meaning lurks in the simple word *too*—an awareness that each and every day the father rose early to a cold house and either went off to work or, worse, to seek work. The following five lines are linked by a beautifully crafted chain of echoes underlining the hardship of the father's life: "clothes . . . blueblack cold . . . cracked . . . ached . . . weekday weather . . . banked . . . blaze . . . thanked . . . wake . . . breaking." Only in the second stanza, once the cold abates and the boy rises to dress, is this pattern dissolved into the comforting sounds of *warm, call,* and *slowly.*

It is the third stanza, though, to which I would draw particular attention for its tact and generosity. To have "driven out the cold" might seem enough; to have "polished my good shoes as well" reaches, without losing credibility, toward a higher goodness. If we changed this line to read something like "and ironed my Sunday clothes as well," the poem would evaporate. Not only does polishing his foster-son's shoes show a deep humility (especially when blacks have often been reduced to such menial tasks for whites), but it carries the suggestion, however slight, of Jesus washing his disciples' feet. So the father lowers himself to an almost priestly, if not saintly, height. This alone justifies the suddenly elevated language of the last line, crediting the father with "love's austere and lonely offices"—those duties or ceremonial acts that, in themselves, constitute a religious observance.

Yet, despite these literary excellences, it is another quality—one related to the overall argument of the poem—that most attracts me. That is the willingness to say, "I was wrong"—to be shocked at one's own insensitivity. What could more acutely bespeak guilt than "No one ever thanked him" or, more personally, "I would rise . . . Speaking indifferently to him" and, again, "What did I know, what did I know . . . ?" We need not draw attention to the myriads of accusatory and self-justifying poems one sees almost daily—poems meant to prove that "I am right to hate whom I hate"—to recognize this poem's humane warmth and a humility comparable to the father's. It is this, I think—or dare to hope—that has made it Hayden's best-known poem.

One might argue, however, that Hayden's broad humanism and awareness of other existences, other viewpoints than his own, while informing the subject matter and attitude of this poem, do not express themselves through its technique. There is little in its style or structure idiosyncratic to Hayden—in these qualities it seems not unlike certain poems by Thomas Hardy, William Stafford, and, more recently, Len Roberts. Something quite different happens in such a poem as "Night, Death, Mississippi."

The first of the poem's two sections presents a rural white Southerner who overhears a lynching in the woods near his house and regrets that he cannot be there with "Boy"—probably his son. Two voices are heard, the narrator and the old man, though neither punctuation nor typography distinguishes them. Some of the lines describing the old man's thoughts or recollections—

> A quavering cry.
>
> White robes like moonlight
> In the sweetgum dark

—seem too literate for a man who refers to his son merely as "Boy."
Such lines, I think, represent the old man's perceptions as filtered
through the narrator's richer consciousness.

No doubt, some of those who attacked Hayden's work would
find it offensive that he devotes such vivid realization to this vio-
lent and ugly old man, not to a condemnation of lynching or to a
contrastingly admirable figure, probably black. Yet, though the
poem may appear detached and objective, at no point do we doubt
Hayden's opinion or values. From the first the narrator has estab-
lished a disgust for the old man's crudity:

> The old man in his reek
> and gauntness laughs—

Later we find much the same tone:

> He hawks and spits,
> fevered as by groinfire.

The word *groinfire,* of course, openly defines the subject's driving
sadism. But we have heard that even more clearly in the man's own
words:

> Unbucked that one then
> and him squealing bloody Jesus
> as we cut if off.

When a man has so clearly damned himself from his own mouth,
any commentary could only weaken the portrait's force by sug-
gesting some element of self-interest in the writer.

The second section creates a musical construct based on the ma-
terial of the first but as seen from different perspectives. Williams
sees the three primary stanzas as constituting a single scene, con-
tiguous with the first section: the first two being Boy's tale when he
comes back from the lynching; the third spoken by a woman, prob-
ably the old man's daughter, telling the children to bring water so

"Paw" can wash the blood off Boy. At the same time, if one read the third stanza to mean that Paw should wash the blood off himself, one could take these stanzas as pertaining to other lynchings, other characters. In either case a horrifying irony is created by the contrast between the family's solicitude for a family member and the virulent exultation shown over the victims of his savage violence.

These stanzas are interrupted and balanced, however, by three separate lines given in italics, much as a refrain might be. These lines both associate the victim with Jesus' crucifixion and identify the crucial darkness as neither that of the night nor of the Negroes' skin but as that of the lynchers' souls. The tone here is of lyrical lamentation; the antiphonal effect is comparable to a church service where the choir interrupts and punctuates the preacher's text with a series of sung refrains.

Yet there is an important difference: one assumes that the choir and preacher are ultimately in harmony, saying the same thing; here the narrative and the lyrical interjections stand in sharp contrast and opposition. To find a comparable musical effect one would have to turn, I think, to classical music—to something like the first chorus from Bach's "St. Matthew Passion," where the doubts and questionings of the main choir are balanced against the pure faith and certainty of the boys' choir. Or to the slow movement of Beethoven's "Fourth Piano Concerto," where the angry assertions of the lower strings are balanced and finally soothed away by the calm and tender rejoinders of the soloist. Such a comparison may, at first, seem strained; I do not think Hayden would have found it so. Had his eyesight been stronger, he might have become a violinist; an early poem is devoted to "Beethoven." In any case he would have been aware of the principles of opposition between themes upon which all sonata forms are built.

Only by such an example can I indicate the kind of musical construct Hayden is creating. Above all, he is preserving opposed and various parts of his awareness, counterposing them in a structure that does justice to the variousness of experience and imagination. At the same time, he never obscures his own sense of values, of confronting a positive and horrifying evil.

This technique of juxtaposing fragments of scenes and the voices of differing points of view reaches its fullest realization in such poems as "Runagate Runagate" and, most especially, in "Middle Passage." The method owes much to Eliot's *The Waste Land,* yet its purpose is, finally, completely different. All the voices one hears in *The Waste Land* are, finally, aspects of one mind, memories retained by, or emotions discovered in, a single personality. The various scenes in "Middle Passage" would not all have been experienced by any one character; the various voices one hears belong to a multiplicity of characters, each having a disparate and independent existence. Not only do they not speak for Hayden or his narrator, several are allowed, once again, to damn themselves from their own mouths. *The Waste Land's* final aim is to concretize and explore the sensibility of its speaker and his sense of meaninglessness, which rises from an affectional and sexual loss. The purpose of "Middle Passage," even though we have some interest in the narrator's meditations, is not to render a state of mind but, rather, to let the reader partake of an experience in the outside world, the horror of the slave trade, then to join in celebrating Cinquez, who fought against it.

To do so, Hayden has collected, during a long period of research, a great variety of materials. His weaving of these into the three sections of the poem is masterful. In part 1, the first group, six stanzas, present and comment on the general scene of the slave ships. First, we encounter a simple list of ships' names, names that would translate, Jesus, Star (with a suggestion of Fate), Hope, Mercy. Immediately, the narrator's imagery, "Sails flashing . . . like weapons, / sharks following . . . / horror the corposant and compass rose," underlines the irony of those pious names and establishes, once and for all, the poem's attitude.

The narrator continues:

> Middle Passage:
>   voyage through death
>   to life upon these shores.

—lines that will be repeated as the last lines of the poem. This is succeeded by a dated entry from a ship's log, recording and concretizing the misery inflicted upon the blacks, another list of ships, the narrator's statement of destination:

> Standing to America, bringing home
> black gold, black ivory, black seed.

This mention of seed reminds the speaker that his own ancestors were brought here by just such ships:

Deep in the festering hold thy father lies,
of his bones New England pews are made,
those are altar lights that were his eyes.

The mention of pews and altar lights brings the poem into a new grouping of stanzas, another scene—a New England church where the congregation sings a hymn befitting mariners:

Jesus Saviour Pilot Me
Over Life's Tempestuous Sea

We continue with the smarmy hypocrisy of the sermon and a repetition of the hymn's opening, "Jesus Saviour." This time, however, the hymn may be taken also as the narrator's prayer as he imagines the sufferings of the cargo blacks.

The ensuing pair of stanzas takes us back aboard ship: "8 bells. I cannot sleep, for I am sick / with fear" might well come from that same sailor who wrote the earlier log entry. This much more personal passage, however, must come from a diary or letter he is writing. His fear is not only of a potential revolt of the imprisoned blacks but also of the illness—"Ophthalmia: blindness"—which has spread from the slaves to the crew and captain. The ship is still three weeks from port "& there is blindness in the fo'c'sle." "Which one of us / has killed an albatross?" he asks, so witnessing his own moral blindness to the crimes of his mates and himself.

The following deeply indented and italicized lines, beginning "*What port awaits us, Davy Jones' / or home?*" render the narrator's effort to identify with such a sailor. This particular passage, with its fear of aimlessly drifting with "the jungle hatred crawling up on deck," also serves as a plant for the poem's ending, where Cinquez and the slaves rebel and take command of the *Amistad*.

Another portion from the earlier hymn, "Thou Who Walked On Galilee," brings us to a third scene: the courtroom where we hear the deposition of a sailor who escaped the burning and sinking of the *Bella J.* This was apparently caused by the carelessness of the drunken captain and his sexually rapacious crew, who either fled or perished, leaving the blacks to be burned with the ship. A particular irony is created, however, by the contrast between the formal courtroom language and the horrors depicted:

"Deponent further sayeth . . .

"That there was hardly room 'tween-decks for half
the sweltering cattle stowed spoon-fashion there;
that some went mad of thirst and tore their flesh
and sucked the blood:

"That Crew and Captain lusted with the comeliest
of the savage girls kept naked in the cabins; . . .

"Further Deponent sayeth not."

A final recollection of the hymn "Pilot Oh Pilot Me" closes the section.

I have treated part 1 in considerable detail because its somewhat difficult materials must be fully grasped if we are to realize the overall structure of the poem but also because this seems to me one of the most remarkable structures in American poetry. Read aloud, with the appropriate parts sung (as, incidentally, portions of *The Waste Land* should be), it has an almost overwhelming effect.

Part 2 embodies a single voice; its comparative simplicity is rather like the slow movement of a symphony or other musical composition containing several contrasting parts. The single voice is that of an old slave trader recounting his exotic adventures to a younger man or boy. Several passages—

Twenty years a trader, twenty years . . .
. . . and I'd be trading still
but for the fevers melting down my bones.

—are reminiscent of the old would-be lyncher of "Night, Death, Mississippi":

Be there with Boy and the rest
if I was well again.
Time was. Time was

. . . fevered as by groinfire.

Part 3 returns to the juxtapositions of part 1 but is altogether simpler in construction. It opens with the narrator's brief summation of the significance of the slave trade then goes to a passage, again indented and italicized, in which he turns to a deeper meditation. This, again, includes the attempt to feel his way into the mind of one of the sailors, a man not devoid of pity or guilt:

> *But, oh, the living look at you*
> *with human eyes whose suffering accuses you,*
> *whose hatred reaches . . .*

The climax of this last section, however, lies in the long speech by a Spanish sailor who survived the mutiny aboard the *Amistad* and who asks now that the mutineers, "Cinquez and his accomplices," be sent to Havana for execution. His speech has its eloquence, yet its effect on the reader is tempered by the inclusion of his plea that the court should not heed the words of John Quincy Adams, who, indeed, actually defended the *Amistad* mutineers. The Spaniard's complaint is that Adams would "with his Roman rhetoric weave a hero's / garland for Cinquez." Though intending sarcasm, these lines begin the open celebration of Cinquez as a hero who brings his people, unlike those aboard the *Bella J*, out of captivity.

Where part 1 had ended in the tragic and grisly burning of the *Bella J*, part 3 closes in a moment of triumph. This triumph, however, summarizes and collects much material that went before and subjects it to important ironies. Above all, the fact that this Spanish sailor had served as the blacks' steersman, or pilot, misleading and finally bringing them to America, projects crucial questions backward toward the earlier hymn, "Jesus, Savior, Pilot Me." The blacks, fresh from Africa, cannot serve as their own steersman, yet Jesus—at least that Jesus imagined by the white New England congregation or by the Spanish sailor—cannot save them, may even mislead them into death and slavery. This questioning of Christian guidance must be closely related to Hayden's conversion to the Bahá'í faith.

The poem *does* end, however, on a note of triumph, picking up two lines on the will to freedom from earlier in this section, applying them directly to Cinquez:

> The deep immortal human wish,
> the timeless will:
> Cinquez its deathless primaveral image,
> life that transfigures many lives.

On this tribute the poem closes, incorporating two lines from the poem's very beginning to serve as summation and coda:

> Voyage through death
> to life upon these shores.

Now, however, this line has added ironies, since it is clear that, for many, "life upon these shores" will not be much better than death at sea. Yet some will indeed survive and, especially with such examples as Cinquez's love of freedom, may yet build a better life there.

As might be expected, this did not satisfy many of the extremists. Some criticized Hayden for using his "best" irony to depict the Spanish cause. Yet it is hard to believe that any intelligent or sensitive person could read this passage and think it favored the Spanish side.

That "negative capability" for which Keats so honored Shakespeare is, of course, the breadth of his sympathy, the near universality of his empathy. The honor we bestow upon our greatest poet, Walt Whitman, is again because of that inclusive humanity—that he can identify not only with the victim, with the wounded slave, but also with the overseer and the patroller.

It may be that the only good poet is a dead poet. It would seem that Robert Hayden has now been dead long enough that we might pay him some part of the respect and honor that he so painfully and patiently earned.

HARRYETTE MULLEN
STEPHEN YENSER

Theme and Variations on Robert Hayden's Poetry

4 July 1996

Dear Harryette,

The evening of Independence Day, a crepitation of fireworks in the distant west. What else to do, as I sit here amid stubbornly sanguine, inevitably white, and ineradicably blue thoughts of *liberté* and Crispus Attucks, John Brown, and *égalité, fraternité,* and Harriet Tubman, but drop a line to you about Robert Hayden? I really do want to ask, now that you have looked at the new edition of the *Collected Poems,* how you feel about Hayden. I want to hear because, although your background is different from mine, I feel a certain kinship and because I know that hitherto, like me, you have not been intimately acquainted with his poems and because my own reactions to this edition have been so—vivid? Those reactions include a strong sense of belated discovery (though I was taught in college that Hayden somehow belonged to the canon), with its attendant delight, alloyed only with some little chagrin at the suspicion that Hayden was canonized precisely because he so decorously did not belong, if you take my meaning.

One thing—if it's not itself many—that distinguishes Hayden's work, as Rampersad suggests, is its heterogeneity. There are several Haydens, often heard together. There is the modernist Hayden, the ultra-terse, post-Imagist Hayden, who is influenced by Pound and Williams; there is the classically literary Hayden, who alludes to the old canon, from Shakespeare through Keats and Hopkins to Yeats and Spender; there is the idiomatic Hayden, who grew up on the streets of Detroit; and there is the musical Hayden, who learned from jazz and blues what Bartók learned from Hungarian folk

From the *Antioch Review* 55, no. 2 (Spring 1997): 160–74. Copyright © 1977 by the Antioch Review, Inc. Reprinted by permission of the Editors.

dances or perhaps what Satie learned from ragtime. In "A Ballad of Remembrance" Hayden contrasts what he calls his "true voice," which speaks in tones that are "meditative, ironic, / richly human," with the off-key voices of New Orleans at Mardi Gras.

> the sallow vendeuse
> of prepared tarnishes and jokes of nacre and ormolu,
> what but those gleamings, oldrose graces,
> manners like scented gloves? Contrived ghosts
> rapped to metronome clack of lavalieres.

In fact, however, this "baroque" mode (to use Hayden's term) is just one element in his own "richly human" presence, and even after he recalls coming to himself amid those eldritch voices, he incorporates their lovely grotesqueries in his concluding dedication to an old friend and academic:

> And therefore this is not only a ballad of remembrance
> for the down-South arcane city with death
> in its jaws like gold teeth and archaic cusswords;
> not only a token for the troubled generous friends
> held in the fists of that schizoid city like flowers,
> but also, Mark Van Doren,
> a poem of remembrance, a gift, a souvenir for you.

There's no question, it seems to me, that he revels in the densities, the crossroads, sonic and otherwise, of "arcane city . . . archaic cusswords" and "the fists of that schizoid city like flowers" and that the pleasure he takes is in large part responsible for his "true voice."

It might even be that on occasion he is overly fond of the precious—or the semiprecious—term.

Well, I have more speculations, but by now it's after midnight, cloudy and murky, and I need some orientation. You'll be my polestar.

Yours,
Stephen

7/18/96

Dear Stephen,
Years ago, when I lived for six months in Taos, the proximity of Los Alamos influenced my dreams. For several weeks my sleep was disturbed by nightmares of nuclear Armageddon.

Enclave where new mythologies
of power come to birth—
where coralled energy and power breed
like prized man-eating animals.
Like dragon, hydra, basilisk.

Reading "Zeus over Redeye," I know I share some of Hayden's
fears about the national fascination with violence and apocalypse.
This nation that began in violence seems to return to it again and
again for a sense of self-definition and catharsis, as if determined
that we should end as we began, with a scourging destruction.

This volume of Robert Hayden's collected poems offered me
some unexpected pleasures and surprises. There is pleasure in the va-
riety of Hayden's poetry as well as in the opportunity to observe how
the poems work through recurring preoccupations. When I first
sampled his work, as a student, it seemed most useful to me for ex-
panding the possibilities of what and how an African-American poet
might write.

He wrote, among other things, about black life, and even his
poems devoted to black subjects are marked by a distinctive poetic
idiom that is not strictly bound to African-American oral tradition.
It is, like the poetry of Gwendolyn Brooks, a purposefully literary
language, owing much, as Arnold Rampersad suggests, to the King
James Bible and the canon of British literature as well as to Amer-
ican modernist poetry. Trying to remember my earlier response to
his work, I think that I found it more temperate and virtuous than
risky or showy, despite the occasional ornate or arcane word. Hay-
den was nowhere as fanciful as, say, Wallace Stevens, whose work at-
tracted me in my student days, even though I was disappointed by
the casually racist attitude I found there.

For me Hayden had always seemed restrained, contained. He
seemed to me a poet who shied away from extremes. I felt that his
deliberation prohibited the kind of exuberant expression I was seek-
ing in poetry. But, as you point out and Rampersad's introduction
indicates, there are several different Haydens, and this collected vol-
ume edited by Frederick Glaysher allows us a retrospective view of
those poems of Hayden's that are less likely to be included in an-
thologies of African-American poets or anthologies of American
poets in which Hayden is included as a representative black poet.

This anthologized Hayden is the poet who wrote "Middle Pas-
sage," "A Letter from Phillis Wheatley," "Crispus Attucks," "Frederick

Douglass," "Runagate, Runagate," "The Ballad of Nat Turner," and "El-Hajj-Malik El-Shabazz" for Malcolm X as well as "Those Winter Sundays," a stern poem of familial love and duty, "of love's austere and lonely offices" set against "the chronic angers of that house" in which Hayden grew up in the care of foster parents. "Those Winter Sundays" demonstrates Hayden's self-restraint, scrupulous judgment, and sense of balance—qualities that he also brings to his poems dealing with black culture and historical subjects. His poems about those figures who have become familiar to us, through our now routine acknowledgment of black history, are never merely celebratory. In each the poet holds himself accountable to complex human truths often shrouded in legend, as Hayden considers, along with each historical character, our persistent need to make mythic heroes and heroines of exemplary figures as well as those, like Crispus Attucks, who are history's chance victims.

Robert Hayden was certainly not alone among his contemporaries in pushing the boundaries of what was acceptable thematic and aesthetic territory for a black poet to explore. Melvin Tolson seems bolder than Hayden in his poetic ambition to rank among the modernists. Jean Toomer, before he became a mystic, was more robustly earthy and more innovative in technique: he was born nineteen years earlier than Hayden. Bob Kaufman, only twelve years younger than Hayden, seems far more contemporary in spirit.

In "Full Moon" Hayden expresses disillusionment that the moon has lost its enchantment, no longer "a goddess to whom we pray" but reduced to "the white hope of communications men . . . a mooted goal and tomorrow perhaps / an arms base." In contrast, Kaufman's response to the space race was flippantly antiromantic: "i shall refuse to go to the moon, / unless i'm inoculated, against the dangers of indiscriminate love."

That for Hayden the moon, stripped of its romantic haze and mythic significance, is imagined as a "white hope" might suggest a possible association of hubristic reliance on technology with the white supremacy that has in part fueled the exploratory expeditions of the West. On the other hand, in "O Daedalus, Fly Away Home," Hayden adapts an archetypal Western myth of technological hubris, making Daedalus a flying African whose desire conjures imaginary wings to take him home to the motherland.

In words he attributes to a slave trader (in "Middle Passage"), "I write, as one / would turn to exorcism," Hayden perhaps identifies one motivation for his own incantations. Rather than desiring to

be "released from the hoodoo of this dance," as Hayden feels res-
cued (from its lure?) and free to claim his "true voice" upon the ar-
rival of that utterly civilized poet and critic, Mark Van Doren, many
younger black poets (Ishmael Reed and Ntozake Shange come im-
mediately to mind) claimed their own voices as they threw them-
selves into that spirited dance of Africa's diaspora.

While Rampersad seems to affirm that Robert Hayden
achieved the goal of transcending his racial identity, Hayden is
more complexly multiple than is suggested by a simple dichotomy
of the "black" poet versus the "transracial" poet. (Of course, it is cu-
rious that white poets are not routinely judged by their ability to
transcend their race.) I want to think about this more in my next
letter; but, for now, I'm looking forward to your second round.

Still mulling it over,
Harryette

21.viii.96

Dear Harryette,
I was just thinking about an eccentric project of mine, a kind of
commonplace book interspersed with glosses and meanderings and
minicritiques, and was suddenly diverted back to Hayden by way
of a little meditation on enantiosemes. Sorry to be precious myself,
but I don't know a word except Barthes's (his coinage?) for the
phenomenon I have in mind: single words that mean or imply con-
trary things. I'm thinking of words like *raveling, pall,* and *wan.* (As
in that last case, the opposition can develop over time.) The in-
stance that turned me back to Hayden might not even be a true
enantioseme, since, although its cloven meanings are both homo-
phonic and homographic, they seem to derive from different
sources. As soon as I type it, you'll know the word I mean: *cleave.* A
husband should "cleave to his wife," the Bible tells us, as the mar-
riage ceremony instructs us that no one should put asunder the
union of bride and groom; but then the Bible also tells us that "our
bones are scattered at the grave's mouth, as when one cutteth and
cleaveth wood upon the earth," and in this last case the meaning of
to cleave is precisely "to put asunder." That the latter usage is in the
(King James) Old Testament, so called, whereas the former is in the
(KJ) New Testament, might give us pause—if not much further in-
sight—and might even suggest that those two biblical halves
"cleave together."

In any event *cleave,* with its two meanings, has called to mind

237

one of my favorite Hayden poems—which nonetheless seems to me representative. I'll quote it entire. Note especially line 11:

O DAEDALUS, FLY AWAY HOME
(*For Maia and Julie*)

Drifting night in the Georgia pines,
coonskin drum and jubilee banjo,
Pretty Malinda, dance with me

Night is juba, night is conjo.
Pretty Malinda, dance with me.

Night is an African juju man
weaving a wish and a weariness together
to make two wings.

O fly away home fly away

Do you remember Africa?

O cleave the air fly away home

My gran, he flew back to Africa.
just spread his arms and
flew away home.

Drifting night in the windy pines;
night is a laughing, night is a longing,
Pretty Malinda, come to me.

Night is a mourning juju man
weaving a wish and a weariness together
to make two wings.

O fly away home fly away

I remember your saying in your last letter that you thought Jean Toomer might be "more robustly earthy and more innovative in technique than Hayden." While that might well be, the poem I've just quoted seems to me to have qualities, sensuous and especially innovative, that I also admire in Toomer's poems. I'm thinking especially of Toomer's "Song of the Son," "November Cotton Flower," and "Tell Me" and some of the sound poems, in which he combines elements of an African-American heritage with elements of a European legacy. In Hayden's "O Daedalus, Fly Away Home" those two influences are incipient in the title, one on either side of the comma. There's first the classical reference to the Athenian architect and inventor and then the allusion to the folk song ("Ladybug, ladybug, fly away home, / Your home is on fire, and your children will burn"). This poem's title, in sum, looks to me like a real *cleaving*, in both senses at once.

The "two wings" appear in Hayden's third stanza: "Night is an African juju man / weaving a wish and a weariness together / to make two wings." The twinning adumbrated sonically by *juju*, which refers us to West African magic, works itself out in "a wish and a weariness," contraries bound together by the alliteration on *w*—itself carried on in *weavings* and in *wings*—a letter that patently looks like wings. And who would have both wish and weariness if not the African American, a forced exile (like Daedalus on Crete) who must devise an ingenious means of liberation? The African-American descendant of slaves, then, is our contemporary artificer, working not with feathers and wax but with "coonskin drums and jubilee banjo." (If *jubilee* comes from a Hebrew root meaning "to conduct," which is to say "to lead together," whereas *banjo* evolves from an African-American pronunciation of *bandore*, many spirituals have the same diverse parentage.)

So maybe it comes to seem that there's no end to duplicity, to "wish and weariness," to "laughing" and "longing"—to *cleaving*, in a word (or is it two?). In Hayden's poem Africa is Daedalus' Athens, the biblical Eden, the blissful place from which we have all been ostracized and can only (and cannot but) recall. What can we do? Well, for one thing we can write airs, cleaved, cleft, or cloven, that call up slave songs on the one hand and Sapphic stanzas on the other—but *basta!* So rarely do I catch a train of thought these days that I'm reluctant to get off one once I've done so. Everything human is mixogamous. (Which is probably why Terence could say [as Cicero quotes him], "*Homo sum: humani nil a me alienum puto*" [I'm a person: nothing human is alien to me].) It probably follows from my premise that no writer can be, in Rampersad's term, "transracial." To be transracial would be to have arrived at some quintessentially human (or even superhuman, since humans are "racial") point of view, *n'est-ce pas?* But—on my tentative premise—no point of view can be quintessential.

What do *you* think?

Yours,
Stephen

Dear Stephen,

I tried, in my last letter, to follow a thread into the labyrinth of Hayden's poetry, from his sense of history as violence and myth to his view of nuclear and space technologies as expressions of humankind's linked urges of aspiration, exploration, and destruction. His several poems occasioned by our search for intelligent life in the universe—divine, humanoid, or utterly alien life form—alert the reader to the poet's sense of himself as alien, if not quite extraterrestrial.

In the collected poems one finds recurrent references to those whose difference, whether by choice or by circumstance, makes them, like the Gypsies of "Elegies for Paradise Valley" who are "like us" African Americans, "pornographers of gaudy otherness: / aliens among the alien." The presence of the alien pervades his work, as does the related persona of the freak. These figures of stigmatized deviation reveal the poet's capacity for empathy as well as difficult aspects of Hayden's identity as an African American, as an artist, and as a thoughtfully religious man struggling to reconcile his sexuality with his spirituality.

It is the spiritual journey and its relation to the intense, violent life of Malcolm X that most interests Hayden in "El-Hajj Malik El-Shabazz," as indicated by the title, referring to Malcolm's move toward traditional Islam in his pilgrimage to Mecca.

> He fell upon his face before
> Allah the raceless in whose blazing Oneness all
> were one. He rose renewed renamed, became
> much more than there was time for him to be.

The poem suggests striking resemblances, as well as marked differences, between the poet and his subject. With Malcolm X, Hayden shared a midwestern background, a disrupted family history, an altered identity, conversion to a "raceless" religion, and a preoccupation with violence. Hayden, who received a college education Malcolm might have envied, lived an outwardly more peaceful life, and the two men chose divergent paths to personal transformation. Malcolm's final conversion connected him to the ancient sources and global diversity of Islam, but it in no way diminished his race consciousness as an African American. While Malcolm X made his individual metamorphosis a public model for a redefinition of the meaning of blackness, Hayden worked for most of his life in relative obscurity and, as he became more visible through his poetry, moved further from an identification of his writing with his race.

Hayden's identity was formed at a time when blackness and African-American culture were more severely stigmatized than they are today, and his work is marked by residual attitudes of the nineteenth century that black Americans strove to eradicate, at least from our own psyches, in the decades of the 1960s and 1970s. If the mantras of racial self-esteem were unconvincing to Hayden, it was perhaps because his ambivalence about race was more complicated than a psychosocially comprehensible internalized racism. Certainly, given the history that formed him, it was a significant resistance that motivated Hayden (like Toomer) to insist on the priority of his identity as an American, particularly if it was self-evident to a scholar of the literature that "he so decorously did not belong" to the canon of American poetry, as you put it in your opening letter.

William Meredith's book jacket blurb is somewhat misleading in its insistence that Hayden "would not relinquish the title of American writer for any narrower identity," as is Arnold Rampersad's explanation of Hayden's desire to be counted as an "American" rather than a "black" or "African-American" poet. No doubt, they accurately represent Hayden's preference; but why does neither question that the title of American should be considered more inclusive, given that more people of African descent inhabit the earth than "Americans" (if that term designates U.S. citizens), and "African-American nationalism" has always been linked to a pan-African awareness of the global black diaspora?

Notwithstanding the critic's complicity in constructing the reputation of a "transracial" artist or the poet's conversion to the supposedly color-blind Bahá'í religion, Hayden does not so much transcend race as he employs racial identity as a metaphor for the opacity of the self. Race is one of myriad differences that might make a human being appear alien to another, one of the assorted labels that could cause an individual to feel estranged from others as well as from himself.

Hayden's poetry offers an array of possible responses to alienation, from that of the tattooed man, "Born alien, / homeless everywhere," to the poet's reveling in his alien status as a kind of freedom, in "Kodachromes of the Island": "Alien, at home, as always / everywhere I roamed." Like the extraterrestrial visitor of "[American Journal]," Hayden "passed for an american," but claimed an identity more universal, as a denizen of the cosmos.

Astrally yours,

Harryette

P.S. I'd already written this letter when I heard on the news that scientists have found evidence of a Martian life form. Small galaxy, isn't it?

Labor Day 1996

Dear Harryette,

Without knowing what the other one was up to, each of us mused on Hayden's literary relationship to Toomer, both of us called into question the notion that Hayden is a "transracial" poet, and both of us got drawn into the metaphors of labyrinth and flight. In fact, I was *so struck* by what I took to be a chord that *we* had struck that I almost called you. But a telephone call might spoil the nature of this old-fashioned exchange, and I fended off the impulse. Maybe I'm wrong, but it looks to me as though we dovetail when I venture that Hayden is not really transracial, although his Eden (in "O Daedalus, Fly Away Home") is "the blissful place from which we have all been ostracized" and when you argue that "Hayden does not so much transcend race as employ identity as a metaphor for the opacity of the self." If my ostracized self is one with your self rendered opaque, I'm delighted, as I rarely am by agreement.

What I want to turn to for a moment is your quotation from the so-called scholar to the effect that Hayden was canonized these several decades ago "because he so decorously did not belong." Since it's not quite clear to me how you read my sentence, or even how I wrote it, I want to clarify it here, to wit: my suspicion is that Hayden's name was carved into the (old) "canon" when it was because his poetry was handsomely indebted to what have since been called mainstream Eurocentric traditions at the same time that it was markedly affected by his African-American heritage. In his preface to Hayden's *Collected Prose* (1982) Frederick Glaysher begins by noting, "Hayden is now generally recognized as the most outstanding craftsman of Afro-American poetry." In this dubious respect (as who should say "she is the most outstanding technician among Chicana poets") Hayden seems to me different from, say, Amiri Baraka, Sonia Sanchez, Bob Kaufman, and the later Gwendolyn Brooks, who are less inclined to play by conservative cultural rules, even though Hayden was himself enlarging the playing field and changing its proportions. I should add that any alteration of rules in medias res strikes me as eminently "American," though that impression might itself be chauvinistic of me. But I think I take *American* to mean something less sharply defined than some of the influential anthologists of the 1950s took it to mean. I've just been reading David W. Stowe's essay "Uncolored People" in the new *Lingua Franca,* and I'm glad to be reminded by it of Albert Murray's belief that American culture is, "regardless of all the hysterical protestations of those who would have it otherwise, incontestably mulatto." I think that's what I believe. (I understand my term *mixogamous,* in my last letter, to be closely related to Murray's *mulatto.*)

Among Hayden's poems that you mention in connection with alienation is his later "The Tattooed Man." As you say, it is a poem about a man who was "Born alien, / homeless everywhere," whose subsequent epidermal enhancements only confirmed that he is indeed a "grotesque outsider" who does not "belong." The literary antecedent that springs to my mind is Djuna Barnes's tour de force in *Nightwood* in describing Nikka, "the nigger who used to fight the bear in the *Cirque de Paris,*" who is elaborately "tattooed from head to heel with all the *ameublement of* depravity." Did Hayden know Barnes's novel? Surely he did—as I suspect Elizabeth Alexander would have known both when she wrote "The Venus Hottentot"—but, in any case, his "Tattooed Man" shares with Nikka a paradoxical inclusivity.

Barnes's paragraphs, too long for quotation entire at this juncture, adumbrate Hayden's tattooed man, with his "jungle arms, / their prized chimeras" and "birds-of-paradise / perched on [his] thighs." Barnes's Nikka seems to me a version of Othello, partly because "it [his penis] at a stretch . . . spelled Desdemona" and partly because he brings together other contraries: for example, "over his belly was an angel from Chartres; on each buttock, half public, half private, a quotation from the book of magic, a confirmation of the Jansenist theory, I'm sorry to say and here it is." Hayden's performer seems at first also to represent simply the other, the abject, the "grotesque outsider whose / unnaturalness / assures them they are natural, they

243

indeed / belong." In the penultimate verse paragraph the tattooed man worries that his own corporeal artworks "repel the union of / your [the paying customer's] flesh with mine." In fact, however, his tattoos *proclaim* such a union. They include tattoos of "gryphons," creatures half-lion and half-eagle, and there is one of "naked Adam / embracing naked Eve," and what is evidently the largest tattoo pictures "the Black Widow / peering from the web / she spun, belly to groin." What manner of creature could *escape* this generative web? The poem's conclusion seems at first blush to insist on the speaker's singularity and the audience's alterity, but at every step it undercuts itself, beginning with the doubling, "I yearn I yearn," which iterates the poem's opening lines, "I gaze at you / longing longing," and thus reinforces those lines' latent identification by mirroring the *I* and the *you*. The crux of the matter here is in Hayden's lines, "I do not want / you other than you are. / And I—I cannot / (will not?) change." Which is to say, first, "I want *you* to be *other*, as you are," and, second, "*I* must/will be *other* to you." The implied vows are symmetrical. And then, when the poem ends with the Yahweh-like, seemingly monolithic assertion, "I am I," the reader cannot but feel that the *I* is such precisely because of the splitting manifest in the formulation: "I—I." The self, that is, is in expanded form the self-that-longs-because-incomplete.

But I've overstayed my welcome and will put on hold all related gossamer projections.

Yours in Shangri-L.A.,
Stephen

9/19/96

Dear Stephen,
Your richly elaborated reading of "O Daedalus, Fly Away Home" suggested to me another manifestation of the double consciousness signaled by the contradictory dual signification of the predicate *cleave*. Looking at the poem again, following your explication, I noticed that, if the title and dedication are counted as lines, the poem divides into halves hinged by the provocative question, "Do you remember Africa?" Like Countee Cullen's "What is Africa to me?" this line poses the vexed question of the African American's divided identity. Here it highlights a generational difference and a crucial break separating captive Africans with a memory of "home" from their offspring born into American slavery. The latter remember Africa only indirectly, through the memory of their ancestors.

The legends of flying Africans always involved those with a recent memory of a home elsewhere, to which they walked, swam, or flew over the ocean trusting in traditional African spiritual beliefs that the souls of the dead return to their birthplace. The speaker in the poem has reconciled himself to his alienation, and only the memory of the grandfather's faith suggests the possibility of some alternative existence. The African-American's determination to build a life and create a culture in the "New World" is a commitment his legendary flying ancestor refused to make. The grandfather who flies away versus the grandchild who remains, together, figure the internal struggle that Du Bois termed "double consciousness."

All of us who are Americans of African descent know this place as home while at the same time knowing that our claim to belonging here continues to be contested. The ancestor cutting his losses and cutting loose for Africa, cleaving the air, and the descendant cleaving to his earthly existence as dearly as he clings to the consolations of myth and music dramatically represent Du Bois's concept of double consciousness, as two halves of the "one dark body" whose dogged strength is the only thing that prevents its being torn asunder. Double consciousness describes the psychic constitution of African Americans who are at home neither in Africa, where we are foreigners, nor in the United States, which declined to assimilate us in its melting pot. We who cleave to a home that was never fully ours, regardless of our labor, faith, and blood, are divided from ourselves by our compulsory awareness of how others see us. We are reminded every day that we are aliens here, and so we keep alive in ourselves the memory of the Middle Passage and the ancestors' flight.

For Hayden a further aspect of double consciousness seems also reflected in the poet's attempt to reconcile the presumption of Western literacy with the presumption of African-American orality—or, put in somewhat different terms, the presumption of the master's literacy and the slave's illiteracy. Traces of the strain of these interlocking presumptions are apparent in the body of Hayden's poetry.

Particularly useful for this discussion would be a comparison of "Middle Passage" with "The Dream." With its references to the written documents of slave traders, to passages excerpted or paraphrased from the letters, journals, and ships' logs of those who bought and sold Africans, to transcribed records of court testimony from the disgraced captains and wretched crews of ships embarked on disastrous voyages, and even with its parody of a song from Shakespeare's *The Tempest,* "Middle Passage" eloquently illustrates the problem of representing or reconstructing the history of the subjugated from the writings of the dominant culture.

In "Middle Passage" the Africans themselves are wordless, if not silent—their speech unintelligible to their captors. What is reported is their "moaning" and "shrieking," their "crazy laughter" and their singing. Even Cinquez, the leader of a successful slave mutiny aboard the *Amistad* and the only captive African here mentioned by name as an individual historical subject, is merely "that surly brute" in the eyewitness account of the slave trader. Hayden takes quite a different approach in "The Dream," a Civil War narrative from the point of view of two black Americans, an illiterate slave in the South and a soldier from the North, literate in African-American vernacular, who has joined the Union Army to defeat the Confederacy. Here again we find "laughing crying singing" black folks but also the free indirect discourse of Sinda, a slave disappointed with the brusque white Yankees: "Marse Lincum's soldier boys . . . were not the hosts the dream had promised her." Her narrative alternates with passages from a letter written by Cal, a black soldier who might be related to Sinda, sending news of the war home to kin in the North. Cal, who has "listed" in the army to make sure that "old Jeff Davis muss be ketch an hung to a sour apple tree," fulfills Sinda's dream that she might one day greet an army of black soldiers fighting for freedom.

Together these poems suggest some of the difficulties and creative strategies of the poet seeking to forge a literary language of disparate cultural materials. Hayden's orchestration of folk speech and song with the written language of slaveholders, slaves, fugitives, and free people of color had been enabled by other African-American writers who had reclaimed black vernacular from its debased use and abuse in American popular culture. Hayden's work might be seen in relation to a history of arguments and experiments of black poets, from Dunbar to James Weldon Johnson, from Cullen to Hughes and Sterling Brown, from Toomer and Tolson to Kaufman and Baraka. As Henry Louis Gates argues persuasively in *Figures in Black,* African-American poets had to reconcile a Western poetic tradition built on a foundation of classical texts with a maligned African-American tradition of orality that had been forcibly uprooted from its ancient sources in Africa.

White American writers and entertainers had heard the fresh invention of African-American speech, which they stole and warped in order to ridicule the speakers. With the exploitation of black dialect by others, most of whom created works demeaning black people, African-American writers felt that they had lost a possible avenue of expression. In addition to their alienation from a literary tradition that excluded African Americans, black writers also had reason to feel estranged from the African-American vernacular. Only by reclaiming and remaking it as a literary language with attention to its particular expressive potential and also by claiming and "mastering" the language of the dominant literary tradition were black poets able to overcome the presumed stigma of black English as well as the presumed alienating effects of Western literacy.

So this is it, the end of our summer correspondence. I have certainly enjoyed it and found your comments always stimulating as well as eloquent.

Your pen pal,
Harryette

PART FOUR *Essays on Individual Poems*

DAVID HUDDLE

The "Banked Fire" of Robert
Hayden's "Those Winter Sundays"

For twenty years I've been teaching Robert Hayden's most fre-
quently anthologized poem to undergraduate poetry-writing stu-
dents. By *teach* I mean that from our textbook I read the poem
aloud in the classroom, I ask one of the students to read it aloud, I
make some observations about it, I invite the students to make
some observations about it, then we talk about it a while longer.
Usually, to wrap up the discussion, I'll read the poem through once
more. Occasions for such teaching come up about half a dozen
times a year, and so let's say that during my life I've been privileged
to read this poem aloud approximately 240 times. "Those Winter
Sundays" has withstood my assault upon it. It remains a poem I
look forward to reading and discussing in my classroom. The poem
remains alive to me, so that, for hours and sometimes days after it
visits my classroom, I'm hearing its lines in my mind's ear.

Though a fourteen-liner, "Those Winter Sundays" is only loosely
a sonnet. Its stanzas are five, four, and five lines long. There are
rhymes and near-rhymes but no rhyme scheme. The poem's lines
probably average about eight syllables. There are only three strictly
iambic lines: the fourth, the eighth, and (significantly) the four-
teenth. It's a poem that's powerfully informed by the sonnet form;
it's a poem that "feels like" a sonnet—it has the density and grav-
ity of a sonnet—which is to say that in its appearance on the page,
in its diction and syntax, in its tone, cadence, and argumentative
strategy, "Those Winter Sundays" presents the credentials of a
work of literary art in the tradition of English letters. But it's also
a poem that has gone its own way, a definite departure from that
most conventional of all the poetic forms of English and Ameri-
can verse.

From *Touchstones: American Poets on a Favorite Poem*, ed. Robert Pack and Jay Parini
(Hanover: University Press of New England, 1995), 81–83.

The abstract issue of this poem's sonnethood is of less value to my beginning poets than the tangible matter of the sounds the poem makes, especially those *k*-sounding words of the first eleven lines that one comes to associate with discomfort: "clothes . . . blueback cold . . . cracked . . . ached . . . weekday . . . banked . . . thanked . . . wake . . . cold . . . breaking . . . call . . . chronic . . . cold." What's missing from the final three lines? The *k* sounds have been driven from the poem, as the father has "driven out the cold" from the house. The sounds that have replaced those *k* sounds are the *o* sounds of "good . . . shoes . . . know . . . know . . . love . . . lonely offices." The poem lets us associate the *o* sounds with love and loneliness. Sonically, the poem tells the same story the poem narrates for us. The noise of this poem moves us through its emotional journey from discomfort to lonely love. If ever there were a poem that could teach a beginning poet the viability of the element of sound crafting, it is "Those Winter Sundays."

Quote its first two words, and a great many poets and English teachers will be able to finish the first line (if not the whole poem) from memory. Somewhat remarkably, the poem's thesis—that the office of love can be relentless, thankless, and more than a little mysterious—resides in that initially odd-sounding two-word beginning, "Sundays too." The rest of the line—the rest of the independent clause—is ordinary. Nowhere else in Anglo-American literature does the word *too* carry the weight it carries in "Those Winter Sundays."

Not as immediately apparent as its opening words but very nearly as important to the poem's overall strategy is the two-sentence engineering of the first stanza. Because they will appreciate it more if they discover it for themselves, I often maneuver Socratically to have my students describe the poem's first two sentences: long and complex, followed by short and simple. It almost always seems to me worthwhile to ask, "Why didn't Hayden begin his poem this way: 'No one ever thanked my father for getting up early on Sundays, too'? Wouldn't that be a more direct and hospitable way to bring the reader into the poem?" After I've taken my students that far, they are quick to see how that ordinary five-word unit, "No one ever thanked him," gains meaning and emotion, weight, and force, from the elaborate preparation given it by the thirty-two-word *Sundays too* first sentence.

So much depends on "No one ever thanked him" that it requires the narrative enhancement of the first four and a half lines.

It is the crux of the poem. What is this poem about? It is about a son's remorse over never thanking his father not only for what he did for him but also for how (he now realizes) he felt about him. And what is the poem if not an elegantly fashioned, permanent expression of gratitude?

"Those Winter Sundays" tells a story, or it describes a circumstance, of father-son conflict, and it even makes some excuses for the son's "Speaking indifferently" to the father: there was a good deal of anger between them; *chronic angers of that house* suggests that the circumstances were complicated somewhat beyond the usual and ordinary conflict between fathers and sons. Of the father we know that he labored outdoors with his hands. Of the son we know that he was, in the classic manner of youth, heedless of the ways in which his father served him.

Though the evidence of his "labor" is visible in every stanza of this poem, the father himself is somewhere else. We don't see him. He is in some other room of the house than the one where our speaker is. That absence suggests the emotional distance between the father and the son as well as the current absence, through death, of the father on the occasion of this utterance. It's easy enough to imagine this poem as a graveside meditation, an elegy, and a rather impassioned one at that, "What did I know, what did I know?"

The grinding of past against present gives the poem its urgency. The story is being told with such clarity, thoughtfulness, and apparent calm that we are surprised by the outburst of the repeated question of the thirteenth line. The fourteenth line returns to a tone of tranquillity. Its diction is formal, even arch, and its phrasing suggests an extremely considered conclusion; the fourteenth line is the answer to a drastic rephrasing of the original question: *What is the precise name of what as a youth I was incapable of perceiving but that as a life-examining adult I now suddenly understand?*

I tell my students that they may someday need this poem, they may someday be walking along downtown and find themselves asking aloud, "What did I know, what did I know?" But what I mean to suggest to them is that Hayden has made them the gift of this final phrase like a package that in ten years' time they may open and find immensely valuable: "love's austere and lonely offices." Like "the banked fires" his father made, Hayden has made a poem that will be of value to readers often years after they've first read it.

"Those Winter Sundays" has articulated a treasure of an insight and preserved it for me until I was old enough to appreciate it. The poem always has the power to move me, to make me understand something so subtle that apparently I need to be reminded of it again and again. Hayden's poem is a banked fire that holds its warmth and allows me to rekindle my spirits whenever I come back to read it.

"Those Winter Sundays" honors a much-criticized figure in American culture of the 1990s—the withdrawn, emotionally inexpressive, and distant (and probably unhappy and angry) father. The poem makes its way toward perceiving the emotional life of such a man. The poem *realizes* love as it lived in such a man. That my own father was somewhat similar is perhaps why the poem particularly affects me, but I have witnessed its affecting so many others that I must assume either that such fathers exist in multitudes or that the poem cuts across vast differences of background in its instruction to the reader to reconsider the lives of those who helped us make our way into adulthood.

Whenever I teach "Those Winter Sundays," I face a dilemma of personal, political, and pedagogical consequence. Do I tell my students that Hayden is an African-American poet? That fact *does* make a difference in how we read the poem: the "cracked hands that ached / from labor in the weekday weather" may be seen in a context of a racial-economic circumstance, and thus "the chronic angers of that house" may also be seen as a result of racially enforced poverty. There are, however, manual laborers and poor families of all ethnic backgrounds, and so one need not necessarily read "Those Winter Sundays" as a poem that has anything to do with racial issues. It might even be argued that to read the poem as being about race is to give the poem a racist reading.

My students are almost always white, they are only beginning to learn about modern poetry, and they aren't likely to be acquainted with any African-American poets. If I tell them that Hayden was an African American, am I practicing a subtly racist bit of pedagogy? On the other hand, if I don't tell them that the man who wrote this poem is an African American, aren't I denying them a piece of knowledge that is essential not only for the understanding of this poem but for their general poetic education? (One wonders what the equivalent might be for another poet. To omit telling students of a Robert Frost poem that he lived for most of his life in New England? To say nothing about Walt Whitman's homosexuality? To leave unmentioned Emily Dickinson's reclusiveness? Is there really any equivalent?)

I'm a teacher; I almost always look for a positive approach to such dilemmas. I see an admirable ambiguity and psychological complexity in the fact that the poem can be read in both ways, as a poem that has nothing to do with race and as a poem that is somewhat informed by the circumstance of racial injustice. I do tell my students that the author was an African American, but I tell them only after we've read it a couple of times and talked about it. That piece of information is very nearly the last thing that I tell them before I read it to them the last time, the reading in which once more I journey in my own voice through the words, the lines, the stanzas, down through the cold house into the waiting warmth it always offers me, that necessary, inspiring insight it delivers to me again and again, that the duties of love (like the duties of poetry) are often scrupulously carried out in invisible and thankless ways.

LAURENCE GOLDSTEIN

The Greatest Poem in the
World ["Perseus"]

My teasing title mimics one by Herbert Read, from a collection of
newspaper leaders he published in 1945, *A Coat of Many Colours*.
The title of his journalistic piece is "The Greatest Work of Art in
the World." Because Read was an influential aesthetician who had
helped to shape the English-speaking world's response to the inno-
vative art movements of the century, his tantalizing headline must
have aroused skeptical curiosity in any reader, lay or specialized,
who took up the newspaper that morning. By what right and with
what criteria does any critic assert the absolute primacy or sover-
eignty of any single work of art? Whether the choice turned out to
be some canonical masterpiece or some daring minor work res-
cued by Read's discerning taste from neglect, his choice would cer-
tainly outrage almost everyone. Indeed, there is something not only
subversive but heretical in isolating for exclusive praise a sample of
the fine arts tradition. What Copernican hubris would dare to set
one sun, one divine icon, at the center of a system no previous
critic had imagined in such a bizarre configuration?

Read had anticipated all of these reactions, of course. His article
begins as a memory narrative set in July 1939. He, with some
other(s) identified under a general *we,* enter the city of Florence bur-
dened by an onset of the melancholy of the overcivilized. "I brought
to everything a tired, disillusioned eye," he writes, and later speaks of
his "fit of boredom." He is weary of the obligation every traveler in
Italy feels to honor the Renaissance by visiting each revered mu-
seum piece and echoing four hundred years of praise for its great-
ness. In a mood that clearly owes something to the retrospect upon
Italian fascism in the intervening years, Read expresses repugnance
at the grandiloquence, the pomposity, the pretension, of the great
tradition enshrined in the Uffizi, the Accademia, and the Pitti

From *The Southern Review* 35, no. 4 (Autumn 1999): 774–88.

Palace. And so he wanders into the Museo Archeologico, attracted as much by the shade as by its assemblage of ruined artifacts.

And there he sees it, "a small object," unlabeled, in a glass display case with a jumble of other objects. It is a bronze, "the head of a negro boy, probably an African slave—and it seemed to shine there like a glowworm in the darkness of my mood." Only two or three inches high, of uncertain date and culture, it appeals to him by both its scale and its novel subject. The work is an anti-masterpiece; it makes no claims upon him and therefore stands all the brighter:

> Whatever he was, and whenever he lived, this artist created something without age or epoch, something so elementally simple and fresh that it had the power, in my sophisticated mind, to rouse the highest pleasure and to prompt—as an aftermath— the deepest questionings.

The work does not possess the hegemonic cultural power of a figurehead for Empire, for Civilization, even for Art. It is a modest fragment. "What is greatest in art is also at the same time the least," Read remarks and then corrects himself to affirm that the greatest art escapes all categories of measurement or value. Therefore, in the spirit of Wordsworth declaring that the meanest flower that blows can bring thoughts too deep for tears, Read proclaims this bronze the greatest work of art in the world.

On one level the essay offers a recognizable, indeed hoary, sentiment, one we might place under the rubric of primitivism. It is reminiscent of the assertion by John Fowles's protagonist in *The Magus* that the lyric "Come live with me, and be my love" is the greatest poem in our literature, superior to all the grandeur of Shakespeare's plays. Wherever tradition exerts its authority by high rhetoric, complex form, and monumental style, we can expect gestures of resistance, defiant preference for the intimate, the unassuming, the humble. Read's chief criterion for his revisionist version of greatness is that the object or text "persist through the busy and distracted years that follow." Nature and culture provide each of us with these memorial objects in abundance; one must recognize and lay claim to them, free from the intermediary and intimidating influence of scholastic authority.

I have lingered on Read's charming and obscure essay because it so fetchingly embodies and enacts its message; it is a fugitive piece of commentary unlikely to arrest the attention except by accident.

257

It serves a heuristic function, in the sense of "stimulating interest as a means of furthering investigation." But the common reader is less likely to further investigate the writings of Herbert Read (or bronzes of undecidable period) than to apply Read's lesson to him- or herself: What small art object might I settle on in my own experience that has fulfilled the criteria set forth by Read? What haunting image or text have I carried with me many years that has provided the special illumination that comes from aesthetic (re)cognition, the pleasure derived from a deepening understanding of the human condition endowed by the remittent force of a brief text?

It would do the world good if every learned person stepped forward with an example. Some have done so in the book *Touchstones: American Poets on a Favorite Poem,* edited by Robert Pack and Jay Parini. Yet the commentaries tend to the explicative, rarely consulting the larger contexts or emotional imperatives summoned by the poems. My project in this essay is to investigate as deeply as I can a poem that has haunted me for decades, and (like Read, though at greater length) to assert a centrality for the poem in our contemporary culture. I have chosen Robert Hayden's poem "Perseus," first published in 1955. I came upon it in 1966 when the author's *Selected Poems* appeared. I was not, like Read, in a state of boredom but the polar opposite. The Vietnam War and the civil rights struggles of that era had driven me to a degree of simmering anger and vindictiveness toward my nation, its history and political leaders, that I would not have imagined possible even two years before. I was on the brink of engaging in the kind of countercultural acts shared by my generation: marching in protest down the boulevards of New York City, sitting in against CIA recruitment on my college campus, declaiming against my government as part of the "armies of the night" gathered in Washington, D.C. In this manic state, and ever afterward, Hayden's poem informed my thoughts and helped to temper my actions. For the help it has repeatedly given me in dark times, I declare it the greatest poem in the world.

PERSEUS

Her sleeping head with its great gelid mass
   of serpents torpidly astir
burned into the mirroring shield—
   a scathing image dire

as hated truth the mind accepts at last
and festers on.
I struck. The shield flashed bare.

Yet even as I lifted up the head
and started from that place
of gazing silences and terrored stone,
I thirsted to destroy.
None could have passed me then—
no garland-bearing girl, no priest
or staring boy—and lived.

It is notable that when Herbert Read settles on an artwork that
he will proclaim to have such redemptive powers that it can be
called "the greatest," it is the head of an African slave. One feels this
to be not an incidental but an essential reason for his valuation. The
"negro boy" remains sufficiently outside the social and imaginative
experience of Europe that Read's eye is refreshed by his otherness;
he is off-center, peripheral to the self-glorifying world of Floren-
tine humanism. Of course, we see that Read's appropriation of the
boy's image is in some sense a patronizing act of colonization. The
child is a noble savage, a cultic figure of simplicity, the uncivilized,
the unhistorical. Read exhibits the fascination for the exotic that
he shares with his favored Romantic artists and with the surrealist
painters he credited with rescuing modern art from drab mimetic
figuration. And yet this reaching out to the stranger crossing his
path unexpectedly in the heart of Florence strikes the reader as a
healthy impulse, the foundation of an aesthetic that makes black-
ness visible to a white majority. It is a species of encounter that bore
fruit in later decades.

Likewise, Hayden's choice of the Perseus legend is part of his
strategy to integrate what was considered in the 1950s a "main-
stream" tradition of Eurocentric poetry with the African-American
tradition (beginning with Paul Laurence Dunbar and gathering
strength from the Harlem Renaissance) of privileged attention to
black history and black experience on the American continent. An
African-American poet like Hayden who writes a poem about a
Greek myth makes a statement of solidarity with white modernist
writers who explore their heritage and identity through the agency
of classical stories. An anthology of 1971, *Hero's Way: Contemporary
Poems in the Mythic Tradition,* edited by John Alexander Allen, gath-
ers nearly five hundred pages of poems of this kind. (None is by a

black author.) Here are poems, not all of them "contemporary," on the various gods and goddesses of the Trojan War, on Orpheus, the Chimera, Lorelei, Narcissus, the Minotaur, Ariadne, Danaë, and many others, each interpreted as an archetype of the collective unconscious in the manner sanctioned in this period by C. G. Jung's and Erich Neumann's psychoanalytical theory and in the literary criticism of Northrop Frye and his followers. The anthology, which includes only a small portion of the myth-centered poems of the postwar period, reminds us how powerful the impulse was at that time to speak parabolically rather than directly about both personal and historical experience. (A widely read critical text of the same year, Lillian Feder's *Ancient Myth in Modern Poetry*, theorized the ubiquitous presence of mythic figures and allusions in the work of modernist poets like Yeats, Eliot, Pound, and Auden.)

Hayden claimed in an interview that "Perseus" was written in response to the execution of Julius and Ethel Rosenberg in 1953, which stirred in the poet a memory of injustices in his own racial history. He had recently written in his landmark poem "Middle Passage" an account of some brutal events of that history, setting documentary-style accounts of voyages like the *Amistad's* in ironic relation to the prayers and songs of white preachers, sailors, and merchants who conducted the slave trade as well as to Ariel's song in *The Tempest* and allusions to works like Coleridge's "The Rime of the Ancient Mariner" and Melville's *Benito Cereno*. "Middle Passage" and "Perseus" are linked not only by theme but by keywords. The altered refrain of Ariel's song in "Middle Passage" reads:

> Deep in the festering hold thy father lies,
> the corpse of mercy rots with him,
> rats eat love's rotten gelid eyes.

Here we see the original of Medusa's "gelid" mass of serpents and the obsessive way that her image "festers" in the imagination of the poet. Each new atrocity reopens the wound inflicted by the primal horror of one's first awakened consciousness of the Medusa head of History itself. For a great-souled author like Hayden there can be no question of choosing one realm, one racial history, rather than another. The Perseus myth belongs exclusively neither to whites nor to blacks but to all races, because it illuminates the tragic experience of all races.

In the poem, more an abbreviated first-person testimony by

Perseus than an account of his adventures, the reader is compelled to share an angle of regard upon the murder of Medusa that is intimate and immediate. In effect the reader reenacts along with Perseus the ritual act of violence and its psychic impact. Perseus shapes his confession into two matching seven-line stanzas of iambic verse, evoking the compression of the sonnet. Everything is tightly wrought in this brief narrative, which begins in medias res with Perseus' astounded perception of Medusa in the mirror of his shield. We see that the speaker is an allegorizer; he no sooner glimpses the Gorgon's "scathing image dire" than he compares it to "hated truth" the mind cannot escape. The last line of the first stanza begins, "I struck." His blow seems to be directed as much at "hated truth" as at the monster. It is a reflex gesture of denial, of obliteration of consciousness. And, sure enough, the shield flashes bare. The "scathing image dire" is gone. (The *Oxford English Dictionary* traces *dire* back to 1567 and cites, among others, *Paradise Lost* 2.628: "All monstrous, all prodigious things, Gorgons and Hydras and Chimeras dire.")

The first word of the second stanza is the ever-resonant conjunction *Yet*. Perseus discovers that, in the act of severing Medusa's head from her body, he internalizes her murderous power as part of his identity. "I thirsted to destroy," he remarks in the terse, emphatic style appropriate to stolid heroes. Now he has the power of a god to kill at will, simply by showing the head and turning his enemies to stone. In allegorical terms, once he has introjected the scathing image he is fated to reproduce it, to extend its mordant effect everywhere. As artist, Perseus displays his consciousness of history's horrors to generations of readers or spectators still unborn. He contaminates their imagination and initiates them into the condition of humanity. None can escape, no matter how innocent—indeed, the innocent, figured as the garland-bearing girl and the staring boy, are most susceptible. In Hayden's case those who know little of the slave trade are educated by "Middle Passage"; those who neglect the Holocaust are introduced to the "childhood foreclosed" of the girl in the concentration camp in "Belsen, Day of Liberation." Bitten by the snake himself, Hayden witnesses the succession of horrors in the 1960s he calls "the mourning time" in order to infect others with the genuine felt history of his era. Like the ancient mariner whose spellbinding story acquaints the wedding guest with hated truths about the perilous condition of fallen humanity, Perseus stands ready for new victims, of whom alert readers of this poem must be counted.

In later poems on Greek myths, such as "Sphinx" and "Richard Hunt's 'Arachne,'" Hayden performs a radical revision of the original myth. But "Perseus" does not seek to discover something in the story of this ephebic hero that the myth itself does not clearly imply. When Perseus holds up the head of Medusa to vanquish Atlas or the sea monster that threatens Andromeda (in some versions, though not in Ovid's) or Phineus and his followers at the wedding feast, he has *become* Medusa; they are paired twins, transposed heads, mirror images. The myth tells us something fundamental about the nature and effects of violence, how ineluctably we transform ourselves into the monstrous figure of our enemy when we strike at it. The hero's tragic fate is often to see the culture he has saved metamorphose, thanks to his action, into a variant form of the destructive force he triumphantly battled. And, make no mistake, this is bitter truth, hated truth. Were readers in 1955 prepared to hear that the crusade against Hitler had changed America into a simulacrum of Nazi Germany and that the Rosenberg executions proved the point? Or that the lynchings and castrations described in poems like "Night, Death, Mississippi" had transmogrified some white Christians into satanists, worse than anything that white racists could even imagine of black people?

Myth criticism was undergoing a new surge of popularity in the 1950s and 1960s, and no doubt we owe "Perseus" in part to the broad appeal of psychological commentaries on the fundamental myths of the culture. But what made the poem attractive to me was that it militated against the monomyth that so many of these critics tried to construct. That monomyth is usefully synthesized by John Alexander Allen, the editor of *Hero's Way,* from a variety of scholarly texts, of which Joseph Campbell's *The Hero with a Thousand Faces* (1949) is probably the most celebrated and influential. In the general version of the myth, according to Allen, the hero's quest involves the search for unity, completeness, and the reconciliation of opposites. He seeks "the Boon of Understanding" and fights through obstacles of all kinds—a "Road of Trials" that includes plentiful monsters and tyrants—as a means of reaching "the inexhaustible source of life." Some myth critics, like Northrop Frye, are more candid than others in specifying the Christ story as the foundation narrative of their appreciative commentaries. In the biblical account of human history, according to Frye, man begins as a semidivine creature in a perfect garden, falls into a wasteland of experience, and then is redeemed by the heroic Christ, who slays the Whore of Babylon and Satan in order to restore the garden as a great city, Jerusalem.

For Frye, T. S. Eliot is the central figure of twentieth-century literature—following the lead of Dante, Spenser, Milton, and Blake—precisely because he adheres to, while extending in a modernist manner, this central spiritual story of the Western canon. Frye's book on Eliot focuses on works like *The Waste Land,* "Ash Wednesday," and *Four Quartets* that repeat the major elements of the triumphal myth of Christianity. Frye concludes his book by asserting, "The greatness of [Eliot's] achievement will finally be understood, not in the context of the tradition he chose, but in the context of the tradition that chose him." *Greatness* is best defined as submission to an overpowering discourse that writes with or through the individual talent, inscribing itself with a period flavor even in a cultural milieu suspicious of tradition and rebellious against it.

Hayden might be said to adhere more to the practice of those who choose their tradition. The heroes that interest him are not those who submit and sacrifice themselves, as in Eliot's narratives, but those who act and survive. It is not Jesus but Cinquez who represents, at the close of "Middle Passage," the "deathless primaveral image, / life that transfigures many lives." Hayden's movement into the Bahá'í faith early in his career suggests that he found Christianity insufficient as ideology and blemished in its historical performance by arrogance, hypocrisy, and cruelty. His test case might well have been *The Waste Land,* which surveyed the inferno of Western history without noticing the plight of the black person. In "Middle Passage," a poem clearly derived from Eliot's example, the boats of the slave trade have Christian names—"*Jesús, Estrella, Esperanza, Mercy*"—and the traders are the pillars of the church: "*Deep in the festering hold thy father lies, / of his bones New England pews are made, / those are the altar lights that were his eyes.*" Hayden parodies Eliot's already ironic use of Shakespeare's lines from *The Tempest* in order to put the blame for slavery on a historical force somewhat more specific than the universal "burning" of unsatisfied desire. Hayden's poem is both an homage to Eliot, in its use of the collage form for its sequence of episodes, and a critique of Eliot's verse, Eliot's tradition, and Eliot's religion.

"Greatness" for Hayden might be said to consist in this: an enactment in narrative, mythic or otherwise, of a triumph over evil, at the same time that the narrative strips away the illusion of triumph from the act and reveals its "dire" consequences. "Great" poems of Hayden's time that undertook an analysis of the reciprocal effects of struggles between good and evil tended to the monumental: W. H. Auden's *For the Time Being,* William Carlos Williams's *Paterson,* and Robert Penn Warren's *Brother to Dragons.* "Perseus" is a counterexample, one of those cameo lyrics that seem, in the way Herbert Read describes, off the contemporary mark, recondite, even a little evasive until read in the light of Hayden's other poems and the cultural terrain of the 1950s. Perseus "starts" from his landscape of "terrored stone" as Adam does from the Garden, marked by the memory of a terrible crime. Popular culture will misread his achievement as heroic (see the movie *Clash of the Titans* as a paradigm), but the elite culture must perform the thankless task of pointing up the subversive implications of the Perseus story. Perseus perpetuates his crime in the same manner as Medusa, petrifying enemies, purported enemies, and innocent bystanders alike. What a moment of clarity it was in the 1950s to hammer out, like the twisting of the tiger's sinews on the anvil of art, this angry message for readers nourished on the oversimplifications of hero movies and myth criticism alike. Of such poetic acts does greatness consist.

And what of Medusa? When Robert Lowell visited Florence he gravitated not to the Museo Archeologico, like Herbert Read, but to Cellini's famous statue of Perseus, his wavy locks curled like serpents, holding the head of Medusa. "Pity the monsters!" he was moved to say:

> My heart bleeds black blood for the monster.
> I have seen the Gorgon.
> The erotic terror
> of her helpless, big bosomed body
> lay like slop.

The Greeks understood that Medusa was once an innocent, a garland-bearing girl, a priestess who aroused the lust of Poseidon and, after being raped, became a monster whose poisonous thoughts turned to serpents on her skull. Lowell sees that the story of Perseus and Medusa is fundamentally about the violence of sexuality, the vindictive fury of the afflicted and abused. Medusa is the feminine wrenched by sexual violation into the masculine prerogatives of warfare. The serpents that sprout from her head manifest her new-found carnal knowledge, and her murderous gaze mimics her new and dangerous vision of mankind. Perseus commits the second and ultimate rape upon her impure lower body, transforming it from a beauty of nature to "slop," an unthreatening heap of waste.

More than this. Medusa is imaginable, Eleanor Wilner claims in an essay in *TriQuarterly* 88, as Nature itself receiving its death wound from the male energies empowered by the sky god Athena, goddess of intellect. (Athena transforms Medusa into a monster and aids Perseus in his victory over her.) The myth, then, enacts "the demonizing of [an] older form of the sacred." This form, according to Wilner, exalted the figure of the feminine, of (re)productive nature, as central to the life of the culture. Perseus is the advance guard of a warrior spirit that Wilner, no less than Hayden, traces to the political forces emblematized in our era by the Pentagon, by a Cold War ideology that seeks transcendence and triumph in technological power. Indeed, no recent poem exposes this tendency more effectively than Hayden's "Zeus over Redeye," in which the poet wanders through the Redstone Arsenal:

> In soaring stasis rocket missiles loom,
> the cherished weapons named for Nike
> (O headless armless Victory),
> for Zeus, Apollo, Hercules—
> eponyms of redeyed fury
> greater, lesser than their own.

Perseus belongs in this company, though no rocket has (yet) been named for him. Here again, Hayden's critique resonates with the countercultural discourse of the 1950s and 1960s, with texts like Lewis Mumford's *The Pentagon of Power,* Herbert Marcuse's *Eros and Civilization,* and Norman O. Brown's *Life against Death.* In such books the remedy for "one-dimensional man," man the warrior, was the force of Eros, and specifically Eros as naturalized desire, as the repressed power of what Nature had come to signify since the Romantic era. Likewise, Wilner calls attention to the fact that in Greek mythology "Athena took the severed but still dreadful head of Medusa and affixed it to the breastplate of her armor, taking unto herself the ruined powers of her enemy, making of nature and the lower world the captured emblem of her own chilly aegis." In Medusa is the possibility of transformation back to a sacred worship of nature, and nobody knows this better than the psyche that slays her again and again yet may in the end yield to her erotic fascination, her welcoming of instinct and desire, and join with her to redeem the world.

Analysis of Hayden's fragment-like poem, then, needs to begin with the responsive testimony of Medusa herself, allowing the fiendish Gorgon to recall the innocent girl before her transformation into a killer. Ann Stanford's "Medusa," from *In Mediterranean Air* (1977), is spoken by the erstwhile maiden who attends Athena's altar and suffers there the outrage that triggers the mythic narrative:

> I stood as he walked—the old man—up from the shore.
> He climbed the temple stairs. He praised my grace.
> I had never seen a god before.
> He seized and raped me before Athena's altar.
>
> It is no great thing to a god. For me it was anger—
> no consent on my part, no wooing, all harsh
> rough as a field hand. I didn't like it.
> My hair coiled in fury; my mind held hate alone.
> I thought of revenge, began to live on it.
> My hair turned to serpents, my eyes saw the world in stone.

The sinuous syntax and elevated diction of Hayden's poem are appropriate to the hero's self-estimation; Medusa, on the other hand, speaks here in the simple declarative sentences of the traumatized. She does not aspire to turn her experience into poetry but into a kind of angry anti-poetry, the plain truth of the unsophisticated ("I didn't like it"). To be traumatized is to be arrested in perception and understanding, to see the world in stone, to repeat forever the speech of the abused teenager. As in Louise Bogan's classic poem, "Medusa," violator and violated share the same fate, to remain ontologically in a state of fixed identity, oblivious to the change of seasons and the passages of social experience. Ann Stanford's victim can never change, except through death. And yet change stirs in her, for she is pregnant with the creature Pegasus. The poem ends:

> And now the start,
> the rude circling blood-tide not my own
> that squirms and writhes, steals from me bone by bone—
> his monster seed growing beneath my heart,
> prisoned within my prison, left alone,
> despised, uncalled for, turning my blood to stone.

As her thoughts turn to the horse of the Muses, the figure of poetry, her language begins to take on shapeliness, enhanced rhyme, syntactic complexity, causality. Her body must deliver this figure of transformation, engendered by violence, as part of her sacrifice, a woman made into slop. She becomes, unwittingly, the primal Mother of the afflicted imagination, a figure of Memory itself.

One virtue of Hayden's making his poem a dramatic monologue is that we do not expect Perseus to understand the dynamic of revenge that Stanford enforces on us. Perseus is as ingenuous as a garland-bearing girl, a fool and tool of the gods, especially Athena, who aids him by giving him the shield. Were Hayden to tell this story in his own voice he might be tempted to conceive Medusa as he does the Aztec goddess Coatlicue in his poem "Idol," part of a sequence based on his travels through Mexico. She is a Kali figure, a goddess of death who exacts from her believers ritual human sacrifices as the price of a sacred relation to her: "the heart wrenched / from the living breast, / . . . the raw meaty heart quivering in copal." No hero has killed Coatlicue, and so she reigns in cultural memory as a vital icon of the savage world, a precedent for modern violence enacted by a community of believers. She functions something like Helen of Troy in Ezra Pound's *Cantos*. Pound quotes on several occasions Aeschylus' epithets for Helen—"ship-destroying, man-destroying, city-destroying"—and generalizes in what seems to be the voice of Odysseus, in Canto 29:

> the female
> Is an element, the female
> Is a chaos
> An octopus
> A biological process

Circe and Helen are the principal referents here, but Medusa, too, is associated, as the daughter of ocean gods and the chosen of Poseidon, with the sea, the element inimical to man. Seas are man destroying, the widow maker; thus Amy Clampitt in her poem on Medusa asserts that this doomed figure enforces on us "Terror of origins: the sea's heave, the cold mother / of us all." When Sylvia Plath seeks to annihilate her mother's influence she identifies the noxious antagonist as "Medusa" (in the poem of that title), a sea creature with eely tentacles. In so doing, she reaffirms her status as a heroic poet, though a reading of Hayden's poem would have reminded her that she has only introjected her mother's slimy creatureliness into her own imagination. In Plath's poems of the watery depths, such as "Full Fathom Five" and "Lorelei," and in her obsessive poems about the enviable status of statuary, we hear the desire to become one of Medusa's victims. Likewise, in Radcliffe Squires's eerie poem "The Garden of Medusa" the poet approaches the Gorgon's dwelling with two options, both of them appealing: to slay the monster and achieve fame—"newspapers will tingle with the shock of your name"—or "choose to forget the mirror and / See what the face really looks like." Always the poet chooses the strategy of mediation over the unmediated vision of the sublime figure Death.

Perseus as poet. We keep returning to this formulation and need to consider it at more length. Hayden gives us the cue in a ruminative essay he wrote upon returning to his childhood haunts in Detroit:

No, this was no nostalgia "trip" for him. He felt today no sadness, no regret, remembering things past. These were all in the poem ["Elegies for Paradise Valley"], and poems for him were often a means of catharsis, a way, he often thought, of gazing upon the Medusa without being turned to stone, the poem being his mirror shield.

This quotation reminds us that the events in "Perseus" occur within a human consciousness. Medusa is the victimizing world that cannot be stared at directly but must be represented at one remove in a psychic process that requires the absorption of its full horror ("the shield flashed bare") and then its refiguration in art. According to recent theorists like René Girard, Hélène Cixous, and Julia Kristeva, not only art but language has its origin in the crisis resulting from confronting the abomination and signifying it for the community. Many of Hayden's poems—"The Rabbi," "The Whipping," and especially "Tour 5," with its recoil from the "Shrill gorgon silence" of the rural South—anatomize the relation of language, history, and the poetic task.

Implicit in this view of the myth is the assumption that the poet, or more generally the artist, must ruthlessly destroy in him- or herself the power of the noncreative self, the presence of the world, figured as a threatening (but ultimately redeeming) monster. As Tobin Siebers points out in *The Mirror of Medusa*, the exchange of identities and powers of fascination between Medusa and Perseus guarantees that the moral categories of good and evil remain in uncertain flux. Whole cultures, especially warrior cultures like our own, can trace their ambiguous history to the primal myths of shared guilt derived from violent actions represented in seminal texts. For male authors the shadow antagonist of the virile hero is often cast as a feminine figure, or anima: Mother, Maiden, Temptress, or Witch. It is the world that bewitches, enthralls, fascinates, that fixes its dangerous and evil eye upon the artist who lashes out in resistance, determined to remake or reenvision fate on his terms, hardly aware of the extent to which those terms are dictated by the informing nature of the force he annihilates and the effects of the fact of annihilation. The Perseus myth is instantly recognizable by all aspiring authors as an enabling narrative of the upwelling of creative life.

Youth and the Bright Medusa. The title of Willa Cather's 1920 collection of stories, which includes "Paul's Case," calls attention to the numinous countenance of the potent world that every young person confronts upon reaching maturity. To avoid being slain by its power one must inflict a disabling blow upon it, the very act that shuts the gates upon the state of innocence. That Perseus is a monster as well as Medusa is not only the key insight in Hayden's poem but one of the fundamental and dire truths of literary history in this century. How many biographies of artists render them, wittingly or unwittingly, as monsters! One hears the note in the following elegiac tribute to F. Scott Fitzgerald by his friend John Peale Bishop:

> None had such promise then, and none
> Your scapegrace wit or your disarming grace;
> For you were bold as was Danaë's son,
> Conceived like Perseus in a dream of gold.
> And there was none when you were young, not one,
> So prompt in the reflecting shield to trace
> The glittering aspect of a Gorgon age.
> . . . .
> Was it that having shaped your stare upon
> The severed head of time, upheld and blind,
> Upheld by the stained hair,
> And seen the blood upon that sightless stare,
> You looked and were made one
> With the strained horror of those sightless eyes?
> You looked, and were not turned to stone.

This poem was written for inclusion in the posthumously published book of Fitzgerald's late writings called *The Crack-Up*. Bishop's poem uses as an epigraph a famous sentence from the title essay: "In the real dark night of the soul it is always three o'clock in the morning." Bishop traces the now familiar trajectory of Fitzgerald's life from his emergence as a young ambitious hero of the creative life to his ultimate subjugation as a hack in Grub Street, subdued by the destructive element of modern American society, "a Gorgon age." Fitzgerald's life, then, is readable, at least by Bishop, as a gradual transformation of Perseus into Medusa. "You looked and were made one / With the strained horror of those sightless eyes," he writes in the poem's key lines. Yet Fitzgerald was not turned to stone, was not silenced or blinded; he continued to reflect back to a large readership the horrors he had internalized as both a penalty and nurturing requirement of his art. The dark night of his soul became ours; his version of the bitch goddess Success experienced at three o'clock in the morning, *The Great Gatsby*, is our nation's fundamental modern text, the "greatest" American novel of this century, according to a recent poll of writers and editors commissioned by the Modern Library, and sooner or later every young person in the educational system is exposed to it.

One could multiply such examples indefinitely. Obviously, Hayden's "Perseus" belongs in the Uffizi of our public imagination, part of the central story of the culture we keep telling ourselves in narrative after narrative. Though the poem has been overlooked and proves a revelatory surprise to those who stumble across it, it can no longer, in Read's formulation, be called "great" or "the greatest." Ours is an era suspicious of the idea of greatness, worried that such a label represents a hegemonic claim upon us. This essay is offered in the spirit of rebuttal, an endorsement of hyperbolic praise of fugitive pieces needful for the vexed spirits of their audiences. "Perseus" implicates us in the massive and monumental themes of our most studied modern literature, even as it seems to be nothing more than a slight lyric about an ancient legend. This archaic story is indeed "without age or epoch," and, as we have seen, it "prompts . . . the deepest questionings." When it seized my imagination in 1966, at the inception of my own career as a writer, it clarified psychological and historical issues that had clouded my understanding. It had the brevity and force of a sacred inscription, even as it pretended to be nothing more than a gloss on a legend I had nearly forgotten from my high school reading of Edith Hamilton's *Mythology*. Now

I am more sympathetic to the view, expressed by Paul Valéry and seconded by Geoffrey Hartman in *The Unmediated Vision,* that Perseus better represents the modern poetic self than Narcissus or Apollo or Orpheus. "Perseus" is the specular instrument in which artists of today can discover, as a rite of initiation, the ambiguity of their creative powers. I propose to place it at the center of our canon, the sun that illuminates our thorny path toward the future.

FRED M. FETROW

Robert Hayden's "Frederick Douglass": Form and Meaning in a Modern Sonnet

John Keats in 1819 used a sonnet to call for more freedom in the treatment of the sonnet form. In "On the Sonnet" he urged poets to unfetter the sonnet from traditional rigidity to allow it to find its own organic form.[1] Keats in that poem, and in other sonnets, practiced what he preached. Later poets heeded the call; several experimented with the form and structure of the sonnet. Gerard Manley Hopkins, for example, notably stamped the sonnet with his unique approach to meter, syntax, and usage. Hopkins, with his "sprung rhythm" and syntactical innovation, adapted the traditional form to his "modern" impulse. Neither Keats nor Hopkins merely tinkered; the success of their efforts can be partially measured by the results. Both authors achieved a close and functional relationship between the altered structure and the meaning of their sonnets, which eschew many conventional elements of form.

Among contemporary poets who have produced sonnets on their own terms, none is more candid in admitting his debt to Hopkins than Robert Hayden.[2] Hayden's best-known sonnet, "Frederick Douglass," initially published in 1947, does indeed exhibit Hopkins's influence, but, more important, the poem also shows the viability of the sonnet form when practiced by a modern poet capable of transcending the inherent limitations of a traditional form. As such, the sonnet is a good example of a modern response to the alleged tyranny of form. Hayden has his cake and eats it too, as he divests himself of practically all the traditional formal conventions associated with the sonnet yet successfully retains the reinforcement relationship between form and meaning, a relationship in the past often facilitated by elements of conventional

From *CLA Journal* 17, no. 1 (September 1973): 78–84. Reprinted with permission of the College Language Association.

form such as rhyme, specified meter, and prescribed structural divisions.

Hayden accomplishes optimum coherence by devising an alternate structural method for establishing and exploiting the form-meaning correlation. He constructs "Frederick Douglass" with careful choices of sentence type, sentence structure, syntax, and diction, all of which coordinate and combine to fuse inseparably the form and the meaning of the sonnet. A close reading of the poem, quoted here, reveals Hayden's method and his accomplishment:

> When it is finally ours, this freedom, this liberty, this beautiful
> and terrible thing, needful to man as air,
> usable as earth; when it belongs at last to all,
> when it is truly instinct, brain matter, diastole, systole,
> reflex action: when it is finally won; when it is more
> than the gaudy mumbo jumbo of politicians:
> this man, this Douglass, this former slave, this Negro
> beaten to his knees, exiled, visioning a world
> where none is lonely, none hunted, alien,
> this man, superb in love and logic, this man
> shall be remembered. Oh, not with statues' rhetoric,
> not with legends and poems and wreaths of bronze alone,
> but with the lives grown out of his life, the lives
> fleshing his dream of the beautiful, needful thing.

On a first reading this poem may seem a sonnet in name only. The lines do not rhyme; the meter is clearly not iambic pentameter; although the poem has the "required" fourteen lines, it appears non-structured or at least free of structural restraint. But the appearance is deceiving; the sonnet is in fact highly structured.

One structural innovation is Hayden's inversion of the conventional octave/sestet pattern of the Petrarchan sonnet. Nineteenth-century practitioners, including Keats in "On First Looking into Chapman's Homer" and Hopkins in "God's Grandeur," followed guidelines set out in the medieval period by which the sonnet's opening eight lines present and elaborate on an idea or emotion, and then the subsequent six-line unit, changing the rhyme sounds, comments on the initial passage by extending it, modifying it, or even quarreling with it. Hayden opens his poem with a six-line unit beginning "When it is finally ours" and follows this dependent clause with an implied [then] passage of eight lines: "[then] this man . . . / shall be remembered. . . ." The revision of customary Petrarchan practice keeps the reader off balance, alert. By violating habitual expectations, Hayden joins a group of twentieth-century poets who experimented with the sonnet structure for a variety of rhetorical effects and thematic purposes: Wilfred Owen, e. e. cummings, Edna St. Vincent Millay, John Wheelwright, W. H. Auden, Dylan Thomas, and John Berryman, to name a few.

Another primary structure is sentence type and arrangement. The sonnet consists of only two sentences. The first of these covers lines 1 through the midpoint of line 11; the second sentence spans the remainder of the poem. Both are periodic sentences, with the vital element withheld until the last moment. This choice of sentence type allows Hayden to build toward the ultimate point of the sentences (and the poem) while controlling the tone of the preceding clauses. In the first periodic sentence the poet twice utilizes parallelism, whereby he first presents and expands his conception of freedom and then follows with a personal and historical profile of Frederick Douglass. The second sentence concludes the poem by distinguishing between tributes to the memory of Douglass and the ultimate nature of his legacy.

The parallel structure of the first sentence is used to define freedom repeatedly and progressively. Hayden, with a series of descriptive terms, forms a progression that moves "freedom" from the realm of the abstract to the concrete and real. This movement mirrors and thus reinforces the movement and meaning of the entire sonnet. The series contains words made equivalent (but not identical) with freedom: in line 1 *this freedom* is followed by *this liberty,* which expands the conception of freedom only slightly, from one abstraction to another (albeit more specific) abstraction. "This beautiful and terrible thing" advances one step farther toward the concrete.[3]

That this seemingly indescribable "thing" is being methodically defined becomes apparent with the next step in the progression, a shift to freedom's elemental function. This shift (a use of Aristotle's *final cause*) images freedom as graspable as dirt; freedom is "needful to man as air," and, although air is invisible, the concreteness of *usable as earth* brings *freedom* full scale to an elemental reality. Just as Hayden with parallel structure and descriptive diction moves freedom from abstraction to reality, so his poem contends that Douglass's legacy ultimately will be the reality of freedom lived rather than just freedom only conceived. The delayed climax of this lengthy periodic sentence thus exhibits, in miniature, the thrust of the entire poem. The form is the function is the meaning.

The repetition, anaphora fashion, of the initial *when* in those successive clauses also establishes the tone of yearning for that freedom so copiously delineated in the first sentence. The instinctive longing is more specifically conveyed by lines 4 and 5. There Hayden presents a list to emphasize the elemental necessity of freedom: "when it is truly instinct, brain matter, diastole, systole, / reflex action." In accordance with the other structural components, even this brief catalogue proceeds from abstract to concrete. After the abstract *truly instinct,* we are led through *brain matter, diastole, systole, reflex action.* The concreteness of this series is then contrasted with the abstract nonreality of the "gaudy mumbo jumbo of politicians," which, through connotation, may be an ironical comment on perverse white conceptions of black "style."

Examination of the poem's first sentence also reveals the nature and method of Hayden's metrical system. He does use meter but in an unconventional way. In the interview previously cited he describes the metrical pattern and indicates the effect he was seeking: "'Douglass,' then, is not in iambic pentameter. Certain words in each line receive accent, and there are usually five stresses in each line." Later he remarks, "The poem is tightly constructed, taut and wound up like a spring."[4] This stress system produces a beat that reverberates through the periodic parallelism of the first ten lines. The systole-diastole regularity of the accentuation in those lines coincides with the repetition of diction and pulsing progression toward the climax of the sentence. This "doubling" effect, a modern example of what Alexander Pope meant by "the sound must seem an echo to the sense," is especially evident in the characterization of Douglass. Note the repetition and stress pattern in the parallel phrases, "This man, this Douglass, this former slave, this Negro . . . this man . . . this man / shall be remembered." In their entirety these phrases constitute a historical portrait of Douglass, and the increasing emotional intensity of the content gathers momentum from the conjunction of the sentence structure and the relentless beat of Hayden's version of stressed verse.

The brief list of Douglass's personal qualities also fuses the real and the abstract and thus once more reinforces the larger thought of the poem. Hayden describes the man whose vision will produce "real" freedom as a balanced combination of emotion and intellect. Douglass was "superb in love and logic"; the poet here implies that Douglass's love produced the vision, while Douglass's gift for abstract logic helped move his vision closer to reality.

The final sentence climaxes the sonnet and completes the portrait by clarifying *how* Douglass will be remembered *when* freedom is real rather than abstract. Hayden again uses a parallel structure, this time to facilitate antithesis. He creates a set of balanced contrasts that distinguish the real but artificial heritage from the living, breathing fulfillment of Douglass's dream. The real heritage left by Douglass is not fame commemorated or maintained with artifacts but, rather, the living progeny of his example. The items in the *not* phrases are contrasted with the items in the *but* phrases as rhetorical strategy for clarifying the difference between superficial reality (statues, legends, poems, wreaths) and living reality ("lives grown out of his life, the lives / fleshing his dream"). This assertion of how Douglass shall be remembered thus culminates the movement of the poem as it completes the overall progression from the abstract to the real. This conclusion derives organically from the general "when . . . then" premise of the sonnet.

The imbedded question of exactly when this reality of freedom will be fully realized is answered implicitly in the concluding lines. The proximity of this fulfillment and the present absence of it are both suggested by the paradox inherent in Hayden's assertion. He claims Douglass will not be remembered with poems, yet what is Hayden here doing? The ultimate point of this apparent contradiction, whether it is deliberate paradox or subconscious irony, seems evident. The poet is not naive enough to assume that his conception of freedom "has arrived," but he hopefully longs for a time and a reality of freedom when his poem, and other tributes to Douglass like it, simply will be superfluous.

This poem, in addition to its intrinsic merit, shows that the sonnet in the hands of a modern poet attentive to his craft can be used to posit laminated layers of meaning with individualized rather than conventional form. With parallelism, antithesis, repetition, and a personalized stress system, Hayden accomplishes what his more renowned predecessors achieved with rhyme, iambic pentameter, and prescribed structures. Robert Hayden wrote "Frederick Douglass" while in the process of learning his craft. The resultant poem can now teach us "moderns" to appreciate the adaptability of "old" forms. Hayden, in the instance of "Frederick Douglass," may not have completely unfettered the sonnet form, but his sonnet is (as Keats recommended so long ago) "bound with garlands of her own."

NOTES

1. John Keats, *Poetical Works,* ed. H. W. Garrod (London: Oxford University Press, 1956), 371. Keats was not, of course, the first poet to experiment with the sonnet form. For an account of sonnet experimentation prior to and including that of Keats, see Lawrence J. Zillman, *John Keats and the Sonnet Tradition* (1939; rpt., New York: Octagon Books, 1966).

2. Hayden, in a recent interview, states, "Well, when I was working on my own sonnets I was also studying Hopkins, and under his influence I decided to experiment with stressed verse." For the context of these remarks, see "The Poet and His Art: A Conversation" in *How I Write / 1* (New York: Harcourt Brace Jovanovich, 1972), 191.

3. In assigning this contrasting duality to freedom, Hayden perhaps has in mind Douglass's own initial conception of freedom, described in his autobiography: "Liberty, as the inestimable birthright of every man, converted every object into an asserter of this right. I heard it in every sound, and saw it in every object. It was ever present to torment me with a sense of my wretchedness. The more beautiful and charming were the smiles of nature, the more horrible and desolate was my condition." *Life and Times of Frederick Douglass* (1892; rpt., New York: Macmillan, 1962), 86.

4. *How I Write 1,* 191.

BRIAN CONNIFF

Answering *The Waste Land:*
Robert Hayden and the Rise of the
African-American Poetic Sequence

April 1966 was one of the most eventful and paradoxical months in
the history of twentieth-century American poetry. At the Third
World Festival of Negro Arts in Dakar, Senegal, Robert Hayden's
A Ballad of Remembrance was awarded the Grand Prix as the best re-
cent volume of Anglophone poetry. In at least some international
literary circles the prestige of this award roughly matched its
Olympic title. The first such event to be held on "independent
African soil," the festival was sponsored by Léopold Sédar Senghor
in conjunction with UNESCO and the Société Africaine de Cul-
ture and was attended by over ten thousand people from thirty-
seven nations. The other finalists in the poetry competition were
Derek Walcott's *In a Green Night* and Christopher Okigbo's *Limits.*
Langston Hughes was one of the judges. Also in attendance were
Aimé Césaire, Léon Damas, Alioune Diop, Yevgeny Yevtushenko,
and Duke Ellington. André Malraux, then French minister of cul-
ture, seems to have captured the prevailing spirit when he praised
the festival as an indication that Senghor's cultural program was
about to shape the "destiny of a continent."[1]

For Hayden, though, the Grand Prix was wildly unexpected. He
had not yet published a book with a commercial or university press
in the United States, and he was still teaching fifteen hours each se-
mester as an associate professor in the English department at Fisk
University. Even the Grand Prix itself, when it first arrived, seemed
to do him as much harm as good.

In fact, within a few days, while his poetry was being praised in
Senegal as the centerpiece of international negritude, back home
in Nashville Hayden was being attacked as the scapegoat of choice
for a new generation of African-American poets.[2] At Fisk's First

From *African American Review* 33, no. 3 (Fall 1999): 487–504.

Black Writers' Conference a group of writers and students, led by Melvin Tolson, assailed Hayden as the stooge of exploitative capitalists and, all in all, a traitor to his race. For the most part Tolson and his supporters endorsed the "Black Cultural Nationalism" of Ron Karenga, with its declarations that "all art must reflect and support the Black Revolution" and that "any art that does not discuss and contribute to the revolution is invalid." Hayden's crime was that he refused to be labeled a "Negro poet." From the beginning of the conference, and much to the dismay of most of his audience, he insisted that he should be considered, instead, "a poet who happens to be Negro." When he reiterated his position at a panel discussion—which also included Tolson, Arna Bontemps, and Margaret Walker—the advocates of Black Cultural Nationalism reacted as though they had come face to face with the enemy. Tolson's response was perhaps most characteristic. Among other things he declared that "when a man writes, he tells me which way he went in society." "I'm a black poet," he continued, "an African-American poet, a Negro poet. I'm no accident—and I don't give a tinker's damn what you think."[3] One member of the audience even accused Hayden of contributing to the "delusion" of the "young black people" studying at Fisk. In the following months students on the Fisk campus—almost all of whom, as Hayden was well aware, were from backgrounds more privileged than his own—continued to refer to him as an "Uncle Tom" or an "Oreo," believing that he should use the prestige granted by the Grand Prix to authorize and advance their political positions.

I begin with these events for three reasons. First of all, it is in these few days that studies of Hayden almost inevitably find their critical center—and, unfortunately, Hayden's defining moment.[4] From a conventionally biographical perspective this focus might seem reasonable. In the years immediately following the Third World Festival of Negro Arts, Hayden was granted a brief flurry of academic and otherwise official interest. From 1967 to 1969 he was offered a couple of visiting professorships, a permanent position at the University of Louisville, a recording at the Library of Congress, and, finally, the position at the University of Michigan that he would accept and then occupy for the rest of his life. Nonetheless, it is safe to say that even by the end of the 1960s, soon after the Grand Prix and his auspicious association with the negritude movement, and at least until very recently, Hayden would regain and retain his status as, in Julius Lester's words, "one of the most underrated and unrecognized poets in America." This neglect is largely the result of a collective choice—usually implicit but nonetheless clear—that academic critics have made in their descriptions of Hayden's career. Hayden's poetry has rarely been considered in terms of its rich affiliations with the work of major international poets—including Walcott, Okigbo, and Césaire, among many others—as suggested at the Third World Festival. And his poetry has never been seriously considered, at least by mainstream critics, in relation to the major works by younger African-American poets, who have found it a rich resource and an inspiration.[5] Rather, his poetry has been viewed—by his detractors and most of his supporters—as somehow determined by his one-line answer to the "Negro question," as it was framed by his opponents at the Fisk conference. For Tolson and the younger writers of the emerging Black Arts Movement, Hayden eventually came to be viewed as a poet of some ability—and some minor historical significance—whose work is irreparably limited and dated because it is not sufficiently concerned with issues of race. Even Arna Bontemps, who was often sympathetic with Hayden's work, would conclude after the Fisk conference that Hayden "doesn't really like that Negro thing." Meanwhile, for a handful of more conservative critics and editors Hayden's poetry has also maintained a kind of marginal interest—and, ironically, for much the same reason. For instance, in the influential *Norton Anthology of Modern Poetry* Richard Ellmann and Robert O'Clair begin their introduction to Hayden's poetry by stating that Hayden "did not subscribe to any esthetic of Black poetry." They describe his poetry in terms of his interest in the work of Countee Cullen, Carl Sandburg, Edna St. Vincent Millay, and "the English classics," and then include a selection of Hayden's poetry that would seem to suggest, to a reader unfamiliar with his career, that he must have been trying to write a kind of race-free poetry. In either case Hayden's critical reception has served, more than anything, to obscure and diminish his most formidable accomplishments.

Second, when viewed in the context of the history of American poetry over the past thirty years, the events of April 1966 point to an even more striking neglect. Recent criticism has remained oblivious to one of the most remarkable developments in contemporary literature: the rise, in part out of Hayden's poetry, of the African-American poetic sequence. Because of their particular moment in history, I think, the conferences in Dakar and Nashville were bound to have mixed legacies. Despite the notable absence of the more politically "radical" American writers, the Third World Festival of Negro Arts did help make the rich history of negritude known beyond the cultural centers of Paris and Dakar. At the same time, as a formative moment in the American debate over a "black aesthetic," bringing together a number of still neglected writers on the verge of academic awareness—if not legitimacy—Fisk's First Black Writers' Conference helped expand the audience of such poets as Margaret Walker and Amiri Baraka, among others, and the second conference of 1967 would generally be recognized as the impetus for Gwendolyn Brooks's movement toward African poetic forms and what has been called a "new Black consciousness."[6] Nonetheless, the universalizing grandeur with which Hayden was praised, on the one hand, and the vehemence with which he was attacked, on the other, suggest that the two conferences, like most events that end up being reconstructed as defining moments, obscured just about as much as they revealed. After all, the often contentious politics surrounding the emerging postcolonial African and Caribbean literature—still loosely grouped at the Dakar conference under the title "négritude"—was just about as foreign to Hayden's sensibilities as the cultural politics of the Fisk conference.[7] A Bahá'í by faith, Hayden was committed to abstinence from partisan politics of any kind. Beginning just about a decade later, however, American poets would be better prepared to draw directly from the legacy of Hayden's poetry—at once individualistic and engaged, local and international, highly crafted and improvisational. Clearly conscious of Hayden's example, in recent years such poets as Michael S. Harper, Jay Wright, and Brenda Marie Osbey have been writing highly ambitious poetic sequences, firmly grounded in history, that invoke distinctly heterogeneous heritages with a wide range of formal experimentation.

Third, if the events of April 1966 are located in the context of a more extensive literary history, Hayden becomes an even more significant figure. His career spans a crucial period, from the early 1940s through the early 1970s, and his poetry eventually plays a major role in the emergence and development of what I have come to call "posttraditional" poetry. This poetry is largely informed by its author's paradoxical stance toward literary tradition. The posttraditional poet is certainly conscious—in fact, often intensely conscious—of tradition. At the same time, though, he or she manages, in one way or another, to view any distinctly literary tradition as historically contingent. Most often, the posttraditional poet uses this sense of contingency to construct from disparate sources a personal heritage—provisionally, heterogeneously, willfully—in order to address some perceived historical crisis or, especially in recent years, some immediate social need.

Posttraditional poetry has its most conspicuous origins in the mid-1920s, when, just about simultaneously, the leading canonizers of high modernism began to take radical measures to address what seemed to them a profound schism between their most revered traditions and their peculiar historical interpretations of postwar Europe. At this time, writing in Venice, Ezra Pound began to juxtapose paradisal visions with Dante's *Inferno* and Major Douglas's economics. At the same time, in London, T. S. Eliot, recently established as a cultural icon, began his second "career" as poetry editor at Faber and Gwyer, redefining himself as a "reactionary" man of letters in what was in effect an elaborate attempt to counterbalance his own philosophical uncertainty with a millennial vision of Christian culture. Meanwhile, in Ireland William Butler Yeats set out on his first deliberate effort to distance himself from his early romantic nationalism—a truly strange journey, by way of a highly personal reclamation of an Anglo-Irish heritage, that would eventually lead him, in the last days of his life, to the striking embrace of common humanity in "The Circus Animals' Desertion" and "Cuchulain Comforted."

By the middle of their careers these poets were writing as though tradition—as they knew it—was about to come to an end, under the assault of a debased and debasing culture. They cultivated their notions of historical crisis in ways that resulted not only in reactionary cultural politics but also, eventually, in an understanding that, if the sense of literary culture they so cherished could be threatened and even destroyed by the forces of history, then any canon, indeed any culture, might be considered radically contingent.

Of course, at least since the Bollingen Prize controversy of 1949, the efforts of later poets and critics to come to terms with this legacy—especially its disturbing mixture of poetic innovation and reactionary politics, its vast international influence and intense Eurocentrism—has amounted to a kind of collective anxiety attack. By now, though, it has become clear that these often embarrassing ancestors have contributed largely—and, politically speaking, despite themselves—to the rise of a posttraditional poetry that has been growing at least since the mid-1980s, more explicitly heterogenous and more international, both in its sources and its influence, in such works as Adrienne Rich's *Your Native Land, Your Life* (1986), Seamus Heaney's *Station Island* (1983), and Derek Walcott's *Omeros* (1990). Considered more broadly, a distinctly posttraditional stance has become increasingly apparent in the linguistic heterogeneity of contemporary Irish poets like Nuala ni Dhomhnaill and Medbh McGuckian, in the communal heritage evident in the prison poetry and autobiographical writing of Jimmy Santiago Baca, and in the remarkable emergence of contemporary poetry by American Indians. For these later poets any approximation of a tradition—any communal or even personal heritage—is conceived pragmatically, as one instrument among many others with which they can engage a world that is at once overwhelmingly various and desperately in need.

In this essay I will focus primarily on Hayden's "Middle Passage," the long early poem that would remain his most significant contribution to the development of posttraditional poetry. In "Middle Passage" he developed an experimental poetics that could examine racism, directly and specifically, by telling an episode of its history in a number of contending voices. Even at this early point in his career Hayden was able to challenge the modernists' sense of social crisis and give voice to his personal doubts about modernism's moral limitations—in terms that would not even be suggested at the conferences at Dakar and Fisk. In this sense "Middle Passage" is crucial to any reconsideration of Hayden's career. It anticipates his later "Negro history" poems, including "Runagate Runagate," "The Ballad of Nat Turner," and "Frederick Douglass." It also anticipates a number of Hayden's poems in widely varied historical contexts—most notably "A Ballad of Remembrance," "Night, Death, Mississippi," "Belsen, Day of Liberation," "El-Hajj Malik El-Shabazz," and the important later sequence, "Words in the Mourning Time"—in which he explores, often in brutal detail, the psychology and consequences of racism and xenophobia. Throughout this poetry, as William Meredith has put it, "there is scarcely a line of his which is not identifiable as an experience of Black America."[8]

Eliotic Intonations

For American poets of Hayden's generation the development of a posttraditional poetry almost inevitably involved some kind of direct confrontation with received modernism. Hayden was certainly no exception. Beginning his career in the early 1940s, he was conspicuously aware of the previous generation's legacy, particularly as it was perceived in the academy. In this view a few designated "masterpieces," the most conspicuous of which was *The Waste Land,* tended to appear as the culmination—both in the sense of the highest attainment and in the sense of the end—of a predominantly English tradition. The posttraditional impulses in the work of the established modernists—Yeats's provisional reconstructions of his own heritage in his final poems, for instance, or the philosophical and linguistic uncertainty of Eliot's "Little Gidding"—were not yet recognized or had not yet appeared.

Hayden's confrontation with this legacy can be seen in two contrary tendencies of his critical writing. On the one hand, he was prone to monumentalize Eliot's work—as would most academics of his time—by locating it at the end of the Great Tradition. In an overview of "Twentieth Century American Poetry," written for a 1973 textbook entitled *The United States in Literature,* he begins with a surprisingly conventional narrative account of modern poetry in which he acknowledges "the supremacy of Auden and Eliot" in the 1940s and then finds his conclusion in a description of "The Love Song of J. Alfred Prufrock" and *The Waste Land* as expressions of "the spiritual emptiness of industrialized civilization."[9] On the other hand, having been raised in Detroit's Paradise Valley, Hayden was also unusually aware, for an academic of his time, of the persistence of folk culture, jazz, and popular song throughout modern poetry. So even in his textbook account he mentions, along the way, the influence of these populist forces on the work of Edwin Arlington Robinson, Robert Frost, Carl Sandburg, Edgar Lee Masters, and the writers of the Harlem Renaissance—among many others.

Only on rare occasions in his critical writing could Hayden put aside this characteristic ambivalence—and, in doing so, move beyond the positions of both the "academicians and purists" and the Black Cultural Nationalists. Near the end of his career, in an address to the Library of Congress, he was finally able to articulate a more nuanced and culturally grounded understanding of "poetry as a medium, an instrument for social and political change":

Poetry *does* make something happen, for it changes sensibility. In the early stages of a culture it helps to crystallize the language and is a repository for value, belief, ideals. The *Griot* in African tribes keeps names and legends and pride alive. Among the Eskimos the shaman or medicine man is a poet. In ancient Ireland and Wales the bard was a preserver of the culture.

From a perspective with this range of cultural and historical reference, the conventional academic canon of the midcentury—which usually seemed, with Eliot in his place, so complete—suddenly appears temporary, limited, and relatively inconsequential. So, in the same passage, Hayden is able to reconsider poetic tradition in terms that are personal, pragmatic, provisional, and moral:

> A point to consider: What would I as a poet do if my people were rounded up like the Jewish people in Germany under the Nazis? Claude McKay's sonnet "If We Must Die"; the poems of the Greek poet Yannis Ritsos that were recited and sung by men and women fighting in the streets for the freedom of their country; Pablo Neruda, William Butler Yeats, Emily Sachs, Muriel Rukeyser, Gwendolyn Brooks, Walt Whitman; they stand out as poets even if you dislike their politics. To be a poet, it seems to me, is to care passionately about justice and one's fellow human beings.[10]

In this construction of a living poetic heritage Hayden no longer sees tradition as a "line of development" leading toward an inevitable poetic conclusion. He is arranging writers, in heterogeneous combinations, to address a particular historical problem with a poetic vision of justice and compassion.

One irony in Hayden's situation is that, obvious political differences aside, this general method of overcoming the canon of the day is something he shared not only with a number of his contemporaries but also, in a way he himself never recognized, with the canonized modernists themselves. Like Yeats, Pound, and Eliot—especially in the later stages of their careers—Hayden's most basic tendency was to reconstruct a standard canon and, at the same time, to locate himself outside this canon in a way that highlighted its limitations and, ultimately, its historical contingency. In this sense his method was similar to that of philosophers like Nietzsche and Heidegger, as Richard Rorty has described it, when they redescribed their predecessors in terms of a tradition that seemed, in some sense, to have reached its end. Canon construction then became a strategy for dealing with "the problem of ironist theory . . . the problem of how to overcome authority without claiming authority."[11] In this sense, at least from the mid-1920s on, each of the major modernists eventually came to see himself as Hayden saw Eliot: at the end of the English poetic tradition, as, in some manner of speaking, the last poet.

Still, for those of us who have entered the academy well after the rise of postmodern theory, I think it is difficult to appreciate just how common, and at times overwhelming, the monumentalizing view of Eliot was in the 1940s. Overcoming *The Waste Land* was a problem Hayden shared with such different poets as H.D. when she wrote her *Trilogy,* William Carlos Williams when he wrote the first four books of *Paterson,* and even Charles Olson, early in the next decade, when he began *The Maximus Poems.* As these poets progressed through the 1940s and 1950s, they were not worried, as their predecessors had been, that tradition, as they knew it, was about to end and that therefore there might no longer be anything of significance to write; rather, they were driven, and at times practically inebriated, by a sense of freedom they associated with the end of tradition, in the conventional academic sense of the term. That is why, just when literary criticism was being established in an unprecedented state of institutional security and influence within the academy and mainstream critics were settling on a totalizing view of poetic tradition, a number of American poets were undertaking some of the most ambitiously experimental work of the century.

That is also why, no matter how monumental high modernist poetics might have seemed to be when Hayden began his career, his confrontation with *The Waste Land* should not be construed as the kind of agonistic struggle against "belatedness" imagined by Harold Bloom in books like *The Anxiety of Influence, A Map of Misreading,* and *Agon.* Hayden's revision of Eliot's poetics was far more conscious and strategic than Bloom's Freudian mythology would allow and more engaged with history than Bloom's metaphysics and his preoccupation with private irony have ever permitted him to recognize. In the writing of his poetry, Hayden understood from the start that all acts of literary influence, and most of all those involving any kind of "alternative" tradition, take place in a world in which power is distributed unequally. As Edward Said has written of narrative literature in relation to European imperialism, even the most essentialist accounts of influence always retain, in some form, traces of the relationship between master and disciple, even master and slave.

In "Middle Passage" Hayden's revisionist strategy is calculated most of all to challenge Eliot's poetics by drawing upon historical sources alien to Eliot's social world. He originally meant to use this poem as the opening piece in a volume to be entitled "The Black Spear," in which he would attempt to "correct the misconceptions and to destroy some of the stereotypes and clichés which surrounded Negro history."[12] Though Hayden never finished "The Black Spear," an early manuscript version, without "Middle Passage," won the Hopwood Award for creative writing in 1942 when he was a graduate student at the University of Michigan, and many of the poems later appeared, extensively revised, in the fifth section of his *Selected Poems* of 1966.

Several critics have discussed the significance of "Middle Passage" to Hayden's career-long effort to incorporate revisionist history into his poetry. At the same time, however, most of the critics who have noticed the connections between Hayden's poetry and Eliot's have assumed that Hayden was, at least in matters of poetics, little more than a dutiful disciple, learning matters of technique from the master and in some cases imitating him directly.

In fact, the only readers who seem to have understood the kind and degree of confrontation involved in Hayden's reading of Eliot are those younger poets who have turned to Hayden's poetry as a resource for continuing innovation. For instance, Michael S. Harper has referred to "Middle Passage" as, in part, an "answer" to *The Waste Land*—that is, a poetic and historical challenge rather than a reverent echo. Harper recognizes that Hayden tried, through his knowledge of diverse poetic traditions, to move "beyond many of the experiments steeped in conscious modernism."[13] According to Harper, "Middle Passage" recalls "the schizoid past's brutalities" in order to confront Eliot's poetry with "a broad and pungent social reality." Along similar lines Jay Wright has written that "Middle Passage" alters Eliot's famous claim that a poet's fundamental responsibility is to language—and at the same time answers the criticism of many of Hayden's "younger contemporaries"—by demonstrating that "a language has a history and a relationship to other languages" that is more complex, and far more political, than Eliot ever imagined.[14] To these poets Hayden's view of Anglo-American modernism is much like that of Houston Baker in *Modernism and the Harlem Renaissance:* even though such iconic figures as Eliot and Joyce and Pound confronted the "changed condition of humankind" in the early twentieth century with "seriousness and sincerity," to use Baker's words, they also "mightily restricted the province of what constituted the tumbling of the towers, and they remained eternally self-conscious of their own pessimistic 'becomings.'"[15]

As he worked on the manuscript of "The Black Spear" in New York City during the summer vacation of 1941, Hayden immersed himself in the various histories, journals, notebooks, and ships' logs related to the slave trade in the Schomburg collection. Most significantly, at least for "Middle Passage," he also read the account of an 1839 slave mutiny on a schooner named the *Amistad* in Muriel Rukeyser's remarkable biography of the theoretical chemist Willard Gibbs. Gibbs's father, Josiah, was for most of his life a retiring professor of theology and sacred literature at Yale; in his more daring moments he was an amateur practitioner of the new German philology. But when a group of slaves who had seized control of the *Amistad* mysteriously appeared on Long Island, only to be thrown in jail, the elder Gibbs came to their aid, teaching them some English and finding translators for their legal defense among the African laborers in the ports of New York. He also seized the opportunity to begin a study of Mendi grammar.

Still, Hayden could not effectively use his research to answer *The Waste Land* until he had established a critical understanding of Eliot's poetics. At the end of the summer of 1941 he returned to Michigan, where he continued his research and enrolled in a course taught by W. H. Auden. Under the influence of Auden's teaching Hayden's understanding of modern poetry, and Eliot in particular, was caught in an intellectual landslide. Auden still spoke of Eliot as a close friend, and regarded him as the leading arbiter of current literary taste, but he was also in the midst of a prolonged, difficult moral questioning of his own earlier poetry. Most of all, in 1941 Auden was struggling to reconcile his early leftist politics with his recent reading of modern theology, especially the Christian realism of Reinhold Niebuhr—often deliberately obscuring his earlier positions but still subjecting his poetry to the questions of conscience raised by the rise of Nazism, the fall of the Spanish Republic, and the ongoing war in Europe. Auden's understanding of Christianity was significantly different from Eliot's increasingly millennial vision of a homogeneous Christian culture, and before long, most notably in *For the Time Being*, he would reject Eliot's peculiar fusion of social crisis and reactionary ideology.

Auden's efforts to remake himself as a Christian intellectual led him to challenge the very idea of a stable literary canon. A couple of years before Hayden met him, in his "New Year Letter," Auden had satirized the prevailing concept of literary influence, the idea that anyone who dares to write poetry must face "interrogation" by "the grand constructions of the dead." Dismissing this kind of purely literary anxiety, Auden had claimed for the poet a radical freedom to reshape the canon in order to serve immediate social needs, moral imperatives, and even personal whims:

> Each one, so liberal is the law,
> May choose whom he appears before,
> Pick any influential ghost
> From those whom he admires most.

By the time Hayden came along, Auden's method of teaching involved an apparently endless rearrangement of texts in constellations that were provisional, deliberately unconventional, and often downright playful. Another of Auden's students at Michigan, Donald Pearce, has described Auden's teaching at this time as driven by a "sense of verbal text as interdisciplinary conflux, or event . . . of convergent-and-explosive text."[16] Tossed into one of Auden's textual "confluxes," Eliot's works could never appear as sacred, or as secure, as they were so often made out to be: for instance, in the reading list for Auden's course in the fall of 1941, Eliot's essays and *Family Reunion* appear alongside more than two dozen other books, including Kierkegaard's *Fear and Trembling,* Nietszche's *The Case of Wagner,* and Rimbaud's *Season in Hell.*

As eccentric as they must have seemed to many of his poor students, Auden's exercises in textual convergence were motivated by a developing sense of moral purpose. Mostly through his reading of Niebuhr, Kierkegaard, and Charles Williams, Auden had recently come to believe that the individual is far more capable of moral action than any larger social group can ever be. Primarily for this reason, the undermining and reconstruction of an authorized tradition was more than just the individual poet's prerogative. At the very least it was a moral responsibility. At best it could be a religious vocation.

Before long, all of these revisionary forces—the Negro history, the understanding of tradition as an array of cultural fragments provisionally constructed by an individual writer, the commitment to canon reconstruction as a moral imperative—would provide Hayden with his own means of answering *The Waste Land.*

Though "Middle Passage" was not finished in time for the Hopwood contest, "The Black Spear" manuscript did include a preliminary response to Eliot. This poem is far less impressive than "Middle Passage," but it does suggest just how quickly and systematically Hayden was developing his own revisionary poetics. "Schizophrenia" is a superficially Eliotic poem in two voices, each of which speaks a refrain with variations. The first voice recalls *The Waste Land*'s "heap of broken images" and its nearly exhausted anguish in the face of cultural and spiritual disintegration:

> We were trying to harvest the fragments
> of our scattered spirits,
> but it was the blitzkrieg's year,
> and the bombs were falling.

"The blitzkrieg's year" is only the most obvious among many symptoms of a culture so fragmented, so far beyond any hope of repair, that it seems to have come to the end of its history. The war continues, somehow, beyond human agency; yet, at the same time, it is all too ordinary, something like the weather. "Schizophrenia"'s second voice supplies the predictable metaphoric connection between this cultural catastrophe and personal insanity. For this second voice the falling bombs are little more than background noise for a series of private nightmares: "I saw a man in a cracked gold mirror / and a man in surrealist streets"; "I saw a pale girl, savage of eye, / fondling a headless doll"; and so on. Like a conspicuously modernist Parsifal, he has set out on a quest of some significance, apparently, but he is unable to figure out where he should go or what he should do: "One of these tasks is mine, / and the other is mine, / but which is mine they won't tell me." Needless to say, it is never clear just who "they" might be, these unhelpful shades. But that hardly seems to matter either, since, as it turns out, within a few lines both of the poem's speakers discover that they are locked up "in padded cells."

Poetically, the most basic problem with "Schizophrenia" is that its two voices sound far too much alike to answer each other—let alone anyone else—in any very meaningful way. Even if they are meant to be spoken by the same person, they could hardly support any respectable diagnosis of schizophrenia—perhaps clinical depression or echolalia or some such thing, but not schizophrenia. And, more important, these voices seem to be far too distant from recognizable events for "the blitzkrieg's year" to have any historical resonance, even in a time of war. Both voices echo Eliot's diction, syntax, rhythms, and repetitive phrasing, almost to the point of parody but never to any discernible purpose.

Still, at this early point in Hayden's career I think this little experiment proved to be very valuable: he learned that he could not answer Eliotic despair, in any very useful way, with his own rendition of Eliotic despair. By doing Eliot in two very similar voices—voices that just about any reader of poetry in the 1940s would find familiar—he discovered that all this preoccupation with the "tumbling towers" of some universalized Western culture, the "split shards / of the major illusion," could be patently self-indulgent. In "Schizophrenia" the speakers' vaguely nostalgic longing to recover the "shattered spirit" of the past only hides their mutual impulse to turn the harshest realities of the ongoing war, the falling bombs, into an analogue for some vaguely personal anxiety, just as *The Waste Land*'s compulsive allusions and nervous voices tend to obscure the social conditions of post–World War I London.

"Middle Passage"

For all "Schizophrenia"'s shortcomings—Hayden would never include it in any of his published collections—the poem's halfhearted experiment in Eliotic voices soon developed into a more pointed and far more powerful response. In "Middle Passage" Hayden once again explored the theme of cultural "schizophrenia" but this time within the historical context provided by his research on the slave trade. This historical material gave him the means by which he could abandon the kind of psychological posturing—the inevitable blending of dreams and consciousness, self and other, world war and private neurosis—Eliot's poetry had helped make fashionable.

"Middle Passage"'s most significant element of "social reality," as Harper would put it, was provided primarily by Rukeyser's account of the strange series of events set in motion by the *Amistad* mutiny. When the mutiny occurred, the *Amistad* held fifty-three Africans who had until recently been part of a much larger group, probably captured in one of the local wars fought, in those days, primarily for the acquisition of slaves. They had already been dealt by traders in Sierra Leone, sent under a Portuguese flag to the thriving market in Havana, bought by two Spaniards named Ruiz and Montez, placed in irons, and shipped off once again, this time to Guanaja, the main port of Principe. Their capture and transportation violated the decree of Spain of 1817—and, for that matter, "all the treaties then in existence" among European countries and the United States.[17]

Until the fourth night after the *Amistad*'s departure from Havana, their crossing was much like countless others on the Middle Passage. Hayden makes this point by constructing the poem's main narrative so that it emerges in the midst of fragments drawn from assorted accounts of earlier journeys. In this way he is able to tell the story of the *Amistad* against a background of sickness, madness, fire, rape, and other cruelties:

> "Deponeth further sayeth *The Bella J*
> left the Guinea Coast
> with cargo of five hundred blacks and odd
> for the barracoons of Florida:
>
> "That there was hardly room 'tween-decks for half
> the sweltering cattle stowed spoon-fashion there;
> that some went mad of thirst and tore their flesh
> and sucked the blood:
>
> "That Crew and Captain lusted with the comeliest
> of the savage girls kept naked in the cabins.

On that fourth night, however, the *Amistad*'s journey took an unusual turn. After just about all of the ship's crew had gone to sleep, having spent much of the day battling a storm, the slaves managed to get hold of machetes being sent along to cut sugar cane in the New World. Led by a man named Cinquez, they quickly seized control of the ship, killing the captain and the cook, who had threatened them throughout their journey. Then, because they believed they would need experienced sailors to navigate back home, they decided to spare the lives of Montez, Ruiz, and a cabin boy who had helped them as a translator.

This decision backfired. For sixty-three days Montez and Ruiz managed to delay their return, guiding the ship east by day and then turning northwest by night when they knew their captors would be unable to judge their direction. Zigzagging across the Atlantic in this way, the *Amistad* soon became the subject of local legend, with reports in the American press of a "phantom ship" following a route so incomprehensible that it must be driven by ghosts. When the *Amistad* finally landed at Montauk, Long Island, the Africans were thrown in the county jail. Accordingly, in "Middle Passage" it is Montez and Ruiz, suddenly set free, who tell this part of the story:

> It sickens me
> to think of what I saw, of how these apes
> threw overboard the butchered bodies of
> our men, true Christians all, like so much jetsam.
> Enough, enough. The rest is quickly told:
> Cinquez was forced to spare the two of us
> you see to steer the ship to Africa,
> and we like phantoms doomed to rove the sea
> voyaged east by day and west by night,
> deceiving them, hoping for rescue,
> prisoners on our own vessel, till
> at length we drifted to the shores of this
> your land, America, where we were freed
> from our unspeakable misery.

The story of the *Amistad* provided Hayden with a narrative framework within which he could include accounts of cruelty, from various sources, that make *The Waste Land*'s sense of "horror" seem timid and self-indulgent. But what would turn out to be just as important—at least for Hayden's development as a poet—was Rukeyser's less dramatic account of the series of trials and political maneuvers that began once the *Amistad* had landed on Montauk. This portion of the Gibbs biography, along with courtroom testimony by Montez and Ruiz published a hundred years earlier in John Barber's *A History of the Amistad Captives*, provided Hayden with a vision of a less personal, more historically grounded kind of schizophrenia: the assorted moral duplicities in mainstream American culture that sustained the slave trade. In these accounts he discovered a labyrinth of hypocrisy and rationalization so intricate that, to account for it with any degree of accuracy, he needed to master a more complex and ironic interplay of contending voices.

When the *Amistad* slaves landed on Long Island, they were surprised to discover that their arrival in a "free state" did not mean they would be set free. Of course, they "claimed freedom, charging

Ruiz and Montez with assault, battery, and false imprisonment" (Rukeyser 36–37). Of course, for their part Montez and Ruiz claimed possession of the *Amistad* and its passengers.

Strangely, though, they were not the only ones to make such a claim—not by a long shot. Led by a Captain Green, who lived down the road, a group of Long Islanders also "claimed salvage on the vessel, the cargo, and the slaves," on the grounds that they had been the first to speak to Cinquez and his men when they had come ashore looking for water. Still another claim was made by a certain Lieutenant Gedney who, having seen the *Amistad* approaching Montauk, thinking it must have been a pirate ship and hoping for an opportunity to revive his languishing career, had ordered his own crew to follow. Meanwhile, the Spanish minister, with the support of the pro-slavery press in the United States, claimed the ship and its "cargo" for Spain, arguing that the trials should be held in Cuba since "a 'trial and execution' in Connecticut was not as good." Not to be outdone in a matter of patriotic duty, the local district attorney "claimed that the Africans should be held, according to the 1819 Act, subject to the pleasure of the President." Secretary of State John Forsyth and Attorney General Felix Grundy intervened, trying to keep the proceedings within federal jurisdiction so they might be able to turn the slaves and cargo over to "persons designated" by the Spanish minister. Even President Van Buren considered getting involved—he too was inclined to return the ship and the slaves to Spain—until he realized that he lacked an extradition treaty.

All things considered, it is hardly surprising that, in Hayden's account, Montez and Ruiz are perplexed. Most of all, they have trouble understanding how some Americans—especially the members of the antislavery movement who are sponsoring the Africans' defense—fail to recognize their right to what they consider their own property. When Hayden gives them a chance to speak for themselves, they focus their astonishment primarily on John Quincy Adams, who has taken up the cause of the *Amistad* slaves and will eventually argue for their freedom in their final appeal before the Supreme Court. When the events of the poem take place, Adams is seventy-three years old and returning to court after a thirty-two-year hiatus. Even by his own account, he is not in very good shape, with "a shaking hand, a darkening eye, a drowsy brain, and with all of my faculties dropping from me one by one, as the teeth are dropping from my head." To the Spanish slavers he seems to have been transported from the Roman Empire, rhetorically extravagant and oblivious to the practical demands of their very modern business:

> We find it paradoxical indeed
> that you whose wealth, whose tree of liberty
> are rooted in the labor of your slaves
> should suffer the august John Quincy Adams
> to speak with so much passion of the right
> of chattel slaves to kill their lawful masters
> and with his Roman rhetoric weave a hero's
> garland for Cinquez. I tell you that
> we are determined to return to Cuba
> with our slaves and there see justice done. Cinquez—
> or let us say "the Prince"—Cinquez shall die.

Ironically, it is with this slaver's speech that "Middle Passage" enters a maze of moral contradictions: between the law of New York and the broader political interests of the federal government; between the "Christian" slave traders, whose legacy of violence and lust has been documented throughout the poem, and the so-called apes who have spared their lives; between the slaves' perception of the United States, during the journey, as "mirage and myth" and these strangely "civilized" events that occur once the ship reaches the "actual shore"; between the talk of liberty in the free states and the "roots" of this liberty in slave labor; between the familiar language of Montez and Ruiz, confident in its sense of a culture shared with educated Americans, and the increasing isolation of the poem's main narrative voice, as it traces the history of "dark ships" that move like "Shuttles in the rocking loom of history."

Within this narrative framework Hayden uses his historical sources to turn Eliot's own poetics against his restricted vision of cultural decline. In "Middle Passage" Hayden makes use of *The Waste Land*'s abrupt shifts between multiple voices, its cryptic quotations, its central symbols of fire and water, its references to the sea as the site of transformation, and its mythical hero who must journey through the land of the dead in order to restore a vital society. He even includes a bitter variation on Eliot's variations on Shakespeare. The two passages from *The Tempest* used by Eliot—Ariel's song, "Full fathom five thy father lies," and Ferdinand's lament for his missing father—are displaced from Prospero's magic island, compressed, and relocated in the hold of a slave ship:

> *Deep in the festering hold thy father lies,*
> *the corpse of mercy rots with him,*
> *rats eat love's rotten gelid eyes.*

By establishing this doubly ironic relationship between his poem, *The Waste Land,* and the Shakespearean original, Hayden undermines the cultural nostalgia that Eliot characteristically imposes upon such passages: the search among the ruins for a once-coherent civilization, the pained intimations of moral decline, the longing almost beyond hope for some reconstruction of the fragmented past that might bring spiritual redemption. To put it another way, in Hayden's allusions the passages from earlier texts do not appear as a bulwark against the ruinous forces of modernity; they, too, have been transformed so that they carry the indelible marks of history in their imagery and even in their music. After "Middle Passage"'s accounts of, among other things, ophthalamia, starvation, death by fire, and live people fed to sharks, *The Waste Land's* method of allusion seems painfully literary.

That is the most important difference between "Middle Passage" and "Schizophrenia." In "Middle Passage" Hayden appropriates Eliot's poetics with this distinct purpose—and, in doing so, he develops a morally engaged, pragmatic poetics that would eventually align his work with the posttraditional poetry of a younger generation. Most fundamentally, his answer to *The Waste Land* demonstrates just how Eliot's poem struggles toward moral condemnation, without being able to establish any convincing or consistent moral ground. In this way Hayden is able to exploit a radical philosophical uncertainty that is one of the pervasive features of Eliot's poetry but is typically obscured by Eliot's later pronouncements on culture and religion. At the center of *The Waste Land's* moral universe, as Eliot and others have noted, is the vision of Tiresias, old and blind, "throbbing between two lives." According to Eliot's famous notes, Tiresias is "the most important personage in the poem, uniting all the rest":

> I Tiresias, old man with wrinkled dugs
> Perceived the scene, and foretold the rest—
> I too awaited the expected guest.
> He, the young man carbuncular, arrives,
> A small house agent's clerk, with one bold stare,
> One of the low on whom assurance sits
> As a silk hat on a Bradford millionaire.

Of course, Tiresias' vision turns out to be the most famous—and discouraging—seduction in twentieth-century poetry:

> Flushed and decided, he assaults at once;
> Exploring hands encounter no defence;
> His vanity requires no response,
> And makes a welcome of indifference.
> (And I Tiresias have foresuffered all
> Enacted on this same divan or bed;
> I who have sat by Thebes below the wall
> And walked among the lowest of the dead.)

With its shifts between vatic proclamation and mock-heroic deflation, this passage brings *The Waste Land's* method of allusion close to that of English neoclassical satire, with its characteristic manner of exposing contemporary pretensions by holding them up to the standards of an idealized past that is deceptively made to seem available by the imitation of conventional poetic form. But, as Ezra Pound understood, I think, in some of his revisions of Eliot's typescript, such a method is fundamentally irreconcilable with either the poem's sense of irreparable fragmentation or its striving to give voice to distinctly modern anxieties. On the other hand, without the ironies generated by its classical and neoclassical allusions, this passage would suggest that Eliot's vision of Western civilization's impending doom must somehow wrench its moral authority from a voyeuristic commentary on an uninspired sexual fling—as if sexual boredom were the end of the world.

In "Middle Passage" Hayden places a reply to Tiresias' vision at his poem's center, both spatially and thematically. For Hayden the heart of darkness resides in the speech of an anonymous slave trader who, in the course of twenty prosperous years, has come to view his work, from its basic sources to its net profits, as an ordinary business. Loosely based on Theodore Canot's account of his own career in his *Adventures of an African Slaver,* it is a passage that, I imagine, must have been noticed by the judges at the Senegal conference, given their tendency to view both literature and racism in the context of colonialism:

> Aye, lad, and I have seen those factories,
> Gambia, Rio Pongo, Calabar;
> have watched the artful mongos baiting traps
> of war wherein the victor and the vanquished

Were caught as prizes for our barracoons.
Have seen the nigger kings whose vanity
and greed turned wild black hides of Fellatah,
Mandingo, Ibo, Kru to gold for us.

And there was one—King Anthracite we named him—
fetish face beneath French parasols
of brass and orange velvet, impudent mouth
whose cups were carven skulls of enemies:

He'd honor us with drum and feast and conjo
and palm-oil-glistening wenches deft in love,
and for tin crowns that shone with paste,
red calico and German-silver trinkets

Would have the drums talk war and send
his warriors to burn the sleeping villages
and kill the sick and old and lead the young
in coffles to our factories.

By placing this speech at the center of "Middle Passage," Hayden
also develops the strategy of moral implication he uses when Mon-
tez and Ruiz contrast Adams's rhetoric to the economic realities of
slavery in America.[18] By including this particular slaver's voice, he is
able to widen his net of implication: the speech is effective precisely
because it seems so familiar, the words of a man who has simply
been carried along in a job that leads him to everyone from local
rulers like "King Anthracite" to "factory" workers at the barracoons
to lawyers in New York.

Passages like this one suggest that Hayden's rejection of Black
Cultural Nationalism, almost twenty-five years later, was primarily
determined by the already formidable achievement of his own po-
etry. He would never be a "Negro poet" if that meant—as it cer-
tainly seemed to mean to his audience at the Fisk conference—that
he could not mimic for his own purposes the voices of lynchers
and common slavers. He would never be a Negro poet if that
meant he could not use such impersonations to implicate, among
many others, the African kings whose vanity and greed were so
necessary to the slave trade, especially in its early years when white
men rarely entered Africa's interior. And he would never be a
Negro poet if that meant he could not give full voice to historical
characters like Montez and Ruiz in order to account, accurately

and with sufficient moral complexity, for the contending political and social forces at work when the *Amistad* captives finally landed in New York.

But, even more fundamentally, in his work of the early 1940s Hayden sets out to restore to poetry the sense of contingency by which a particular historical moment—say, for instance, a mutiny aboard a Spanish slave ship—appears vividly uncertain and, for that reason, at that moment, human action is potentially prophetic. The fragmentary narrative in the final lines of *The Waste Land* depends, more than any other passage of the poem, upon the myth of Parsifal, in various incarnations, searching for the Chapel Perilous in his quest to restore, and reconnect, the natural and social orders. *The Waste Land's* other more or less religious allusions—most notably, the vision of the disciples on the road to Emmaus and the ritualistic ending of the Upanishads—are more than anything else variations on this theme. This overarching mythic structure and the poem's dominant narrative voice imply that these apparent fragments are ultimately unified in the refuge of a collective unconscious—or some such half-concealed repository of cultural memory and meaning—where they dwell, in their more complete forms, beyond the changes and challenges of history. In this way Eliot strains poetic metaphysics just about, but not quite, to the point of breaking. Or, to put it another way, in *The Waste Land* Eliot stops just on the verge of the posttraditional.

On the other hand, by rescuing Cinquez from obscurity—that is, by returning him, through poetry, to living history—Hayden asserts the possibility that an unlikely individual, even after one of the most convoluted journeys through the Middle Passage and the American courts, can act in a manner that "transfigures many lives." In the end, despite the eloquence of Montez and Ruiz—and the many others who claimed to own him—Cinquez did not die for his part in the mutiny. Somehow, Adams managed to revive his long-neglected skills as a litigator, and the Supreme Court ultimately ruled that Cinquez should be released to the missionary society for transportation back to Sierra Leone—along with those other slaves who had managed to survive their journey, imprisonment, and legal odyssey. By ending "Middle Passage" with a poetic account of Cinquez's survival, Hayden transforms *The Waste Land's* theme of transformation. He replaces "mirage and myth" with historical revision and continuance. Even more important, in contrast to Eliot's nostalgia for a stable tradition, supported by an equally stable social order, Hayden ends with a prophetic voice capable of resurrecting the suppressed past in, and beyond, the present:

> The deep immortal human wish,
> the timeless will:
>
> Cinquez its deathless primaveral image,
> life that transfigures many lives.
>
> Voyage through death
> to life upon these shores.

And, so, a "deep immortal human wish" finds expression in the poetic image—but what is most important is that the poem does not end there. The couplet at the center of this concluding passage balances two visions of Cinquez: for an instant he is equally a figure within the poem and an individual living in a historical moment. But the sequencing of the couplet's two lines, like the larger movement of this passage, suggests that the poetic image aspires to the status of an individual life, which can transfigure many other lives through prophetic action. The poem and the historical life invest each other with meaning, in a common world, for "life upon these shores."

Hayden and the Contemporary African-American Poetic Sequence

Of all the consequences of the literary politics of April 1966, probably the strangest is that Hayden's poetry—with its radical contingency, historical detail, moral complexity, and formal experimentation—would be so persistently ignored or undervalued by scholars and critics. This neglect can be interpreted within a number of contexts: for instance, the conflict between the cultural politics of New Criticism, in the years of its greatest domination in elite universities, and the Black Arts Movement, as it shaped one generation's discussion of African-American poetry; or the recent ascendancy of African-American novelists like Alice Walker and Toni Morrison; or the declining status of contemporary poetry within the academy over the past forty years or so, with the tendency to relegate poetry to creative writing programs; or the increasing influence of theories that seem to be more readily proved by narrative fiction and, in some cases, popular culture.

But none of these contexts really does much to lessen the irony, or the larger significance, of Hayden's situation. Just as critical approaches more sympathetic to history and issues of race have gained academic acceptance and influence, African-American poets have produced a body of work that is, I think, unprecedented in the degree to which it adapts innovative poetics to address historical and racial issues. Yet the criticism has remained virtually oblivious to the poetry. Hayden himself anticipated this problem when he said, in one way or another, any number of times, that discussions of "race and poetry" always seem to turn into discussions of "race."

So, for the most part it has been left to a younger generation of African-American poets to claim and continue Hayden's legacy. These poets have generally begun their careers with a clear recognition of the limitations of both Black Cultural Nationalism, with its tendency toward the kind of rigid political proscription that led to Tolson's denunciation of Hayden, and New Critical aestheticism, with its tendency to ignore race altogether and treat Hayden as a kind of minor formalist. At the same time, these poets have recovered some of the more useful affinities between African-American poetry and international negritude that were merely suggested by the conference in Dakar.

Most of all, these more recent poets have drawn from the approach to historical poetry that Hayden began to develop in "Middle Passage." By demonstrating that literary tradition—like history itself, as it is actually being lived—is radically contingent, Hayden made it easier for younger poets to view any given tradition as provisional, even improvisational. To put it in the more familiar terms of literary history, these poets have extended many of the poetic experiments of modernism while historicizing the modernists' sense of historical crisis—that is, the peculiar dread of impending chaos and social disruption, the barbarians-at-the-gates mentality, that so often characterizes the later canon formations of Yeats, Eliot, and Pound.

For instance, in his sequence "Debridement" Michael S. Harper extends Hayden's experiments in multiple voices and historical disjunctions. Using a prosody derived in part from jazz, "Debridement" comments upon a more recent but equally "schizoid" episode of the recent past: the Vietnam War, in which the poem's main character inadvertently wins a Medal of Honor, and the years immediately following, in which he returns to the projects, only to be berated by "militants" then shot and killed by a white store manager who is frightened to see "a car filled with blacks" parked in his neighborhood.[19] Shifting, often with the syncopation of a Charlie Parker solo, between Cambodia, the Projects, and the hospital where its main character dies, "Debridement" depends upon a sense of history in which the past remains oddly alive in the present and in which it seems that poetry—in particular, a distinctly posttraditional poetry—can provide the resources necessary to bring this past to judgment in a manner that serves the needs of the present.

Hayden's legacy also endures in the poetic sequences of Brenda Marie Osbey, with their multiple voices, disjunctive narratives, and heterogeneous cultural traditions. In works like "Ceremony for Minneconjoux," *In These Houses,* and most of all the book-length narrative poem *Desperate Circumstances, Dangerous Women,* Osbey's féfé women recreate a local history of New Orleans' Tremé district, in heterogeneous voices rich with the rhythms of island songs, okono drums, hoodoo chants, and "root ends / against tamborines."[20] Fittingly, Osbey begins the final sequence of *In These Houses* with a tribute to Hayden, a variation on his poem "O Daedalus, Fly Away Home." In this poem Hayden adopts a popular legend from Georgia Sea Island: "It was believed there were certain Africans who, after being brought here as slaves, flew back to Africa. They had magic power and, as I say in the poem, they could just spread their arms and fly away."[21] Drawing from the personal reminiscences of former slaves, Hayden recounts these legends in a kind of juba, accompanied by "coonskin drum and jubilee banjo." Osbey's tribute recalls not only Hayden's "Daedelus" but also the end of "Middle Passage":

> amid all the laughter
> i manage to fly away home
> have yet to perish
> in the sea.[22]

In her poetry, as in Hayden's, legend functions as both local history and living literature. A "tradition" of this kind is not something preserved by the purifiers of language against the corrupting influences of common culture—whether within the boundaries established by the range of allusion and other restrictive gestures of modernist poetics or within the institutional practices of the academy. A tradition of this kind is woven by the individual poet from the strands of assorted heritages still alive within her community. It still serves immediate purposes. It is a means of survival.

It seems to me that Hayden's legacy is apparent in similar ways in Melvin Dixon's "Tour Guide: *La Maison des Esclaves,*" Yusef Komunyakaa's "Blues Chant Hoodoo Revival," Elizabeth Alexander's "The Venus Hottentot," and, perhaps most significantly, Jay Wright's *Dimensions of History* and *The Double Invention of Komo.* One way of looking at these works would be to say that they are part of one of the richest—and least appreciated—traditions in modern American literature, a tradition that undoubtedly includes Hayden as a shaping and presiding presence. It is also certainly true that all of these works draw, in one way or another, from what Robert Stepto has called, in a discussion of Wright's poetry, "the tangle of black traditions binding the Americas to West Africa."

But in remarkable ways all of these works point to a more fundamental lesson that should be drawn from the strange events of April 1966, from Hayden's calculated response to Eliot's poetics—and from the kind of reconsideration of Hayden's career that I am advocating. Terms like *tradition* and *influence* can only be applied to this poetry in a manner that is self-conscious and ironic, if at all. This poetry is so highly attuned to historical, social, cultural, and moral disjunctions that it never pretends to resolve, through direct appropriation of an established poetic convention, any injustice or hypocrisy that remains unresolved in the society at large. Instead, this poetry uses improvisation and linguistic heterogeneity as a means of constantly redescribing, and cultivating, human complexity and dignity.

So, I think it would be more accurate and more useful to say that this poetry—which might be called, rather loosely, the contemporary African-American poetic sequence—builds on Hayden's legacy by constantly renegotiating relationships between contending traditions and contending social orders. Each of these poets reconstructs, at will, a heritage that is at once personal and historically grounded, continuous and progressively hybrid, in order to serve immediate social need.

To put it another way, for more than fifty years now Hayden's work has been one of the most persistent forces moving poetry in the direction of the posttraditional.

303

NOTES

1. Janet G.Vaillant, *Black, French and African: A Life of Léopold Sédar Senghor* (Cambridge: Harvard University Press, 1990), 323. Clearly, the significance of the festival's location was not lost on its organizers or its participants. The first festival had been held in 1956 at the Sorbonne—as Vaillant notes, "the center of French scholarship"—and the second in 1959 in Rome, "The Capital of Christian Europe."

2. Rosey Pool, a member of the "Grand Jury" for Hayden's Grand Prix and for many years the leading advocate of his poetry, proclaimed that "at Dakar the words 'Negro' and 'Negritude,' Negro-ness, took on new meaning and dignity." She also used the example of Hayden to invest "negritude," in particular, with unusually extended, personal, and religious overtones: "In light half-nightmare and half-vision he speaks of the face of Baha'u'llah. prophet of the Bahá'í faith, in whose eyes Hayden sees the suffering of the men and women who died at Dachau and Buchenwald for their specific *Negritude."* Rosey Pool, "Robert Hayden: Poet Laureate," *Negro Digest* 15 (June 1966): 39–43. In his keynote address at the Fisk conference Saunders Redding was more upbeat: he drew loud applause by referring to negritude as a "relatively inexplicable mystique." See David Llorens, "Writers Converge at Fisk University," *Negro Digest* 15 (June 1966): 55.

3. See Llorens, "Writers Converge," 62–63. More than a decade later, in his 1978 address at the Library of Congress, Hayden would respond to this particular comment. At one point in a dialogue between "the Poet" and "the Inquisitor" (a figure "more like Chekhov's Black Monk than anything else"), the Poet rebukes his adversary with the phrase, "As if you give a tinker's damn about poetry." Robert Hayden, *Collected Prose,* ed. Frederick Glaysher (Ann Arbor: University of Michigan Press, 1984), 4, 15.

4. The three book-length studies of Hayden, each of which begins with a biographical overview and then proceeds to critical analysis of his poetry, are typical in this regard, though they vary in their estimation of the degree to which the events of 1966 would ultimately shape Hayden's career. Fred M. Fetrow accurately describes the changes in Hayden's critical reception following the International Prize and the Fisk Conference. Pontheolla Williams uses Hayden's response to the conference—his rejection of Black Nationalism and his continued determination not to be bound by any kind of "Black Aesthetic"—as the central message of her "Biographical Sketch" and as the recurrent theme of her critical analysis. John Hatcher entitles his chapter on Hayden's life in the 1960s "The Crucial Years" and begins the critical portion of his book with an attempt to focus Hayden's career by accounting for his response to "The Problem of a 'Black Aesthetic.'"

5. The notable exception is Robert Stepto, who considers Hayden, Michael S. Harper, and Jay Wright as three poets who develop "post-modernist expressions" anticipated by the ending of Ralph Ellison's *Invisible Man.* Robert B. Stepto, "After Modernism, After Hibernation: Michael S. Harper, Robert Hayden, and Jay Wright," in *Chant of Saints,* ed. Michael

S. Harper and Robert B. Stepto (Urbana: University of Illinois Press, 1979), 471. Also, in his introduction to the *Selected Poems of Jay Wright* Stepto suggests that "from the view of literary history" Hayden's "Middle Passage" might be "the poem behind Wright's art," since it anticipates Wright's attention to "the tangle of black traditions binding the Americas to West Africa."

6. D. H. Melhem, *Gwendolyn Brooks: Poetry and the Heroic Voice* (Lexington: University Press of Kentucky, 1987), 154.

7. A general idea of the academic consensus on the dimensions of négritude, at about the time of the Dakar conference, is provided by Lilyan Kesteloot's rather conservative survey, described in chapters 21 and 22 of her book *Black Writers in French: A Literary History of Négritude,* trans. Ellen Conroy Kennedy (Philadelphia: Temple University Press, 1974).

8. William Meredith, foreword to Hayden, *Collected Prose,* vi.

9. Hayden, *Collected Prose,* 45–49.

10. Ibid, 11.

11. Richard Rorty, *Contingency, Irony, Solidarity* (New York: Cambridge University Press, 1989), 105.

12. Hayden, *Collected Prose,* 162.

13. Michael S. Harper, "Remembering Robert Hayden," *Michigan Quarterly Review* 21, no. 1 (1982): 184.

14. Jay Wright, "Desire's Design, Vision's Resonance: Black Poetry's Ritual and Historical Voice," *Callaloo* 10, no. 1 (1987): 18.

15. Houston Baker, *Modernism in the Harlem Renaissance* (Chicago: University of Chicago Press, 1987), 4.

16. Donald Pearce, "Fortunate Fall: W. H. Auden at Michigan," in *W. H. Auden: The Far Interior,* ed. Alan Bold (Totowa, N.J.: Barnes and Noble, 1985), 157.

17. Muriel Rukeyser, *Willard Gibbs: American Genius* (New York: Doubleday, 1942), 18.

18. Hayden uses a similar strategy in "Night, Death, Mississippi," in which a later episode in American racism is described through the voice of one of its villains—an old man who, as his son is out taking part in a lynching, looks back with a nearly sexual excitement to the times when he too could join in the torture and killing.

19. Michael S. Harper, *Images of Kin: New and Selected Poems* (Urbana: University of Illinois, 1977), 110.

20. Brenda Marie Osbey, *Ceremony for Minneconjoux* (Lexington: Callaloo, 1983), 6.

21. Hayden, *Collected Prose,* 174.

22. Brenda Marie Osbey, *In These Houses* (Middletown, Conn.: Wesleyan University Press, 1988), 33.

VERA M. KUTZINSKI

Changing Permanences:
Historical and Literary Revisionism
in Robert Hayden's "Middle Passage"

> And if I dared
> the agonies
> of metamorphosis,
> would I not find
> you altered then?
> —ROBERT HAYDEN, "THE TATTOOED MAN"

In his poem "[American Journal]" Robert Hayden, posing as an alien observer in a culture of "charming savages" and "enlightened primitives," describes America as

> an organism that changes even as i
> examine it   fact and fantasy never twice
> the same   so many variables.

The posture Hayden adopts in this poem seems curious until we remember that the figure of the mysterious stranger appears in his poetry with some regularity. This is true particularly of *American Journal*, which is quite a remarkable collection of "alien" presences flaunting their "gaudy otherness" like the gypsies at the end of "Elegies for Paradise Valley." What Phillis Wheatley, John Brown, Paul Laurence Dunbar, and Paul Robeson share with the Rag Man, the Prisoners, the Tattooed Man, Madam Artelia, Jamaican Cynthia, and other characters in Hayden's "journal" is that they are all more or less grotesque outsiders in a society unable (or unwilling?) to comprehend the nature of their difference. As Hayden astutely puts it in "The Tattooed Man":

From *Callaloo* 9, no. 1 (Winter 1986): 171–83. © Copyright Charles H. Rowell. Reprinted by permission of the Johns Hopkins University Press

Hundreds have paid
to gawk at me—
grotesque outsider whose
unnaturalness
assures them they
are natural, they indeed
belong.

These lines recall yet another of Hayden's aliens: the winged old man ("actual angel? carny freak?") of "For a Young Artist." The list could easily be extended to include a host of historical and fictional characters from *Angle of Ascent*—for example, Nat Turner, Malcolm X, Cinquez, Harriet Tubman, and Frederick Douglass, as well as the "stranger" in "Theme and Variation," who anticipates the words of the alien chronicler in "[American Journal]":

all things alter even as I behold,
all things alter, the stranger said.

Alter, become a something more,
a something less. Are the reveling shadows
of a changing permanence. Are, are not
and same and other, the stranger said.

Both the stranger and the alien observer not only speak for Hayden; even more important, they embody in their own peculiar strangeness the poetic posture Hayden assumes both before history as well as before and within language, that is, the perspective, or *angle,* of perception he brings to bear on his historical and cultural identity and on the language that shapes and textures that identity.

Much has been written about Hayden's fascination with history, and Afro-American history in particular, while relatively little has been said about the links between his historical and his literary revisionism. Always preoccupied with "the sly transience of things," Hayden becomes a chronicler of change, of transformations, of metamorphoses. Writing poetry, for him, is what William Carlos Williams has called "an agony of self-realization,"[1] but the self to be realized in language is so multifaceted that it seems too reductive to speak of it as a single self. When Hayden writes, in "Names," "You don't exist—at least / not legally, the lawyer said," we get a glimpse, not only at the personal anguish caused the poet by the discovery that "Robert Hayden" was not his "real" name but of the absence of a conventional self and of the tenuous presence of a "ghost, double, alter ego" in the blank space marked by the dash. As at the end of the penultimate stanza in "For a Young Artist," this incisive dash is a locus of transformation, the place where "self" metamorphoses into "other." That otherness is something that eludes, as in the story on which "For a Young Artist" is based, "legal" definitions.[2] *Legal,* in this context, signifies constraints imposed upon the poet in the form of social, cultural, or literary conventions, which Hayden appropriately figures as a "barbedwire pen" and a "gilt and scarlet cage" in "For a Young Artist" and "The Tattooed Man," respectively. These conventions, or "laws," are what delimit Hayden's own identity, on the one hand, by imposing on him the name of Asa Bundy Sheffey, and, on the other hand, by labeling him a "black poet." Both, to him, are equally pernicious for very similar reasons: they assign to him fixed institutional identities unable to contain Robert Hayden the poet. These names, or labels, are representative of the legalistic definitions of self Hayden seeks to undo, of the kinds of societal and cultural strictures he struggles to efface in order to inscribe his "other" self or selves in the form of that "ghost," or "double," that defies and eludes the lawyer. For Hayden identity, or selfhood, is a matter of history and of historicity, that is, of change, not of institutional affiliations. He used to say to himself that he was not a "joiner." The implications of that pronouncement for his poetics are of unsuspected complexity.

"Alien, at home—as always / everywhere," Hayden proclaims in "Kodachromes of the Island," and he sets out to explore the dimensions of his otherness. Frequently viewing himself from the double perspective of both native and stranger, which suggests a kind of Du Boisian "double consciousness," he assumes the posture not of a conventional historian chronicling Afro-American history but of a modem anthropologist studying the language and the myths of an unfamiliar culture, in this case North America:

> disguise myself in order to study them unobserved
> adapting their varied pigmentations   white black
> red brown yellow

This posture accounts, at least in part, for Hayden's unrelenting criticism of ethnocentric definitions of poetry despite vehement attacks by Melvin Tolson and proponents of the "Black Aesthetic." Hayden insists on defining poetry as "the art of saying the impossible"[3]—that is, as the art of exercising a freedom of self-definition that effectively penetrates the biases responsible for cultural and intellectual ghettoization. Ultimately, his allegedly apolitical attitude toward poetry emerges not as a weakness but as a strength: rather than making overt political statements and turning his poetry into propaganda, Hayden, in the guise of an inoffensive observer, steadily undermines the ideological foundations of American society to clear a space in which to articulate his own difference. His poetic language does not simply protest or praise; it *transfigures* and, in the process, establishes its own form of self-knowledge.

Hayden's best poems are preoccupied with processes of displacement, both in historical and in literary terms. For example, he displaces traditional concepts of order (unity) and of time (linearity) as they manifest themselves in the form of certain literary and historical (or historiographical) conventions. We may call Hayden's poetry a consistent "experiment in disorder" (to borrow a phrase from Octavio Paz)[4] or incoherence, as long as we do not associate incoherence with unintelligibility. Hayden's incoherence is a strategy to free language from static, fixed meanings. "Middle Passage" is a fine example of this strategy, which, as we shall see, effectively links historical with literary revisionism.

The poem's title already refers to a very specific historical process of geographical, social, and cultural dislocation: the Middle Passage. This context is rendered more concrete by references to the transatlantic slave trade throughout the poem, including lists of actual names of slave ships and lengthy "quotations" from logbooks and other seemingly authentic historical documents.[5] A transition from freedom to slavery, the crossing from Africa to the New World is indeed a "Voyage through death," a "voyage whose chartings are unlove." But Hayden is hardly content to enumerate the horrors of the slave trade and to condemn the injustices of slavery. His is a more ambitious goal: to change the very texture of history, to alter the insidious design the dark ships have created:

> Shuttles in the rocking loom of history,
> the dark ships move, the dark ships move,
> their bright ironical names
> like jests of kindness on a murderer's mouth.

Hayden's use of a metaphor of weaving as a figure for writing is most significant: for him the pattern of crisscrossing lines connecting

Africa with the Americas constitutes the charts, or "chartings," of Afro-American history, that is, its official text(s), represented in the poem by the fragmented "quotations" from what at first glance appear to be historical documents. "Middle Passage" as a whole is a careful reading of those official texts, one that unravels the threads of their fabric to weave them together in very different ways. Hayden is indeed a most diligent and skillful weaver of poetic textures, of designs that revise official historical charts and offer correctives or alternatives to historical documentary. Resituated in a new context, the texts Hayden purports to quote lose not their appearance of authenticity but their historical authority. Broken up into textual fragments, they are no longer capable of offering a coherent, unified historical narrative. They become voices among many other, competing voices or, better perhaps, images of language, of the discourse of slavery, without claims to representational authority and historical truth.

This displacement, and in fact effacement, of authority indicated by the conspicuous absence of a central, controlling consciousness, or "voice," in the poem, is significantly reinforced by the fact that these "documents" are not just general accounts of the slave trade. They all have to do, directly or indirectly, with slave mutinies:

> "10 April 1800—
> Blacks rebellious. Crew uneasy. Our linguist says
> their moaning is a prayer for death,
> ours and their own. . . ."

Hayden has carefully "selected" passages reporting various "misfortunes" that interfere with the steady course of the slavers: ophthalmia ("It spreads, the terrifying sickness spreads. / Its claws have scratched sight from the Capt.'s eyes"); suicides; fires; and stormy seas. All these interferences build up to a lengthy narrative of the famous *Amistad* rebellion (1839) in the poem's final section.

On its way from Havana to Puerto Principe (today's Camaguey), the schooner *Amistad,* with fifty-four blacks and two passengers on board, was taken over by the Africans under the leadership of Cinquez (or Cinque). Their intention was to reverse the course of the vessel, using as navigators the two Spaniards they had spared. But, instead of returning to the African coast, the *Amistad,* after several months of aimless zigzagging due to the deception of its navigators, finally reached the Connecticut shoreline. The mutineers, seized by the local authorities, were taken first to New

Haven and then to Hartford to await the trial that would determine whether they were to be freed or returned to their owners. Due to the involvement of prominent New England abolitionists such as Lewis Tappan, as well as of former President John Quincy Adams, the *Amistad* case became something of an international incident. In short the Court ruled that the Africans be freed and returned to their native land on the grounds that their enslavement and transport to Cuba had been in violation of international treaties banning the transatlantic slave trade.[6]

I am not offering this brief sketch of the *Amistad* affair in lieu of a reading of Hayden's poem, nor is it simply intended as background material. At least some familiarity with this event is crucial to an understanding of the historical bases of Hayden's literary strategies of displacement in "Middle Passage." It should further be noted that the *Amistad* case not only created considerable publicity for the New England abolitionists; it also generated a substantial body of writing in the form of legal documents and newspaper reports, not to mention the numerous historical studies it has inspired since. Finally, it set a legal precedent that literally reversed the direction of the Middle Passage and the "laws" that continued to sanction, albeit implicitly, the illegal trade in slaves.

Hayden's account of the *Amistad* mutiny and the subsequent trial merits detailed scrutiny and proves particularly revealing when compared to the poem's first version, published in *Phylon* in 1945. Although cast in the form of a citation, presumably from Pedro Montez's court testimony, Hayden's narrative bears little resemblance to contemporary transcripts of that report.[7] One of the most striking deviations from those documents is the emphasis Hayden places on the storm that delayed the vessel's scheduled arrival. While this information was obviously not relevant to the trial, Hayden explores the way in which it served to rationalize the success of the mutiny:

> But for the storm that flung up barriers
> of wind and wave, *The Amistad*, señores,
> would have reached the port of Príncipe in two,
> three days at most; but for the storm we should
> have been prepared for what befell.
> Swift as the puma's leap it came. There was
> that interval of moonless calm filled only
> with the water's and the rigging's usual sounds,

then sudden movement, blows and snarling cries
and they had fallen on us with machete
and marlinspike. It was as though the very
air, the night itself were striking us.
Exhausted by the rigors of the storm,
we were no match for them. Our men went down
before the murderous Africans.

While the storm probably did facilitate the revolt, the undue and
apologetic stress the speaker places on that event invests it with a
significance particularly suggestive in connection with Hayden's al-
lusions to Ariel's song in *The Tempest:*

> Full fathom five thy father lies,
>   Of his bones are coral made,
> Those are the pearls that were his eyes,
>   Nothing of him that doth fade
> But doth suffer a sea-change
> Into something rich and strange.
>
> (1.2.397–402)

Charles T. Davis was certainly correct in stating that "the allusion to
Shakespeare's sea-change mocks a less spiritual transformation," that
of "black gold, black ivory, black seed" into "New England pews"
and "altar lights."[8] Both are no doubt products of a hypocritical re-
ligious investment later figured as "the corpse of mercy" and "love's
rotten gelid eyes." Similar ironies resound in the names of the slave
ships listed at the very beginning of the poem: "*Jesús, Estrella, Esper-
anza, Mercy.*" Interestingly enough, the second such list ("*Desire, Ad-
venture, Tartar, Ann*") features names completely devoid of religious
connotations. This change in language is significant in that it repre-
sents the widening chasm between slavery and institutionalized re-
ligion during the early eighteenth century. By 1820, the year of the
official abolition of the transatlantic slave trade, it had already be-
come evident that the Christian doctrine would hinder economic
profits. The increasing secularization of the language of slavery, then,
indicates gradual but profound changes in the ideological makeup
of American slave societies: religious values were displaced by eco-
nomic concerns. The name *Amistad* is, of course, an obvious case.[9]
Further ideological transformations surface as we probe even more
deeply into the way in which Hayden adapts the concept of sea-
change to the historical environment of slavery.

It is worth recalling that the sea-changes in Shakespeare's play are brought about by the tempest that Ariel unleashes at Prospero's command. That tempest signifies a violent upheaval, the disruption of reality through imagination (Ariel's "magic"). In that sense the storm marks the transition from one state of being, or one mode of perception, to another, which is also a "voyage through death." The references to the storm in "Middle Passage" have a very similar function: they signal and anticipate the kinds of violent changes associated with slave mutinies and revolts. The storm physically throws the *Amistad* off its intended course, an act that prefigures the more drastic and violent change of course that results from the mutiny itself. The reversal of the schooner's voyage, then, stands for a reversal of colonial power structures, those of the master-slave relationship. Put differently, the revolt represents a struggle against and a successful dislocation of illegally assumed authority. This, in turn, suggests further parallels with *The Tempest,* where both Prospero and Antonio, each in his own way, are guilty of such injustices: Prospero with respect to both Ariel and Caliban; Antonio with respect to Prospero.

Insofar as the *Amistad* revolt epitomizes the successful struggle against an unjust institution and thus the achievement of freedom from bondage, it serves Hayden as a historical paradigm for throwing off course conventional notions of history and of time. History, for him, is not a unilinear progression, an orderly procession of events regulated by laws of causality. The *Amistad* case is of particular interest to Hayden, the revisionist, because it successfully disrupts the official design of Afro-American history by reversing the direction of the Middle Passage, not just in geographical terms but, even more important, in conceptual ones: it literally changes the conceptual and ideological structures, the "laws," that define the power relationships upon which the slave trade is predicated: the idea of European racial and cultural supremacy. Within this context Montez's fictionalized account of the mutiny becomes a self-indictment mainly because of his attempt to rationalize that ideology as "lawful." What Hayden illustrates brilliantly and subtly in the following passage is a significant discrepancy between lawful and just.

> Now we
> demand, good sirs, the *extradition* of
> Cinquez and his *accomplices* to La
> Havana. And it distresses us to know

there are so many here who seem inclined
to *justify* the mutiny of these blacks.
We find it paradoxical indeed
that you whose wealth, whose tree of liberty
are rooted in the labor of your slaves
should suffer the august John Quincy Adams
to speak with so much passion of the *right
of chattel slaves* to kill their *lawful masters*
and with his *Roman rhetoric* weave a hero's
garland for Cinquez. I tell you that
we are determined to return to Cuba
with our slaves and there *see justice done.* Cinquez—
or let us say 'the Prince'—Cinquez shall die.

(My italics)

The legalistic rhetoric of this passage, particularly evident in the
words and phrases I have emphasized, is clearly a more aggressive at-
tempt at rationalization than the previously employed references to
the storm. A noticeable change in tone announces the shift from the
impressionistic description of the revolt and its presumed causes to
an interpretation of the legal case; Montez's voice in that latter pas-
sage is tellingly conflated with that of the Spanish minister.[10] An im-
portant connection exists, however, between the two rhetorical
modes Hayden employs here. On the one hand, the speaker's strate-
gic emphasis on the storm implies that the uprising of the slaves was
simply another "misfortune," a lamentable interference in the "nat-
ural" course of events; on the other hand, he treats it as a criminal
act that requires punishment. The projected expectation is that order
will be restored, that justice will be done. The question is, what
order and whose justice? This is not an ethical problem, as the
speaker seems to imply; it is a legal and a rhetorical one. Neither the
Middle Passage as representative of the process of enslavement nor
the distinction between master and slave is a natural phenomenon.
Both are social conventions, and the way in which they define the
idea of justice is as paradoxical as the image of the "tree of liberty"
rooted in slave labor. These same conventions define the struggle for
freedom as a crime (as evidenced by the terms *extradition* and *accom-
plices*) against laws that conceive of slavery and, for that matter, of the
proposed murder of Cinquez as acts of justice.

The exposure of the internal contradictions that characterize
the discourse of slavery and result from the confusion and confla-
tion of natural laws with ideological precepts is one of the trade-

marks of abolitionist rhetoric, which provides a kind of subtext in this passage. But even the language of abolitionism is not free from inconsistencies: what is at issue here for Hayden is clearly not the paradox of defending "the right of chattel slaves to kill their lawful masters" but the contradictions inherent in the very distinction between *chattel* slaves and *lawful* masters. Hayden added these two qualifiers (the original reads, "the right of slaves to kill their masters") to strengthen the point he is making: that the rhetoric of slavery seeks carefully to conceal its internal contradictions. If slavery poses as a natural institution (that phrase already a contradiction), then the discourse of slavery poses as a natural language, thus detracting from the ideological assumptions on which it rests. This is precisely what Hayden's subtle changes in language emphasize in this instance.

By making these seemingly authentic texts part of the poem, Hayden draws further attention to the problematic truth-value of historical documents. In the same way that "justice" is a matter of conforming to certain laws, historical truth is a function of rhetorical conventions. "Middle Passage" both exposes and unsettles such conventions in order to redefine and reinscribe the idea of history and historical truth. Consider the following lines in this regard:

> "8 bells. I cannot sleep, for I am sick
> with fear, but writing eases fear a little
> since still my eyes can see these words take shape
> upon the page & so I write, as one
> would turn to exorcism."

What writing supposedly exorcises here is the fear of being contaminated: "'A plague among our blacks—Ophthalmia: blindness— & we / have jettisoned the blind to no avail.'" The spreading of this "terrifying sickness" represents a gradual loss of control, both over the ship's destination and over one's destiny:

> *What port awaits us, Davy Jones'*
> *or home? I've heard of slavers drifting, drifting,*
> *playthings of wind and storm and chance, their crews*
> *gone blind, the jungle hatred*
> *crawling up on deck.*[11]

If writing (here in the form of a slaver's logbook) creates an illusion of control and of an authority already in the process of being eroded, it does so by "exorcising" a threatening reality or, better, by containing the disturbing inconsistencies of reality within the ordered patterns of linearity. The religious overtones of this kind of exorcism are readily apparent, especially in connection with the mocking plea to grant "safe passage to our vessels bringing / heathen souls unto thy chastening." But, if exorcism, in the religious sense, is a form of "chastening," of restoring the purity of the soul and the kind of innocence associated with Christian mythology, it is also, more generally, a way of negating otherness, that is, cultural differences of any sort. Exorcism, then, becomes a *self-imposed* blindness resulting from the failure (or refusal) to acknowledge the legitimate existence of other cultures and creeds in order to avoid being "contaminated" by them. This ironic play on the religious justification of slavery is indeed effective, but Hayden's language penetrates the myth of purity even more deeply. Hayden's language reaches down to the ideological core of American society: its Puritan heritage. The implications of Hayden's attack on the narrow-mindedness and intolerance of Puritanism are clarified by a statement from Octavio Paz's meditations on the same subject. He contends that for the Puritans and their North American descendants "every contact is contamination. Foreign races, ideas, customs, and bodies carry within themselves the germs of perdition and impurity. Social hygiene complements that of the body and soul."[12]

For Hayden the kind of writing to which we generally attribute the status of historical documentary and thus a certain truth-value is characterized precisely by such practices of "social hygiene," which is of course but a euphemism for slavery in its many forms. In this way the written chronicles of the slave ships' voyages render visible in their own rhetoric the underlying ideological structures and strictures of North American imperialism: historiography becomes a mechanism of defense against cultural otherness and difference, against everything, in short, that would challenge ("contaminate") existing social institutions. Hayden's is a struggle not only against historical slavery; his struggle is also against the linguistic vestiges of slavery manifest in the continued confinement of Afro-Americans by a language that denies not only their complex historico-cultural identities but also their humanity: for him the difference between such phrases as *sweltering cattle, chattel slaves,* and *black poet* is one of degree only.

As a poet, Hayden is particularly sensitive to ideological constraints placed upon him by certain forms of language. Sharing the deep immortal human wish, / the timeless will" to freedom that comes to be embodied in Cinquez, Hayden is careful not to replace old shackles with new ones. Nor is his definition of freedom simple and commonsensical. No easy resolutions conclude "Middle Passage." While Cinquez unquestionably evolves into an emblem of freedom in the same way that Frederick Douglass does in the poem of that title, the former's freedom is significantly conceived in terms of a return to his native land. We may say that, in some sense, Cinquez is an epic hero who survives the "Voyage through death" and returns from it a wiser man. But Hayden did not, in the final analysis, write an epic poem. In fact, his revisions of the poem on the whole show that he carefully excised all vestiges of the epic mode from the *Phylon* version of "Middle Passage," most notably the prelude, whose repetition of "It was long, long after . . ." perpetuates the convention of linear temporality. Moreover, as the revisions of the poem's final lines particularly indicate, he was not satisfied with weaving "a hero's garland for Cinquez" in the way that John Quincy Adams did when he renamed Cinquez and his companion Grabeau:

> Cinque and Grabeau [declares Adams] are uncouth and barbarous names. Call them Harmodius and Aristogiton, and go back for moral principle to the fierce and glorious democracy of Athens. They too resorted to *lawless violence,* and slew the tyrant to redeem the freedom of their country. For this heroic action they paid the forfeit of their lives: but within three years the Athenians expelled their tyrants themselves, and in gratitude to their self-devoted deliverers decreed that henceforth no slave should ever bear either of their names. Cinque and Grabeau are not slaves. Let them bear in future history the names of Harmodius and Aristogiton.[13]

Hayden's phrase *Roman rhetoric,* a revision of *lavish rhetoric* that also replaces the line "*Jus suum* is the view of the *viejo* [meaning Adams]" in the poem's initial version, effectively invokes this passage from Adams's elaborate discourse on personal liberty and its allusions to the *sic semper tyrannis* motif. However, as a careful reading of the previous citation reveals, Adams's argument does not advocate the abolition of slavery. By renaming Cinquez, he indeed creates a "superb Homeric image," but this rhetorical gesture and the historical analogy on which it so eloquently draws hardly constitute an attack on the system of slavery. The fact that many slaves in the Americas were actually named after Roman or Greek heroes not only renders Adams's analogy suspicious but also reverses the positive symbolism of his act of renaming: in both historical and rhetorical terms this baptism signifies not liberation but another kind of enslavement. Hayden seems well aware of the inappropriateness of re-dressing Cinquez as a classical hero and promptly eliminates the "superb Homeric image" from the final text of the poem. This specific revision already suggests that Hayden's concept of freedom in "Middle Passage" is infinitely more complex and problematic than Adams's defense of *personal* liberty. This complexity is reinforced by the deletion of the reference to Homer, which removes the poem even further from any possible epic resonances. Let us, then, compare the poem's two endings:

I.   The deep immortal human wish
     the timeless will:
          Cinquez its superb Homeric image,
          life that transfigures many lives
          life that defines our history upon these shores.
     Borne from that land—
          our gods false to us, our kings betraying us—
     like seeds the storm winds carry
     to flower stubbornly upon these shores.

                                        (*Phylon* [1945], 53)

II. The deep immortal human wish
     the timeless will:

          Cinquez its deathless primaveral image,
          life that transfigures many lives.

     Voyage through death
                    to life upon these shores.
                                        (Final version)

As freedom's "deathless primaveral image," Cinquez is now invested with a much broader and more flexible mythological significance than in the previous version. Hayden wrests Cinquez away from Adams's stale neoclassical clichés that detach him from his cultural context to charge him with a different definition of freedom

Hayden thus transforms, as he frequently does, a historical character into a poetic paradigm, into a trope. In the process of transforming, he effaces and invalidates the image of Cinquez that represents Adams's "Roman rhetoric" and, connected with that, the legal rhetoric of the trial that reduces the Africans' identity to the terms *ladinos* and *bozales*.[14] Either inscription of identity, the heroic and the legal, is constraining in that it is conceived from within the rhetorical (and ideological) bounds of slavery. The choice here appears to be between a barbed-wire pen and a gilded cage, to recall two of Hayden's previously mentioned images.

Extracted from its restrictive historical and rhetorical frames the figure of Cinquez emerges as "deathless" and "primaveral." In its resistance to narrow definitions and semantic stability, it comes to embody the very power of transfiguration that characterizes Hayden's language. Cinquez's new identity transforms the conventional meaning of Middle Passage. Although still identified as "Voyage through death," the Middle Passage can now be comprehended as an internal journey, indeed as a *rite of passage,* which is a figure for Hayden's historical imagination. "Middle Passage" is the visible, textual shape of that imagination and thus of Hayden's ability to transfigure the movement from freedom to slavery into its exact opposite. If Cinquez returns to Africa, Hayden returns to "life upon these shores," which are his native land, but the "chartings" of his own journey through history are love not "unlove." Hayden's journey, the writing of "Middle Passage," leads toward an understanding of "the claims the living / owe the dead," to borrow a phrase from Jay Wright,[15] toward an understanding of "our history upon these shores." And it is this understanding that transforms chronicles of death into "something rich and strange." From the scattered fragments of "official" histories that Hayden reassembles emerges a text that changes as we behold it and that changes us in the very act of beholding. *Beholding,* a verb Hayden uses as a figure for reading, creates a strangeness and richness due to the absence of a conventional poetic format, such as the epic, that would arrest the continuous sea-changes in Hayden's language. "Middle Passage" is indeed a "changing permanence," a poem whose linguistic surfaces are as varied as its voices and ultimately as deceptive as the references to calm seas in the slavers' logbooks. The historical (and poetic) truth that emerges from these shifting surfaces is the *limbo* of Hayden's ever-transfiguring poetic imagination.

NOTES

1. *Pictures from Brueghel and Other Poems* (New York: New Directions, 1949), 109.

2. For a more detailed discussion of the relationship between "For a Young Artist" and Gabriel García Márquez's short story "Un señor muy viejo con unas alas enormes," see my essay "The Logic of Wings: Gabriel García Márquez and Afro-American Literature," *Latin American Literary Review* 13 (1985): 133–45.

3. Quoted in John Hatcher, *From the Auroral Darkness: The Life and Poetry of Robert Hayden* (Oxford: George Ronald, 1984), 37.

4. *The Labyrinth of Solitude: Life and Thought in Mexico* (New York: Grove, 1961), 51.

5. For details about Hayden's historical (and literary) sources, see Charles T. Davis, "Robert Hayden's Use of History," in *Modern Black Poets: A Collection of Critical Essays,* ed. Donald Gibson (Englewood Cliffs, N.J.: Prentice Hall, 1973), 96–111; and Fred M. Fetrow, "'Middle Passage': Robert Hayden's Anti-Epic," *CLA Journal* 22, no. 4 (1979): 304–18.

6. The court's reference point was the treaty between England and Spain of 23 September 1817, which set the terms for the abolition of the transatlantic slave trade and designated 30 June 1820 as the legal time limit for the import of Africans *(bozales)* to the Spanish colonies.

7. The *Phylon* version clarifies the speaker's identity: "Cinquez spared Don José and me." The testimonies of both Pedro Montez and José Ruiz can be found in John Warner Barber, *A History of the Amistad Captives* (1840; rpt., New York: Arno Press and the New York Times, 1969), 6–8. Hayden's version of the mutiny and its accompanying circumstances seems very much indebted to Muriel Rukeyser's narrative of the *Amistad* mutiny in *Willard Gibbs* (Garden City, N.Y.: Doubleday Doran, 1942), 16–46, esp. 19–20.

8. "Robert Hayden's Use of History," 102.

9. Manuel Moreno Fraginals has commented at length on the significance of such linguistic changes, both with respect to the naming of slave ships as well as the naming of sugar mills in the Hispanic Caribbean. He suggests that both are indicative of the same clash between religious and economic institutions. See *El ingenio. Complejo económico social cubano del azúcar* (Havana: Editorial de Ciencias Sociales, 1978), 112–26, 264.

10. See Barber, *A History of the Amistad Captives,* 31.

11. In the *Phylon* version these lines are neither italicized nor set off from the preceding quotation.

12. *Labyrinth of Solitude,* 24.

13. John Quincy Adams, *Argument in the Case of United States vs. Cinque* (1841; rpt., New York: Arno and the New York Times, 1969), 86–87.

14. The license of the transportation of the *Amistad* slaves, signed by the captain-general of Cuba, misidentifies them as *ladinos,* a term used for blacks long settled in Cuba, instead of designating them *bozales,* referring to recent arrivals from Africa. This fraudulent document and the accompanying testimony by R. R. Madden, a British abolitionist, concerning the

illegal practices of the Cuban authorities, played a significant role in the court's final decision. See Barber, *A History of the Amistad Captives*, 17–18, 22–24. Rukeyser notes that in the translation of this document *ladino* had willfully been mistranslated as *sound* (*Willard Gibbs*, 47).

15. *Dimensions of History* (Santa Cruz: Kayak, 1976), 7.

CALVIN HERNTON

Shining ["Runagate Runagate"]

For two hundred and fifty years one of the main actions of resis-
tance and survival for slaves was the action of flight. Even after slav-
ery, flight from injustice and violence continued into the twentieth
century as an incumbent feature of being black in the United
States.

Consistent with the African cultural heritage, where art is not
only a reflection of but an integral part of everyday life, flight be-
came a dominant theme in the New World expressions of African-
American people. The theme first appears in the "primitive" sorrow-
and-hope songs, which are the sacred spirituals and secular blues
created by the unlettered black masses. Later on, flight occupies a
major place in the "classical" works of the learned, self-conscious
Negro artists. Robert Hayden's "Runagate Runagate" is one of the
most highly polished examples.

During the mid-1930s Hayden was employed in one of the Fed-
eral Writers Projects, where he researched Negro history and cul-
ture. Eventually, a number of significant works came out of this re-
search. "Runagate Runagate" is one of them. In the first stanza
Hayden captures the danger and terror of Negro flight by weaving
a tapestry of common words without the interruption of punctu-
ation, words that reach out and engage, if not engulf, the reader.
The matrix of words running on for seven rather long lines creates
a forest of language that conjures the thick danger of the chase. The
rush of words suggests both the relentless drive of black vernacular
expression and the indefatigable determination to "keep on going
and never turn back and keep on going." It is more than interest-
ing, more than coincidental, that as an adjective *Webster's New World
Dictionary* defines *vernacular* as belonging to home-born slaves.

From the beginning slaveholders were plagued by the "disease"
that infected their slaves with the alien desire to run away. By 1793
many states began passing laws providing for the capture and pun-

From *Field* 47 (Autumn 1992). 34–40.

ishment of slaves, often stipulating handsome rewards for their return. During the nineteenth century, after the Atlantic Trade was outlawed, the flight of slaves became a serious threat to the entire plantation system in the South, which was now dependent on an internal trade, buttressed largely by plantations, and even whole states, that bred and grew their own slaves. *Runaways, fugitives, escapees, maroons,* and *contraband* were terms that put fear and anger in every slaveholder's heart, and initiated freelance "patterollers," hunters and catchers of Negroes. From about 1830 until the end of the Civil War an unbroken stream of slaves escaped from the South via what had come to be known as the Underground Railroad. The metaphor was inspired by the labyrinthine sundry routes along which many acts of ingenuity, bravery, and sacrifice were transformed into legendary feats of mythological proportions:

> Some go weeping and some rejoicing
> some in coffins and some in carriages
> some in silks and some in shackles.

Ellen Craft was light enough to pass for white; she dressed as a white master and escorted her dark-complexioned husband out of the Deep South in clear view of everybody. Henry "Box" Brown acquired his nickname by having himself sealed in a box and shipped aboard a steamer to a northern port. A mother with babe in arms got trapped on a bridge between catchers on either side; rather than be captured, she leaped to death in the ice-cold waters. The first play written by a black person, *Leap to Freedom,* was based on the legend that grew out of the incident. "Many Thousand Gone" became a familiar phrase in black cultural lore, and various plays, songs, novels, essays, and even paintings have been entitled with it. During the height of Underground Railroad activity Congress passed the infamous Fugitive Slave Law of 1850, to little avail. "Catch them if you can, but it won't be easy. / They'll dart underground . . . / plunge into quicksand, whirlpools, mazes, / turn into scorpions when you try to catch them."

The facts, circumstances, and incidents of the Underground Railroad movement, and the mythology, form a vast reservoir of collective memory that—through word of mouth, tales, rhymes, and songs—is passed on from generation to generation. Hayden's research took him into that great experiential resource of black folk culture that Richard Wright labeled "The Form of Things

Unknown." The entire first part of the poem is composed of words, phrases, song titles, expressions, wanted posters, escaped slave advertisements, all taken from the African–American experiential heritage. "No more auction block for me / no more driver's lash for me / And before I'll be a slave / I'll be buried in my grave" are lines from one of the songs that whites banned the blacks from singing. Hayden is working with the most rudimentary forms and elements of the African–American poetic tradition, which includes call-and-response, improvisations, polyrhythmic sounds, runs, and syncopations, with "bassing" ("Runagate Runagate") as the leitmotif. This tradition is collective rather than individual. There is only one *I* in the entire first part of the poem, and it is a communal *I*. The narrative voice is omnipotent and omniscient because it belongs to everybody, to the many thousands who rise and go, who are crossing over. To where—and to what?

> O mythic North
> O star-shaped yonder Bible city

The flight that informs "Runagate Runagate" is not cowardly running away. The "fugitives" are not fleeing from justice because of heinous acts they have committed. The flight of the runagate is anointed by the call of an unimpeachable quest, the quest for Zion—"star-shaped yonder Bible city"—which is North, which is at once reality, symbol, and metaphor (as North represents freedom and South represents slavery). Both the theme and the phenomenon of flight demand of and imbue the fugitives and those who aid them with the grit and valor of the heroic. The previous couplet as well as the lines "before I'll be a slave / I'll be buried in my grave" are heroic. The price of the quest may very well mean death, but the prize is "the" freedom: *the* signifying an already existing quality of life into which one may enter, if only one can reach that "somewhere morning."

Thus, in the final stanza of part 1 of the poem, *North Star* represents another symbol and metaphor for the reality and mythology of Underground Railroad activity. In 1848 Frederick Douglass named his antislavery newspaper the *North Star*. The Ghanian shipping line is named after the North Star. Marcus Garvey's back-to-Africa fleet as well as many more Negro and African enterprises were named in honor of the North Star. Equated with bonanza gold, the North Star is the compass star by which the runaways steered the train to keep on track. The powerfully understated irony of the line from the Negro song, "oh Susyanna don't you cry for me," is not that they are going to Louisiana with a banjo on their knees but that the runagates are bound for the freedom, "freedom-bound." The hyphenation of *freedom-bound* puts an unbreakable seal on the fugitive's commitment to the quest for freedom, which is precious and valued more than bonanza gold:

> North star and bonanza gold
> I'm bound for the freedom, freedom-bound
> and oh Susyanna don't you cry for me
>   Runagate
>   Runagate

When we come to the second part of Hayden's poem, we realize that the first part is a rather elaborate exposition, a portrayal of the collective experience in a general context. It relies on and emphasizes the communal voice and lore, wherein, along with their collective secular and sacred heritage of signs, symbols, songs, idioms, biblical allusions, and double meanings, the heroic is the folk, and the will and deeds of the collective slave Underground Railroad community constitute the hero.

Swiftly progressing from the general to the specific, the second part of the poem moves from the anonymity of mass folk experience to the singling out of a particular individual. Now the individual becomes the hero, and her deeds are the heroic. In 1829 a bounty was placed on the life of David Walker for publishing his incendiary antislavery pamphlet, the *Appeal*. His "mysterious" death quickly followed. The next most dangerous person to the slave system was declared to be Harriet Tubman, with rewards ranging from ten to forty thousand dollars, which would be millions today. In the second part of "Runagate" Harriet Tubman is named, her credentials are cited, and she is placed at the center of the Underground Railroad movement. As in real life, in the poem she is larger than life, she is "General," "Moses," "Armed," and "Dangerous." She is "Wanted . . . Dead or Alive."

Again as in real life, Harriet Tubman does not drop out of the sky; she does not descend from Mount Olympus. Rather, she "rises from their anguish and their power." Whose anguish, whose power? The collective anguish and power of the masses of slaves who numbered four million at the onset of the war. Nor was Harriet Tubman a house servant slave; she was a field slave with whip scars on her back, a woman of earth who received a "summoning" from God and became herself a "shining," a visionary and soldier. Though only about five feet in stature, she braved the journey back and forth, in and out of the South, dozens of times, freeing hundreds of slaves. Her leitmotif is "mean to be free," signifying unfaltering determination and courage. In the scenario that begins with "and this was the way of it," we witness the General "stealing" slaves, leveling her pistol "glinting in the moonlight"; we see and hear her admonish a discouraged runaway, "Dead folks can't jaybird-talk . . . / you keep on going now or die." Suddenly we get the sensation of the heroic aura of Harriet Tubman retroactively empowering the first part of the poem. "Runs falls rises stumbles on from darkness into darkness / and keep on going and never turn back and keep on going."

Come ride-a my train

Hayden was assailed (by others) with the trick question of whether he was a poet or a Negro poet. This is the albatross around the neck of every African-American writer who has ever lived, as if there is some inherent antipathy between poet and Negro poet. Obviously, Hayden did not recognize or feel any such antipathy. He refused to be limited or ghettoized by others on account of his race; rather, he explored, improvised, and expanded the artificial boundaries that both white racism and narrow black nationalism would impose on him and his work. He meticulously worked with the matter and the elements of his heritage, bringing the labor, instinct, skill, talent, and dedication of an incredibly hard-working poet to bear on every page he wrote. That is to say, there is nothing new or original in "Runagate Runagate," *except* the genius of Robert Hayden and the genius he recognized in the experiences and aesthetic tradition of African-American people. Lines such as "hound dogs belting in bladed air," "over trestles of dew, through caves of the wish," and "tell me Ezekiel, oh tell me do you see / mailed Jehovah coming to deliver me?" are wrought from exquisitely controlled feelings of poetic passion. Consider the first half of each of the four lines beginning with "Hoot-owl calling in the ghosted air":

> Hoot-owl calling . . .
> five times calling to . . .
> Shadow of a face in , , ,
> shadow of a voice in . . .

Now the second half of these same lines:

> the ghosted air,
> the hants in the air.
> the scary leaves,
> the talking leaves.

Then the five lines in italics that are connected to and by the bass (conductor's call) lines before and after, rather like the cars of a train with an engine at the front and one at the rear:

> Come ride-a my train
>
> *Oh that train, ghost-story train*
> *through swamp and savanna movering movering,*
> *over trestles of dew, through caves of the wish,*
> *Midnight Special on a sabre track movering movering,*
> *first stop Mercy and the last Hallelujah.*
>
> Come ride-a my train

Hayden does what Ellison does in *Invisible Man*. He employs the tools and modes of the African–American oral tradition, right along with the Western intellectual tradition, to create an incredibly rich and moving matrix of meanings. Robert Hayden was a big man, well over six feet with big bone structure and big hands. He was the kindest man I have known, courteous and charitable, and exuded a warmth that only humility can convey. Much like a diamond cutter hovering over his desk with magnifying glass in his eye, he turns uncut stones into icons and signs of precision. From carefully selected words and their structure on the page, he gives us a jewel of precious perfection. But "Runagate Runagate" is more than a mechanical work of art. Brimming with people, places, incidents, bits of songs, lore, and tales, the poem is a living, moving organism. From the first word, *Runs,* to the last word, *free,* Harriet Tubman's heroic motif is the triple-powered driving force behind the unalterable quest:

> mean mean mean to be free.

ANTHONY WALTON

The Eye of Faith
["Monet's 'Waterlilies'"]

The current perception of Hayden's achievement manifests itself in the inability of many critics and tastemakers to look at *all* of his poems, to let him out of a ghetto, as it were, of "black" poetry, or, more accurately, of being a black who wrote very well. As Hayden is increasingly included in anthologies, the poems are too often the same four or five "Black History Month" poems that convey only a sliver of Hayden's wide-ranging skills and interests.

His own words are helpful here: "There's a tendency today— more than a tendency, it's almost a conspiracy—to delimit poets, to restrict them to the politically and the socially or racially conscious. To me, this indicates gross ignorance of the poet's true function as well as of the true function and value of art. . . . I resist whatever would force me into a role as politician, sociologist, or yea-sayer to current ideologies. I know who I am, and pretty much what I want to say."

In the spirit of the foregoing, I have chosen to look at Robert Hayden's poem "Monet's 'Waterlilies.'" To my mind, this is a "raceless" poem, if such a thing is possible. On its most obvious level it is a testament from one artist to another. It's interesting that Hayden, a child of the inner city, thought that this painting of a bygone French countryside carried him to some restorative past. Monet fought his entire artistic life for a certain kind of light, what he called the "light that pervades everything," and Hayden found spiritual, psychological, and emotional sustenance in the products of those efforts.

Hilton Kramer describes the painting:

a world in which sky and clouds and mists and water-lilies and river grass and willows and underwater flora all converge, un-

From *Field* 47 (Autumn 1992): 48–51.

hampered and undivided by horizon lines or by spatial demarcations derived from fixed perspectives. All elements are consumed in their own reflection and counter-reflection on the pond's surface and by their own proliferating refraction in the air above and the water below. As these convergences become more and more intricate, the surfaces of the pictures lose their details. . . . To define this order we must go beyond these proliferations of light and shade, object and atmosphere, to the vaster subject which pervades these paintings . . . nothing less than the fluidity of experience itself. (*The Age of the Avant-Garde*)

Correlating the citations of "Selma" and "Saigon," we can infer that the "today" of the poem is somewhere in the first half of March 1965. In the preceding three months the Selma, Alabama, campaign of the civil rights movement had raged through the national media, featuring photos and news footage of a silver-helmeted Sheriff Jim Clark of Selma and his deputies brutalizing black women and children, throwing Martin Luther King, Jr. in jail, Malcolm X (who would be assassinated two weeks later) making speeches, and badly wounded NBC reporter Richard Valeriani broadcasting his report from a hospital bed.

On 7 March Alabama State Police attacked marchers on the Edmund Pettus Bridge. NBC broke into regular programming to broadcast the carnage. On 9 March white minister James Reeb was killed. That's some of the news from Selma that Hayden was thinking about. The news from Saigon wasn't any more comforting. By that March the Vietnam conflict had been escalating for several months. In late 1964 the Viet Cong had attacked Bien Hoa, killing five and wounding seventy-six Americans. In February there was a VC massacre at Pleiku and a bombing at Qui Nhon that killed twenty-three young soldiers. At this time the United States was not an active, or stated, participant in the civil war, and in March 1965, at the same time Selma was in chaos, the VC bombed the American embassy in downtown Saigon, killing twenty; marines landed at Da Nang; Operation Rolling Thunder—the saturation bombing of North Vietnam—commenced; and theater commander William Westmoreland requested 300,000 combat troops.

These were the public events Robert Hayden carried in his mind as he walked into the Museum of Modern Art; we'll assume it was a brisk, clear late winter afternoon. Hayden is explicit about the turmoil events thousands of miles away were causing him. His choice of the word *fallout* drags in the third public crisis of that time, the constant possibility of nuclear conflict. In two clear and deceptively offhand lines Hayden has positioned the poem squarely at the center of the three consuming moral dilemmas of the day.

Hayden was a member of the Bahá'í faith, which emerged in the mid-nineteenth century in Iran. Its adherents are nonviolent and believe that humanity is "young," slowly maturing toward an egalitarian world order built on the elimination of prejudice and superstition. Bahá'ís strive to "see" clearly; sight, vision, and, most important, light are the constant metaphors of their religious texts. It can be argued that looking at this "serene great picture" was a religious experience for Hayden. Monet's work became a shrine of art and light into which he could retreat. Human evil, for him, was the result of misunderstanding the continuum of space, time, and light, the seamless universe that all humans are equally a part of. He believed in one ultimate light, a light that was explained by physics as composed of all the colors of the spectrum, for him an appealing metaphor. Looking at Monet's painting, Hayden was able to view this light with his "eye of faith" and be restored. He describes this transformation explicitly in the second stanza. *Iridescence,* strictly defined, is the partial reflection of white light. Hayden was able to stand in front of Monet's painting and be carried, emotionally, from the painting itself and from his psychic distress, through "flesh of light" (in a beautiful phrase) to a timeless state, the original state, Eden.

And there we find Hayden in the final stanza, grieving and miles from Eden:

> O light beheld as through refracting tears.
> Here is the aura of that world
>   each of us has lost.
> Here is the shadow of its joy.

The "lost world" of the poem can be childhood, worldly innocence, or simply good memories, but it is a place that "time" has carried us through "space" away from, irrevocably. For a moment, in the presence of great and redemptive art, a "shadow of its joy" can be revisited and reclaimed.

Read in this fashion, "Monet's 'Waterlilies'" stands as a statement of lyric feeling in the tradition of "Lines Composed a Few Miles above Tintern Abbey" and "Dover Beach," a romantic mixture of idealization and lament. It belongs equally to the American tradition of Whitman and Stevens, blending humanitarian concerns with metaphysical explorations. And it suggests the larger context in which Hayden's work must be viewed if his achievement is to be fully understood and appreciated.

YUSEF KOMUNYAKAA

Journey into "[American Journal]"

In 1975, after years of admiring such poems as "The Ballad of Sue Ellen Westerfield," "Night, Death, Mississippi," and "Homage to the Empress of the Blues," I was fortunate to meet the formidable Robert Hayden. After his Friday night reading at Colorado College in Colorado Springs, we made plans to meet on Saturday afternoon.

I had no idea what I'd say to him. A barrage of elusive questions plagued me throughout the night. The next day I phoned Alex Blackburn, the founding editor of *Writers Forum,* and asked him if he wished to meet Hayden. Alex was elated, and I got off the hook. That afternoon we visited the Garden of the Gods.

Of course, years later, when Michael S. Harper gave me a copy of Hayden's *American Journal,* in early 1981, I was surprised by the title poem. I remember how it rekindled sensations and images of that Colorado afternoon; I read the poem repeatedly, each time feeling Hayden's presence intensifying. The man had a penetrating, indecorous eloquence—so does his poetry. I felt linked to this poem personally. "[American Journal]" taught me how language and imagination can transform a physical landscape into a spiritual one. We had talked about how the Garden of the Gods parallels a moonscape, something otherworldly. It was from there that Hayden began to orbit his imaginative tableau. Where many of us would have written a realistic narrative to recreate that day as we gazed out at the rocky formations called Kissing Camels and proximated an unknown that resonates with an almost-observed realism. It seems as if the narrator is on a spiritual quest, that this voyage into the brutal frontier of the American experience is a confrontation with his own alienation. He is transported through the power of reflection (the mind as spacecraft) in order to arrive at the scary truth of his species.

The poem's syntax suggests that everything is fused by a stream of consciousness—people, situations, ideas. Its satire is enhanced be-

From *Field* 47 (Fall 1992): 56–58.

cause numerous contradictions coexist, a tabulation of positives and negatives that insinuate: "new comers lately sprung up in our galaxy . . . yet no other beings / in the universe make more extravagant claims / for their importance and identity." The crude, egotistical Americans are attractive and repulsive; they are redeemable only if they can name their crimes and insanities or if someone can speak on their behalf—a seer, a poet, or a Christlike sympathizer. The poem's fractured syntax also highlights the narrator's alienation, as if spoken by a foreigner striving to grasp the structure and nuances of a new language.

Indeed, the "humanoid" among us narrates as might an early Western anthropologist, descending into the wilds of his galaxy to do fieldwork. He uses outdated jargon—*charming savages* and *enlightened primitives*—to describe us. Of course, this is the same ethnocentric lingo used by early anthropologists to dehumanize various peoples throughout the world. The narrator, however, employs the oxymorons in a satirical, almost cynical way, to articulate the supreme contradiction of our culture, the American Dream.

After interviewing an "earth man" at a tavern, who maintains he still believes in the dream, "irregardless of the some / times night mare facts we always try to double / talk our way around," the narrator, after further investigation of our society, records the American Dream as a great lie—a cultural materialism based on illusions and paradoxes. The idea that "every body in the good old u s a / should have the chance to get ahead . . . three squares a day" pales under the narrator's witnessing of "the squalid ghettoes in their violent cities." Like a mortified anthropologist, the narrator renames our dream as *vaunted liberty* and typically compares America with the more evolved society from which he traveled: "we are an ancient race and have outgrown / illusions cherished here."

As an outsider himself, he is able to ridicule this illusion, orchestrated by our mythmakers, because he, a humanoid, like others who are physically or culturally "different," are not welcomed into American society, let alone given access to the means of attaining the Dream. The narrator can only exist in the American context if he prostitutes his individuality through "mimicry" and assimilation: "though i have easily passed for an american . . . exert greater caution twice have aroused / suspicion returned to the ship." The speaker is raceless, without gender or genus, but knows this fearful sense of otherness that had driven most Americans into the psychological melting pot.

The narrator speaks as an insider/outsider, a freak in an elastic limbo, whose sensitivity is violated by "unbearable decibels." This investigator knows the impending tragedy programmed by America's love of technology—its machine-oriented existence: "more faithful to their machine-made gods / technologists their shamans." Similarly, he records the cultivated national ignorance that protects and facilitates America's collective ego: "earth men / in antique uniforms play at the carnage whereby / the americans achieved identity."

Is the poet an anthropologist also? Are we responsible for what we witness? Perhaps the speaker is also an artist, one who must not only record the patterns of the universe one finds oneself in but decode, translate, and critique them also. In any case, for me this poem gains more and more authority and significance as the last piece in Hayden's *Collected Poems*. It is a perfect summation and coda to his career as a poet. He always saw himself and his work as totally *American*. Yet I believe he identifies with the displaced speaker in "[American Journal]"—the outsider.

Selected Bibliography

Collected Works

Heart-Shape in the Dust. Detroit: Falcon, 1940.
The Lion and the Archer (with Myron O'Higgins). Nashville: Hemphill, 1948.
Figure of Time: Poems. Nashville: Hemphill, 1955.
A Ballad of Remembrance. London: Paul Breman, 1962.
Selected Poems. New York: October House, 1966.
Words in the Mourning Time. New York: October House, 1970.
The Night-Blooming Cereus. London: Paul Breman, 1972.
Angle of Ascent: New and Selected Poems. New York: Liveright, 1975.
American Journal. Taunton: Effendi Press, 1978.
American Journal. Expanded ed. New York: Liveright, 1980.
Collected Prose. Edited by Frederick Glaysher. Ann Arbor: University of Michigan Press, 1984.
Collected Poems. Edited by Frederick Glaysher. 1985. Reprint. New York: Liveright, 1996, with introduction by Arnold Rampersad.

Correspondence

"Robert Hayden and Michael S. Harper: A Literary Friendship." Edited by Xavier Nicholas. *Callaloo* 17, no. 4 (1994): 976–1016.
"A Selection of Letters." Edited by Xavier Nicholas. *Michigan Quarterly Review* 31, no. 3 (Summer 1992): 305–17.

Anthologies Edited

Kaleidoscope: Poems by American Negro Poets. New York: Harcourt, Brace, 1967.
Afro-American Literature: An Introduction (with David J. Burroughs and Frederick R. Lapides). New York: Harcourt Brace Jovanovich, 1971.

Dramatic Works

"Go Down, Moses." Edited and introduced by Robert Chrisman. *Michigan Quarterly Review* 37, no. 4 (Autumn 1998): 782–802.

Books about Hayden

Aubert, Alvin, ed. Special 210 page issue devoted to Hayden [essays, memoirs, and poems]: *Obsidian: Black Literature in Review* 8, no. 1 (Spring 1981).

Fetrow, Fred M. *Robert Hayden.* Boston: Twayne, 1984.

Hatcher, John. *From the Auroral Darkness: The Life and Poetry of Robert Hayden.* Oxford, U.K.: George Ronald, 1984.

Williams, Pontheolla T. *Robert Hayden: A Critical Analysis of His Poetry.* Urbana: University of Illinois Press, 1987.

Essays on the Work

[excluding those in the present volume]

Bontemps, Arna. "Negro Poets, Then and Now." *Phylon* 11 (Fourth Quarter 1950): 356–57.

Boyles, Ann. "'The Angle of Ascent': Process and Achievement in the Work of Robert Hayden." *Journal of Bahá'í Studies* 4, no. 2 (December 1991–March 1992): 1–28.

Collins, Michael. "On the Track of the Universal: 'Middle Passage' and America." *Parnassus: Poetry in Review* 17, no. 2, and 18, no. 1 (1993): 334–59.

Cooke, Michael G. "Robert Hayden: At Large, At Home in the World." *Afro-American Literature in the Twentieth Century.* 137–57. New Haven: Yale University Press, 1984.

Davis, Charles T. "Robert Hayden's Use of History." *Black Is the Color of the Cosmos: Essays on Afro-American Literature 1942–1981.* Edited by Henry Louis Gates. New York: Garland, 1982.

Faulkner, Howard. "'Transformed by Steeps of Flight': The Poetry of Robert Hayden." *CLA Journal* 21, no. 1 (1977): 282–91.

Fetrow, Fred M. "'Middle Passage': Robert Hayden's Anti-Epic." *CLA Journal* 22 (June 1979): 304–18.

———. "Portraits and Personae: Characterizations in the Poetry of Robert Hayden." *Black American Poets between Worlds, 1940–1960.* Edited by R. Baxter Miller. Knoxville: University of Tennessee Press, 1986.

Friedlander, Benjamin. "Robert Hayden's Epic of Community." *Melus* 23, no. 3 (Autumn 1998): 125–43.

Greenberg, Robert M. "Robert Hayden." *African American Writers.* Edited by Valerie Smith, Lea Baechler, and A. Walton Litz. New York: Charles Scribner's Sons, 1991.

Hansell, William H. "The Spiritual Unity of Robert Hayden's *Angle of Ascent.*" *Black American Literature Forum* 13 (Spring 1979): 24–31.

Henderson, Stephen. *Understanding the New Black Poetry: Black Speech and Black Music as Poetic References.* New York: Morrow, 1973.

Jones, Norma R. "Robert Hayden." *Afro-American Writers, 1940–1955.* Edited by Trudier Harris and Thadious M. Davis. Detroit: Gale Research, 1988.

Nielsen, Aldon L. "The Middle Passage." *Writing between the Lines: Race and Intertextuality.* 114–34. Athens: University of Georgia Press, 1994.

Novak, Michael Paul. "Meditative, Ironic, Richly Human: The Poetry of Robert Hayden." *Midwest Quarterly* 15 (Spring 1974): 276–85.

Oehlschlanger, Fritz. "Robert Hayden's Meditation on Art: The Final Sequence of *Words in the Mourning Time.*" *Black American Literature Forum* 19 (Autumn 1985): 115–19.

O'Sullivan, Maurice J. "The Mask of Illusion in Robert Hayden's 'The Diver.'" *CLA Journal* 17 (September 1973): 85–92.

Parks, Gerald. "The Bahá'í Muse: Religion in Robert Hayden's Poetry." *World Order* 15 (Spring–Summer 1981): 37–48.

Pool, Rosey E. "Robert Hayden: Poet Laureate." *Negro Digest* 15 (June 1966): 39–43.

Rice, William. "The Example of Robert Hayden." *New Criterion* 8, no. 3 (November 1989): 42–45.

Stepto, Robert B. "After Modernism, After Hibernation: Michael Harper, Robert Hayden, and Jay Wright." *Chant of Saints: A Gathering of Afro-American Literature, Art and Scholarship.* Edited by Michael S. Harper and Robert B. Stepto. 476–80. Urbana: University of Illinois Press, 1979.

Wright, John S. "Homage to a Mystery Boy." *Georgia Review* 36 (Winter 1982): 904–11.

Bibliography

Nicholas, Xavier. "Robert Hayden." *Bulletin of Bibliography* 42, no. 3 (1985): 140–53.

New titles

Tess Gallagher, *Soul Barnacles*
Linda Gregerson, *Negative Capability*
Philip Levine, *The Bread of Time*
Larry Levis, *The Gazer Within*
William Matthews, *The Poetry Blues*
Charles Simic, *A Fly in the Soup*

Recently published

Rachel Hadas, *Merrill, Cavafy, Poems, and Dreams*
Yusef Komunyakaa, *Blue Notes*
Philip Larkin, *Required Writing*
Alicia Suskin Ostriker, *Dancing at the Devil's Party*
Ron Padgett, *The Straight Line*

Also available are collections by

A. R. Ammons, Robert Bly, Philip Booth, Marianne Boruch,
Hayden Carruth, Fred Chappell, Amy Clampitt, Tom Clark,
Douglas Crase, Robert Creeley, Donald Davie, Peter Davison,
Tess Gallagher, Suzanne Gardinier, Allen Grossman, Thom Gunn,
John Haines, Donald Hall, Joy Harjo, Robert Hayden,
Edward Hirsch, Daniel Hoffman, Jonathan Holden,
John Hollander, Andrew Hudgins, Josephine Jacobsen,
Weldon Kees, Galway Kinnell, Mary Kinzie, Kenneth Koch,
John Koethe, Richard Kostelanetz, Maxine Kumin, Martin
Lammon (editor), David Lehman, Philip Levine, John Logan,
William Logan, William Matthews, William Meredith, Jane Miller,
Carol Muske, Geoffrey O'Brien, Gregory Orr, Marge Piercy,
Anne Sexton, Charles Simic, Louis Simpson, William Stafford,
Anne Stevenson, May Swenson, James Tate, Richard Tillinghast,
Diane Wakoski, C. K. Williams, Alan Williamson, Charles Wright,
and James Wright